CodeIgniter Web Application Blueprints

Develop full-featured dynamic web applications using
the powerful CodeIgniter MVC framework

Rob Foster

BIRMINGHAM - MUMBAI

CodeIgniter Web Application Blueprints

First published: January 2015

Production reference: 1140115

Published by Packt Publishing Ltd.
Livery Place
35 Livery Street
Birmingham B3 2PB, UK.

ISBN 978-1-78328-709-3

www.packtpub.com

Credits

Author
Rob Foster

Reviewers
Aafrin
Alexandros Dallas
Sharafat Ibn Mollah Mosharraf

Commissioning Editor
Amarabha Banerjee

Acquisition Editor
Nikhil Karkal

Content Development Editor
Rohit Kumar Singh

Technical Editor
Taabish Khan

Copy Editors
Stuti Srivastava
Laxmi Subramanian

Project Coordinator
Mary Alex

Proofreaders
Samuel Redman Birch
Stephen Copestake
Ameesha Green
Clyde Jenkins

Indexer
Rekha Nair

Graphics
Sheetal Aute
Valentina D'silva

Production Coordinator
Melwyn D'sa

Cover Work
Melwyn D'sa

About the Author

Rob Foster has been working in the field of web development for almost 10 years, working for various IT sectors. He has interests in CodeIgniter, Laravel, and iOS programming.

While not hunched over a computer ruining his eyesight, he enjoys drinking good quality wine, appreciates varieties of fine cheese, and has a liking for a pair of comfortable, elastic slacks!

Rob has also written *CodeIgniter 2 Cookbook*, *Packt Publishing*, and was a technical editor for *SUSE Linux 10 Bible*, *Wiley*.

I would like to thank Lucy once again for putting up with all those weekends spent not outside in the lovely summer but inside or for being otherwise bored while I worked on the book—sadly, no *Skyrim* to entertain you this time as that's still in Chloe's garage but you're gunning for top marks on those *Bejeweled* type games so, er, best of luck with that!

Thank you, Rohit at Packt for all your kind help, Taabish for your help with the technical editing—your keen eye for detail caught the errors I missed—and all the reviewers and other editors who helped with this book.

Lastly, thank you friends and family for putting up with me.

About the Reviewers

Aafrin is a self-taught programmer from a cyber security and digital forensic background. He has been actively developing and prototyping web applications since 2003. He codes in various programming languages, including C++, Java, PHP, ASP, VB, VB.NET, and has also worked with frameworks such as EXTJS, CakePHP, CodeIgniter, and Yii. In his free time, he blogs at http://www.aafrin.com and researches on computer security and computer forensics.

Alexandros Dallas studied Applied Informatics in Management and Economy and is now a software test engineer based in Athens.

He has a solid software development background in using PHP, mostly with Codeigniter, and Java. Whenever possible, he spends his time contributing to open source projects. He is well aware of RESTFul Web Services concepts and libraries, such as Jersey and Dropwizard, and has experience in the development, integration, and testing of web APIs.

Alexandros has authored *RESTFul Web Services with Dropwizard, Packt Publishing* (https://www.packtpub.com/web-development/restful-web-services-dropwizard).

Sharafat Ibn Mollah Mosharraf graduated from the University of Dhaka in Computer Science and Engineering. He is currently working as a senior software engineer at Therap Services, LLC. He has expertise and experience in architecting, designing, and developing enterprise applications in Java, PHP, Android, and Objective-C. He loves researching as well as training people on state-of-the-art technologies for the purpose of designing, developing, securing, and maintaining web and mobile applications. He also provides coaching for various teams participating in national software development contests. His areas of interest include user experience, application security, application performance, and designing scalable applications. He loves passing his free time with his family and friends.

I'd like to thank the author for writing such a wonderful book on advanced CodeIgniter applications. I'd also like to thank Mary Alex, the project coordinator of the book. It was a pleasure to work with her. Last but not least, I would like to thank my wife, Sadaf Ishaq, for bearing with me while I dedicated my busy time reviewing the book. It's always been great to have you by my side!

www.PacktPub.com

Support files, eBooks, discount offers, and more

For support files and downloads related to your book, please visit www.PacktPub.com.

Did you know that Packt offers eBook versions of every book published, with PDF and ePub files available? You can upgrade to the eBook version at www.PacktPub.com and as a print book customer, you are entitled to a discount on the eBook copy. Get in touch with us at service@packtpub.com for more details.

At www.PacktPub.com, you can also read a collection of free technical articles, sign up for a range of free newsletters and receive exclusive discounts and offers on Packt books and eBooks.

https://www2.packtpub.com/books/subscription/packtlib

Do you need instant solutions to your IT questions? PacktLib is Packt's online digital book library. Here, you can search, access, and read Packt's entire library of books.

Why subscribe?

- Fully searchable across every book published by Packt
- Copy and paste, print, and bookmark content
- On demand and accessible via a web browser

Free access for Packt account holders

If you have an account with Packt at www.PacktPub.com, you can use this to access PacktLib today and view 9 entirely free books. Simply use your login credentials for immediate access.

Table of Contents

Preface

This book comprises eight projects. These projects are deliberately made with extension and modification in mind, that is, as much as possible, I've tried to build each project in such a way that you can apply your own requirements easily and you don't have to study the code for weeks on end to work out how it functions.

Following each chapter as they currently are will give you a perfectly functioning project, of course, but there is always room to expand and should you choose to extend and add functionality, you can do so easily.

Conversely, each project can be disassembled and specific sections of code can be lifted out and used in completely different projects that are totally separate to this book. I've done this in several ways—as much as possible, the code is kept verbose and simple. The code is kept in small, manageable blocks; I've tried to keep all code as close to the examples of code used in the CodeIgniter documentation (so hopefully, it will follow a familiar flow and appearance).

I've also tried to document each project. The beginning of each chapter will contain wireframes, sitemaps, file tree layouts, and data dictionaries of every table in each project, and in the code itself, I have added explanations of the code.

I try to discuss why something is there rather than just a stale explanation of what something is; this is done in the hope that explaining why something is there will help you understand how relevant the code is to whatever change or amendment you might have in mind.

What this book covers

Chapter 1, *Introduction and Shared Project Resources*, introduces you to this book and documents an initial development environment—installing Twitter Bootstrap, installing CodeIgniter, and developing a few shared common resources used by all chapters throughout the book.

Chapter 2, A URL Shortener, talks about creating an application that allows a user to enter a URL. The application will encode this URL and generate a new, shorter URL with a unique code appended to it—this will then be saved to a database. This URL will be offered to the user for them to distribute and use. Once it is clicked on, the application we will develop will look at the URL, find the unique code in that URL, and look for it in the database. If found, the application will load the original URL and redirect the user to it.

Chapter 3, Discussion Forum, talks about creating an application that will allow users to create an initial question or proposition. This question will be displayed on a type of notice board; this is the beginning of a discussion thread. Other users are able to click on these users' discussions and reply to them should they wish.

Chapter 4, Creating a Photo-sharing Application, talks about creating a small application that will allow a user to upload an image. A unique URL is then generated and saved to the database along with details of the uploaded file. It is offered to the user for them to distribute. Once the URL is clicked on, the uploaded image is fetched from the filesystem and displayed to the user.

Chapter 5, Creating a Newsletter Signup, contains a project that allows a user to register to a database of contacts, in this case, a database of newsletter signups. The user can amend their settings (the settings can be anything you wish: the type of e-mail content they wish to receive or whether they wish to receive HTML or text-only e-mails). The application even supports unsubscribing from future newsletters.

Chapter 6, Creating an Authentication System, contains an application to manage users in a system you might develop and is perhaps the largest chapter in the book. A simple CRUD environment is supplied, allowing you to add, edit, and delete users. In turn, users can register themselves and even reset their password should they forget it.

Chapter 7, Creating an E-Commerce Site, talks about a small but concise e-commerce application that utilizes CodeIgniter's Cart class to support a simple shop. Users can filter products via different categories, add products to their cart, amend items in the carts (adjust item quantities), or remove items from their cart altogether.

Chapter 8, Creating a To-do List, talks about creating an application that allows a user to create tasks that they need to complete. Tasks can be given a due date, that is, a kind of deadline date. The tasks are displayed in an HTML table. The rows of late tasks are given a red background color to indicate their importance. Complete tasks can be set as done and are indicated as being done by being struck through. Finally, tasks can be deleted to remove old and unwanted items.

Chapter 9, Creating a Job Board, talks about creating a job board. Users are encouraged to post an advert on the job board by filling in an HTML form. The contents of the form are validated and added to a database of current available jobs. Other users looking for work can search for these jobs. These users can search through all jobs or enter a search query to see whether a specific job exists.

What you need for this book

The following is what you need:

- You'll need a computer and an *AMP environment (MAMP, WAMP, LAMP, and so on)
- A copy of the CodeIgniter framework

Who this book is for

In short, this book is anyone; you don't have to have previous CodeIgniter experience—however, this will obviously help. That said, this book isn't really aimed at the beginner, but that is by no means a barrier; don't forget, CodeIgniter is an easy-to-use framework and can be picked up quite easily.

Conventions

In this book, you will find a number of text styles that distinguish between different kinds of information. Here are some examples of these styles and an explanation of their meaning.

Code words in text, database table names, folder names, filenames, file extensions, pathnames, dummy URLs, user input, and Twitter handles are shown as follows: "Create or open a .htaccess file."

A block of code is set as follows:

```
$this->load->model('Urls_model');
if ($res = $this->Urls_model->save_url($data)) {
  $page_data['success_fail'] = 'success';
  $page_data['encoded_url'] = $res;
} else {
  $page_data['success_fail'] = 'fail';
}
```

When we wish to draw your attention to a particular part of a code block, the relevant lines or items are set in bold:

```
if ($this->form_validation->run() == FALSE) {
    // Set initial values for the view
$page_data = array('success_fail'   => null,
                   'encoded_url'     => false);
```

Any command-line input or output is written as follows:

```
user@server:/path/to/codeigniter$ php tools/spark install -v1.0.0
  example-spark
```

New terms and **important words** are shown in bold. Words that you see on the screen, for example, in menus or dialog boxes, appear in the text like this: "Enter the following command and click on **OK**."

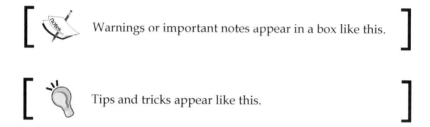

> Warnings or important notes appear in a box like this.

> Tips and tricks appear like this.

Reader feedback

Feedback from our readers is always welcome. Let us know what you think about this book—what you liked or disliked. Reader feedback is important for us as it helps us develop titles that you will really get the most out of.

To send us general feedback, simply e-mail feedback@packtpub.com, and mention the book's title in the subject of your message.

If there is a topic that you have expertise in and you are interested in either writing or contributing to a book, see our author guide at www.packtpub.com/authors.

Customer support

Now that you are the proud owner of a Packt book, we have a number of things to help you to get the most from your purchase.

Downloading the example code

You can download the example code files from your account at `http://www.packtpub.com` for all the Packt Publishing books you have purchased. If you purchased this book elsewhere, you can visit `http://www.packtpub.com/support` and register to have the files e-mailed directly to you.

Errata

Although we have taken every care to ensure the accuracy of our content, mistakes do happen. If you find a mistake in one of our books—maybe a mistake in the text or the code—we would be grateful if you could report this to us. By doing so, you can save other readers from frustration and help us improve subsequent versions of this book. If you find any errata, please report them by visiting `http://www.packtpub.com/submit-errata`, selecting your book, clicking on the **Errata Submission Form** link, and entering the details of your errata. Once your errata are verified, your submission will be accepted and the errata will be uploaded to our website or added to any list of existing errata under the Errata section of that title.

To view the previously submitted errata, go to `https://www.packtpub.com/books/content/support` and enter the name of the book in the search field. The required information will appear under the **Errata** section.

Piracy

Piracy of copyrighted material on the Internet is an ongoing problem across all media. At Packt, we take the protection of our copyright and licenses very seriously. If you come across any illegal copies of our works in any form on the Internet, please provide us with the location address or website name immediately so that we can pursue a remedy.

Please contact us at `copyright@packtpub.com` with a link to the suspected pirated material.

We appreciate your help in protecting our authors and our ability to bring you valuable content.

Questions

If you have a problem with any aspect of this book, you can contact us at `questions@packtpub.com`, and we will do our best to address the problem.

1
Introduction and Shared Project Resources

What is this chapter for? I hope to use this first chapter to act as a primer for all other chapters and projects in the book. I would like you to use the introduction as a common resource containing all of the resources shared by the projects in the book.

The introduction will cover the installation of third-party software, libraries, helpers, and so on, that are required by the projects in the later chapters. By keeping these resources in this chapter, the projects aren't swamped with repetitive code and the project code can be kept as clean and concise as possible.

In this chapter, we will cover the following topics:

- An overview of the book
- Downloading CodeIgniter
- Downloading and installing Twitter Bootstrap
- Creating common header and footer files used for all projects
- Installing Sparks
- Common language items

Common resources

The common resources used in this book are discussed in upcoming sections.

Twitter Bootstrap

Every project in the chapters in this book uses Twitter Bootstrap. We will download Bootstrap and find a good place for it in our filesystem. We will then create the header and the footer files. All projects in the book will call these header and footer files (using the CodeIgniter function `$this->load->view()` to display views). However, these projects will not actually contain the code for the header and footer—only the *working* code between the header and footer (what you might think of as the stuff in between the `<body>` and `</body>` tags) will be detailed in each project.

Headers and footers

The menus will be different for individual projects. In the header file, we will include the code to display the menu, but the actual HTML contents for the menu will be included in each project's chapter. The footer file contains the closing HTML markup for each page.

Downloading CodeIgniter

We'll need a copy of CodeIgniter to start with. This book isn't really aimed at the beginner, so the chances are reasonably high that you already have a copy of CodeIgniter installed or at least know your way around enough to skip this part; however, it does make sense to briefly go through the installation of CodeIgniter so that we have something to talk about in later chapters!

First things first, go to `https://ellislab.com/codeigniter/user-guide/installation/downloads.html`. You'll see something similar to what is shown in the following screenshot. This is the CodeIgniter download page. At the time of writing, the current CodeIgniter version is 2.2.0; this is why the screenshot says **Current version** next to version 2.2.0; however, whichever version is the latest when you're reading this book is the version you want to use.

Click on the **Current version** link, and CodeIgniter will begin to download.

Once it's downloaded, navigate to where you have saved the file; this will be a compressed archive. Unpack it and move the contents of that file to a folder within your web root.

Specific details of routing, configuration, and database use are in each chapter (these details are specific to that particular chapter).

CodeIgniter on newer versions of PHP

You may experience errors if you run CodeIgniter on newer versions of PHP. There is a hack for this that is explained at `https://ellislab.com/forums/ viewthread/244510/`. A poster called *milan.petrak* has described a work around. It can be summed up as follows:

1. Open the `/path/to/codeigniter/system/core/common.php` file and find the line 257.

2. Find the following line:

```
$_config[0] =& $config;
with
return $_config[0];
return $_config[0] =& $config;
```

3. Save the `common.php` file.

This will likely be permanently fixed in later releases of CodeIgniter, but for now, this is the fix.

Installing Twitter Bootstrap

Twitter Bootstrap is a frontend HTML5 framework that allows anyone to easily construct reliable interfaces. At the time of writing, the version of Bootstrap used is version 3.1.1.

We will use Twitter Bootstrap throughout this book to provide the framework for all view files and templates. We will look at how to download Twitter Bootstrap and how to install it in the CodeIgniter filesystem.

Firstly, we will need to download the Twitter Bootstrap files. To do that, perform the following steps:

1. Open your web browser and go to the Bootstrap download link at
   `http://getbootstrap.com/getting-started`. You'll see something similar to what is shown in the following screenshot:

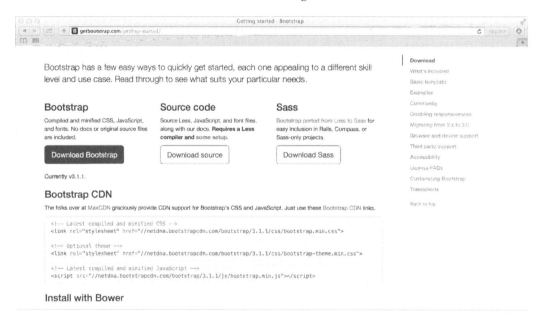

2. Find the **Download Bootstrap** link and click on it (as indicated in the preceding screenshot); the download will start automatically.

Once the download is finished, go to its location on your machine and unpack the archived file. Inside the unpacked file, you should see something similar to what is shown in the following structure:

```
bootstrap/
├── css/
│   ├── bootstrap-theme.css
│   ├── bootstrap-theme.css.map
│   ├── bootstrap-theme.min.css
│   └── bootstrap.css
│   └── bootstrap.css.map
│   └── bootstrap.min.css
├── js/
│   ├── bootstrap.js
│   └── bootstrap.min.js
└── fonts/
    ├── glyphicons-halflings-regular.eot
    ├── glyphicons-halflings-regular.svg
    ├── glyphicons-halflings-regular.ttf
    └── glyphicons-halflings-regular.woff
```

Move the bootstrap folder to your CodeIgniter installation so that the file hierarchy looks like the following:

```
/path/to/web/root/
├── application/
└── views/
    ├── common
        ├── header.php
        ├── footer.php
├── system/
├── bootstrap/
├── index.php
├── license.txt
```

In the preceding tree structure, the application and system directories are to do with CodeIgniter, as are the index.php and license.txt files; however, the bootstrap directory contains the contents of your Bootstrap download.

I have also indicated the location of the common header.php and footer.php files. These files are used throughout the book and act as a wrapper for every other view file.

Removing index.php from the address bar

It is possible to remove index.php from the web browser address bar when CodeIgniter is running. This can be done by following these steps:

1. Create or open a .htaccess file. If a .htaccess file does not already exist, you can create one using the following:

    ○ **Linux/Mac**: Open a terminal window and type the following:

    ```
    touch /path/to/CodeIgniter/.htaccess
    ```

    ○ **Windows**: Create a text file in your CodeIgniter root, naming it file. htaccess. Hold down the Windows key and then press *R* to open the **Run** dialogue. Enter the following command and click on **OK**:

    ```
    ren "C:\path\to\CodeIgniter\file.htaccess" .htaccess
    ```

2. Once your .htaccess file is opened, write the following lines at the top of the file:

```
<IfModule mod_rewrite.c>
RewriteEngine on
RewriteCond $1 !^(index\.php|images|robots\.txt)
RewriteRule ^(.*)$ index.php/$1 [L]
</IfModule>
```

Installing and using Sparks

For a long time, you had to search the Internet and download code from various places—blogs, code repositories, and so on—to find and use extensions, libraries, and other useful snippets of code for CodeIgniter. Useful installations for CodeIgniter were spread across the Internet; as such, they might have been hard to locate. Sparks acts as a single point of reference for extensions of CodeIgniter. It's simple to install and use and contains thousands of useful add-ons for CodeIgniter:

* If you are using a Mac or Linux, then the command-line interface is open to you. Using the terminal application on your system, navigate to the root of your CodeIgniter application and enter the following line:

```
php -r "$(curl -fsSL http://getsparks.org/go-sparks)"
```

If your installation was successful, you should see something similar to the following:

```
user@server:/path/to/codeigniter$ php -r "$(curl -fsSL http://
getsparks.org/go-sparks)"

Pulling down spark manager from http://getsparks.org/static/
install/spark-manager-0.0.9.zip ...

Pulling down Loader class core extension from http://getsparks.
org/static/install/MY_Loader.php.txt ...

Extracting zip package ...

Cleaning up ...

Spark Manager has been installed successfully!

Try: `php tools/spark help`
```

- If you are using Windows, then you will need to download Sparks and unpack it manually; to do that, follow these instructions or check out the instructions on the GetSparks website for the latest version:

  1. Create a folder called `tools` in the top level (root) or in your CodeIgniter directory.
  2. Go to `http://getsparks.org/install`.
  3. Go to the **Normal Installation** section and download the Sparks package.
  4. Unpack the download into the `tools` folder you created in step 1.
  5. Download the Loader class extension from `http://getsparks.org/static/install/MY_Loader.php.txt`.
  6. Rename the file `MY_Loader.php.txt` to `MY_Loader.php` and move it to the `application/core/MY_Loader.php` location in your CodeIgniter instance.

Now that Sparks is installed in your CodeIgniter instance, you can begin to install extensions and packages.

To install a package from Sparks, type the following in the command-line window:

```
php tools/spark install [Package Version] Spark Name
```

Here, `Package Version` is the specific version of the Spark you wish to install. You are not required to state the version and, if you it out, Sparks will download the latest version by default. `Spark Name` is the name of the Spark you wish to install; for example, to install `example-spark` (version 1.0.0), which comes with the default installation, type the following in the command-line window:

```
php tools/spark install -v1.0.0 example-spark
```

If the installation was successful, you should see something similar to the following:

```
user@server:/path/to/codeigniter$ php tools/spark install -v1.0.0
example-spark
```

```
[ SPARK ] Retrieving spark detail from getsparks.org
```

```
[ SPARK ] From Downtown! Retrieving spark from Mercurial repository at
https://url/of/the/spark/repo
```

```
[ SPARK ] Spark installed to ./sparks/example-spark/1.0.0 - You're on
fire!
```

Creating a shared header and footer view

Every project throughout this book will use the common header and footer files that we will create here; navigation menus will be different for each project and, as such, we will build these in the project's chapter themselves. But for now, let's look at the common header and footer files:

1. Create the `header.php` file at `/path/to/codeigniter/application/views/common/` and add the following code to it:

```php
<!DOCTYPE html>
<html lang="en">
  <head>
    <meta charset="utf-8">
    <meta http-equiv="X-UA-Compatible" content="IE=edge">
    <meta name="viewport" content="width=device-width,
      initial-scale=1">
    <meta name="description" content="">
    <meta name="author" content="">
    <link rel="shortcut icon" href="<?php echo
      base_url('bootstrap/ico/favicon.ico'); ?>">

    <title><?php echo $this->lang-
      >line('system_system_name'); ?></title>

    <!-- Bootstrap core CSS -->
```

```
    <link href="<?php echo base_url
      ('bootstrap/css/bootstrap.min.css'); ?>"
      rel="stylesheet">
    <!-- Bootstrap theme -->
    <link href="<?php echo base_url
      ('bootstrap/css/bootstrap-theme.min.css'); ?>"
      rel="stylesheet">

    <!-- Custom styles for this template -->
    <link href="<?php echo base_url
      ('bootstrap/css/theme.css');?>" rel="stylesheet">

    <!-- HTML5 shim and Respond.js IE8 support of HTML5
      elements and media queries -->
    <!--[if lt IE 9]>
      <script src="https://oss.maxcdn.com/libs/
        html5shiv/3.7.0/html5shiv.js"></script>
      <script src="https://oss.maxcdn.com/libs/
        respond.js/1.4.2/respond.min.js"></script>
    <![endif]-->
  </head>

  <body role="document">

<!-- END header.php -->

    <div class="container theme-showcase" role="main">
```

The preceding view file contains the HTML for the head of a document. This is to say that this HTML is used throughout the book for every project, and it contains the HTML markup for everything from the opening `html` tag, opening and closing `head` tags, and the opening `body` tag.

2. Create the `footer.php` file at `/path/to/codeigniter/application/ views/common/` and add the following code to it:

```
    </div> <!-- /container -->
    <link href="<?php echo base_url('bootstrap/css/bootstrap.min.
css'); ?>" rel="stylesheet">

      <!-- Bootstrap core JavaScript
    ================================================= -->
    <!-- Placed at the end of the document so the pages
      load faster -->
    <script src="https://ajax.googleapis.com/ajax/
      libs/jquery/1.11.0/jquery.min.js"></script>
```

```
      <script src="<?php echo base_url
        ('bootstrap/js/bootstrap.min.js');?>"></script>
      <script src="<?php echo base_url
        ('bootstrap/js/docs.min.js');?>"></script>
  </body>
</html>
```

The preceding block of code contains the HTML markup for the footer view file used for every project throughout this book.

Common language items

In each project throughout the book, we will create a specific language file containing specific language items that are relevant to that particular project. However, there are also common language elements that we won't repeat in each project (as there's no need); thus, we can have them here instead.

The language items mostly cover screen elements such as general navigation, general error and success messages, and CRUD actions (edit, delete, and so on).

With that in mind, let's go ahead and create the base language file that will serve as a template for the chapters in this book.

Create the en_admin_lang.php file at /path/to/codeigniter/application/ language/english/ and add the following code to it:

```
// Common form elements
$lang['common_form_elements_next'] = "Next...";
$lang['common_form_elements_save'] = "Save...";
$lang['common_form_elements_cancel'] = "Cancel";
$lang['common_form_elements_go'] = "Go...";
$lang['common_form_elements_go_back'] = "Go back";
$lang['common_form_elements_submission_error'] = "There were
  errors with the form:";
$lang['common_form_elements_success_notifty'] = "Success:";
$lang['common_form_elements_error_notifty'] = "Error:";
$lang['common_form_elements_actions'] = "Actions";
$lang['common_form_elements_action_edit'] = "Edit";
$lang['common_form_elements_action_delete'] = "Delete";
$lang['common_form_elements_active'] = "Active";
$lang['common_form_elements_inactive'] = "Inactive";
$lang['common_form_elements_seccessful_change'] = "Your changes have
been saved";
$lang['common_form_elements_seccessful_delete'] = "The item has
  been deleted";
```

```
$lang['common_form_elements_yes'] = "Yes";
$lang['common_form_elements_no'] = "No";
$lang['common_form_elements_to'] = "to";
$lang['common_form_elements_from'] = "from";
$lang['common_form_elements_history'] = "History";
```

The preceding language items are mostly for HTML forms and tables of data, such as the text for the Submit, Edit, Delete, and History buttons. Also included are general error or success messages. Feel free to add to them if you wish.

Creating the MY_Controller file

All projects in this book make use of the MY_Controller file; this is the same for all projects.

Create the MY_Controller.php file at /path/to/codeigniter/application/core/ and add the following code to it:

```
<?php if ( ! defined('BASEPATH')) exit('No direct script access
allowed');
class MY_Controller extends CI_Controller {

    function __construct() {
        parent::__construct();
        $this->load->helper('form');
        $this->load->helper('url');
        $this->load->helper('security');
        $this->load->helper('language');

        // Load language file
        $this->lang->load('en_admin', 'english');
    }
}
```

As you can see, we load helpers that are common to all projects, such as the form helper and the language helper, among others. The language file is also loaded here.

All the controllers in the project extend from this MY_Controller file rather than the default CI_Controller file.

Autoloading common system resources

We also are autoloading various resources such as support for database access and session management. We need to specify that we're using these resources.

Open the `autoload.php` file from `/path/to/codeigniter/application/config/` in your text editor and find the following line:

```
$autoload['libraries'] = array();
```

Replace this line with the following:

```
$autoload['libraries'] = array('database', 'session');
```

This will ensure that the resources that are required in order to access the database and to manage sessions are always with us.

Security considerations

Whatever you are programming, your two main priorities are security and maintainability; this is to say that your application should be as secure as is necessary and should be written in such a way that someone else can easily program and extend on what you're doing. I can't discuss maintainability—that's up to you—but I can give you guidance on CodeIgniter and security.

However, I should say that no security is 100 percent foolproof. Even banks and security agencies that spend hundreds of millions on systems still get hacked, so what chance do we have? Well, the best we can do is try to reduce the opportunity that someone might do something that could compromise our code or database.

Moving the system folder

You should move your system folder out of your web root. This is to make it as hard as possible for anything other than the web server to access. Take a look at the line in the main `index.php` file:

```
$system_path = 'system';
```

Make sure that you amend the preceding line to this:

```
$system_path = '../system';
```

So, if we moved the `system` folder out of the web root one level higher, we would use the `../` convention, prepending it to `system`.

Error messages

Obviously you don't want to actually display error messages to the outside world. Over time, everyone will gain an understanding of the architecture of your site and where its weaknesses are, especially if you allow SQL errors to be displayed in a production environment.

For this reason, you should change the environment variable in the main `index.php` file from `development` to `production`. This will suppress the reporting errors; 404 and 500 errors will still be caught and displayed normally but SQL errors and other similar errors will be suppressed.

For this, look at the following code in the `index.php` file:

```
define('ENVIRONMENT', 'development');
/*
 *---------------------------------------------------------------
 * ERROR REPORTING
 *---------------------------------------------------------------
 *
 * Different environments will require different levels of error
reporting.
 * By default development will show errors but testing and live will
hide them.
 */

if (defined('ENVIRONMENT'))
{
  switch (ENVIRONMENT)
  {
    case 'development':
      error_reporting(E_ALL);
    break;

    case 'testing':
    case 'production':
      error_reporting(0);
    break;

    default:
      exit('The application environment is not set correctly.');
  }
}
```

Look at the line in bold (the first line). This line has set CodeIgniter to run in development mode; to change to anything else (specifically, a live mode), change the line in bold to the following:

```
define('ENVIRONMENT', 'production');
```

All errors will now be suppressed.

Query binding

Query binding is a good idea; it makes your queries easier to read; queries that use the CodeIgniter binding are automatically escaped, leading to more secure queries. The syntax is simple; for example, consider the following query:

```
$query = "SELECT * FROM `users` WHERE user_email = ? AND user_level =
?";
```

Look at the end of the query; you can see that we use a question mark where we would normally use a variable; this is something that would normally look like this:

```
$query = "SELECT * FROM `users` WHERE user_email = $user_email AND
user_level = $user_level";
```

How does CodeIgniter know what the question mark means, and how does CodeIgniter put the correct value in the query? Take a look at this second line:

```
$this->db->query($query, array($user_email, $user_level));
```

This is how it matches the value to the correct question mark. We use the `$this->db->query()` CodeIgniter function, passing to it two arguments. The first is the `$query` variable (containing the actual query), and the second is an array. Each position in the array matches the position of the question marks in the SQL string.

Summary

Now, you will discover that we are ready to start the book and are all set to tackle each chapter.

Remember that the code for each chapter is available at the Packt website, as is the SQL for each chapter; this will save you from having to type in all this stuff.

2
A URL Shortener

There are quite a few URL shorteners out there on the Internet; however, there's always room for a little fun and sometimes people or companies require their own solutions rather than just using an external provider. The project in this chapter covers just that—developing a URL shortener in CodeIgniter that can be used by anyone.

To make this app, we'll need to do a few things: we'll create two controllers, one to create a shortened URL and one to redirect a shortened URL to its actual location on the Web.

We'll create language files to store text, creating a foundation for multiple language support should you wish to implement it.

We will also make amends to the `config/routes.php` file—this is to ensure that the shortened URL is as short as it can be.

However, this app, along with all the others in this book, relies on the basic setup we did in *Chapter 1, Introduction and Shared Project Resources*; although you can take large sections of the code and drop it into pretty much any app you may already have, bear in mind that the setup we did in *Chapter 1, Introduction and Shared Project Resources,* acts as a foundation for this chapter.

In this chapter, we will cover the following topics:

- Design and wireframes
- Creating the database
- Adjusting the `routes.php` file
- Creating the model
- Creating the views
- Creating the controllers
- Putting it all together

So without further ado, let's get on with it.

Design and wireframes

Before we start building, we should always take a look at what we plan to build.

Firstly, a brief description of our intent: we plan to build an app that will display a simple form to the user. The user will be encouraged to enter a URL into the form and submit that form.

A unique code will be generated and associated with the URL entered by the user. This URL and unique code will be saved to a database.

A new URL will be shown to the user containing the unique code we just generated. That unique code will be appended to the URL of the app we're building. Should the user (or anyone else) click on that link, the app will look up the unique code in the database. If the unique code exists, it will redirect the user to the original URL associated with that unique code.

So, let's take a look at some wireframes to help us understand what this might look like on screen:

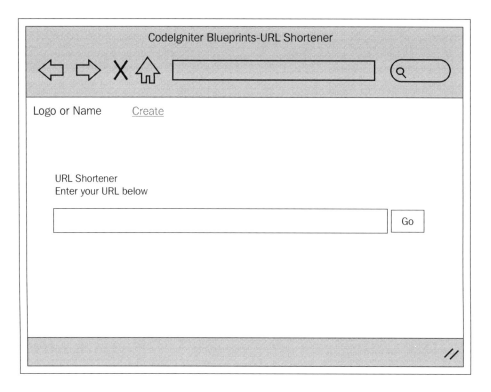

This is the first page that the user will see. The user is invited to enter a URL into the textbox and hit the **Go** button.

The page will be submitted and code will be generated. Both this code and the original URL will be saved to the database. The user will then see the new URL we've just created for them. They can copy that URL to their clipboard (for pasting into an e-mail and so on) or click on it there and then if they wish. This is shown in the following screenshot:

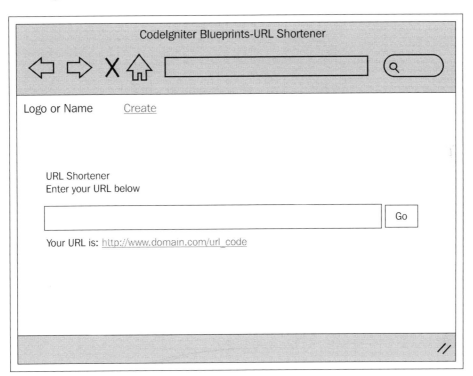

File overview

We're going to create six files for this application, as follows:

- /path/to/codeigniter/application/models/urls_model.php: This file provides access to the database and allows us to create the url_code, save the record to the database, and also retrieve the original URL from the database.

- /path/to/codeigniter/application/views/create/create.php: This file provides us with our interface, the user facing form, and any messages needed to inform the user of their actions or the system's actions.

- `/path/to/codeigniter/application/views/nav/top_nav.php`: This file provides a navigation bar at the top of the page.

- `/path/to/codeigniter/application/controllers/create.php`: This file performs validation checks on the URL inputted by the user, calls any helpers, and so on.

- `/path/to/codeigniter/application/controllers/go.php`: This file provides support for shortened URLs. It gets the unique code parameter from the URI (first segment), sends it to the `Urls_model`, and redirects the user to the associated `url_address` if it exists.

- `/path/to/codeigniter/application/language/english/en_admin_lang.php`: This file provides language support for the application.

The file structure of the preceding six files is as follows:

```
application/
├── controllers/
│   ├── create.php
│   ├── go.php
├── models/
│   ├── urls_model.php
├── views/create/
│   ├── create.php
├── views/nav/
│   ├── top_nav.php
├── language/english/
    ├── en_admin_lang.php
```

Downloading the example code

You can download the example code files from your account at `http://www.packtpub.com` for all the Packt Publishing books you have purchased. If you purchased this book elsewhere, you can visit `http://www.packtpub.com/support` and register to have the files e-mailed directly to you.

Creating the database

Okay, you should have already set up CodeIgniter and Bootstrap as described in *Chapter 1, Introduction and Shared Project Resources*. If not, then you should know that the code in this chapter is specifically built with the setup from *Chapter 1, Introduction and Shared Project Resources,* in mind. However, it's not the end of the world—the code can easily be applied to other situations.

Firstly, we'll build the database. Copy out the following MySQL code into your database:

```
CREATE DATABASE `urls`;
USE `urls`;

CREATE TABLE `urls` (
  `url_id` int(11) NOT NULL AUTO_INCREMENT,
  `url_code` varchar(10) NOT NULL,
  `url_address` text NOT NULL,
  `url_created_at` timestamp NOT NULL DEFAULT CURRENT_TIMESTAMP,
  PRIMARY KEY (`url_id`)
) ENGINE=InnoDB  DEFAULT CHARSET=utf8 AUTO_INCREMENT=1 ;
```

> You don't have to call the database `urls` if you don't want to. Feel free to rename to something else if you wish; just be sure to update the `config/database.php` file accordingly.

Let's take a look at what each item in the database means:

Elements	Description
url_id	This is the primary key.
url_code	This contains the unique code generated by the save_url() function of urls_model.php. This is the code that is appended to the shortened URL.
url_address	This is the actual URL the user entered in the form in the create.php view file. It will be the URL that the user is redirected to.
url_created_at	This is the MySQL timestamp created when the record was added. It is necessary so that we have an idea of when a record was created; also, it gives us a method of clearing old records from the database using a cron script should you wish.

We'll also need to make amends to the `config/database.php` file—namely setting the database access details, username password, and so on.

Open the `config/database.php` file and find the following lines:

```
$db['default']['hostname'] = 'localhost';
$db['default']['username'] = 'your username';
$db['default']['password'] = 'your password';
$db['default']['database'] = 'urls';
```

Edit the values in the preceding lines. Ensure you substitute those values with the ones that are more specific to your setup and situation—so enter your username, password, and so on.

Adjusting the routes.php file

We want short URLs—in fact the shorter the better. The user clicking on a URL would be better served if the URL were as short as possible; for that reason, it would be a good idea if we removed certain things from the URL to make it shorter—for example, the controller name and function name. We will use CodeIgniter's routing functionality to achieve this. This can be done as follows:

1. Open the `config/routes.php` file for editing and find the following lines (near the bottom of the file):

    ```
    $route['default_controller'] = "welcome";
    $route['404_override'] = '';
    ```

2. Firstly, we need to change the default controller. Initially, in a CodeIgniter application, the default controller is set to `welcome`. However, we don't need that; instead we want the default controller to be `create`. So, consider the following line:

    ```
    $route['default_controller'] = "welcome";
    ```

    Replace it with the following code:

    ```
    $route['default_controller'] = "create";
    ```

3. We will also need to set up a route rule for the `go` controller. We will need to remove the controller and function names (usually the first and second parameters in the URI). The following are two lines of code (highlighted in bold); add these two lines below the `404_override` route, so that the file now looks like the following:

    ```
    $route['default_controller'] = "create";
    $route['404_override'] = '';

    $route['create'] = "create/index";
    $route['(:any)'] = "go/index";
    ```

Now, the eagle-eyed among you will have looked at that last line and seen the `(:any)` type; some of you may have wondered what all that was about.

CodeIgniter supports a simple type of regex that makes routing for unknown URLs much easier. The `(:any)` type says to CodeIgniter that any URI pattern not otherwise defined (we're also defining `create`) is to be routed to `go/index`.

Creating the model

The `Urls_model` contains three functions; obviously it contains our `__construct()` function but we're not focusing on that at the moment as it's not doing anything except referencing its parent.

Instead, let's look at the two functions `save_url()` and `fetch_url()`. As their names suggest, one saves information to the database and the other fetches information from it. For now, let's go and create the code and we'll discuss in detail what each function does later:

Create the `urls_model.php` model file and add the following code to it:

```php
<?php if ( ! defined('BASEPATH')) exit('No direct script access allowed');

class Urls_model extends CI_Model {
  function __construct() {
    parent::__construct();
  }

  function save_url($data) {
    /*
    Let's see if the unique code already exists in
    the database.  If it does exist then make a new
    one and we'll check if that exists too.
    Keep making new ones until it's unique.
    When we make one that's unique, use it for our url
    */
    do {
      $url_code = random_string('alnum', 8);

      $this->db->where('url_code = ', $url_code);
      $this->db->from('urls');
      $num = $this->db->count_all_results();
    } while ($num >= 1);

    $query = "INSERT INTO `urls` (`url_code`, `url_address`) VALUES (?,?) ";
    $result = $this->db->query($query, array($url_code, $data['url_address']));

    if ($result) {
      return $url_code;
    } else {
```

```
            return false;
        }
    }

    function fetch_url($url_code) {
        $query = "SELECT * FROM `urls` WHERE `url_code` = ? ";
        $result = $this->db->query($query, array($url_code));
        if ($result) {
            return $result;
        } else {
            return false;
        }
    }
}
```

Let's take a look at save_url(). Notice the PHP construct do...while; it looks something like the following:

```
do {
// something
} while ('...a condition is not met');
```

So that means *do something while a condition is not met.*

Now, with that in mind, think about our problem. We have to associate the URL that the user has entered in the form with a unique value. We will use this unique value to represent the real URL.

Now there's no point using a sequential number (1, 2, 3, … 1000) as our unique value as someone can come along and iterate up through the numbers and get access to everyone's URLs. This may not be such a dreadful security risk as presumably all pages are accessible from the Internet anyway, but it's still not a good idea. So the unique value must not only be unique, it must be random and not easily guessed by passersby. Also, this unique value must only exist once in the database.

To ensure this, we will have to check if the unique value already exists and, if it does exist, make a new unique code and check in the database again.

So, let's look at the do while construct in the save_url() function in a bit more detail. The following is the code:

```
do {

        $url_code = random_string('alnum', 8);

        $this->db->where('url_code = ', $url_code);
        $this->db->from('urls');
        $num = $this->db->count_all_results();
    } while ($num>= 1);
```

We use CodeIgniter's `String` helper and its `random_string()` function (make sure you include the `String` helper using `$this->load->helper('string');` in your controllers' constructor). The `random_string()` function will create (as the name suggests) a random string of characters that we will use for our unique code.

In this case, we're asking `random_string()` to give us a string of characters made up of numbers and uppercase and lowercase letters; that string should be no more that 8 digits in length.

We then look into the database to see if the code `random_string()` has made for us already exists. We'll use the `$this->db->count_all_results();` CodeIgniter function to count up the number of matching results.

If the unique string already exists, then the number returned by `$this->db->count_all_results();` will be equal to 1 (as it already exists). If this happens, we will loop back to the beginning of the `do while` construct and start again by generating a new code.

We keep doing this until we find a code that does not exist in the database. When we do, we break out of the `do while` loop and save that unique code, along with the original URL to the database.

Now let's look at `fetch_url()`. We want to see if there is a record in the database that corresponds to the `$url_code` entered by the user (in this case, they have clicked on a URL). The `fetch_url()` function accepts `$url_code` as a function argument passed to it by the controller and looks for it in the database. If it is found, the entire record (table row) is returned to the controller; if not, it returns false. The controller handles the false result accordingly (it displays an error).

Creating views

We're going to create two view files in this section, as follows:

- `/path/to/codeigniter/application/models/views/create/create.php`
- `/path/to/codeigniter/application/models/views/nav/top_nav.php`

Don't forget that the navigation file (`views/nav/top_nav.php`) is unique to each chapter in this book.

Creating the view file–views/create/create.php

The `create.php` file is the view file that the user creating the shortened URL will see; it contains the HTML form the user will enter the original URL into and any interactive elements such as error or success messages.

Create the `create/create.php` view file and add the following code to it:

```
<div class="page-header">
  <h1><?php echo $this->lang->line('system_system_name'); ?></h1>
</div>

<p><?php echo $this->lang->line('encode_instruction_1'); ?></p>

<?php if (validation_errors()) : ?>
  <?php echo validation_errors(); ?>
<?php endif ; ?>

<?php if ($success_fail == 'success') : ?>
  <div class="alert alert-success">
    <strong><?php echo $this->lang->line('common_form_elements_success_notifty'); ?></strong> <?php echo $this->lang->line('encode_encode_now_success'); ?>
  </div>
<?php endif ; ?>

<?php if ($success_fail == 'fail') : ?>
  <div class="alert alert-danger">
    <strong><?php echo $this->lang->line('common_form_elements_error_notifty'); ?> </strong> <?php echo $this->lang->line('encode_encode_now_error'); ?>
  </div>
<?php endif ; ?>

<?php echo form_open('create') ; ?>
  <div class="row">
    <div class="col-lg-12">
      <div class="input-group">
        <input type="text" class="form-control" name="url_address" placeholder="<?php echo $this->lang->line('encode_type_url_here'); ?>">
        <span class="input-group-btn">
          <button class="btn btn-default" type="submit"><?php echo $this->lang->line('encode_encode_now'); ?></button>
        </span>
```

```
          </div><!-- /input-group -->
        </div><!-- /.col-lg-6 -->
      </div><!-- /.row -->
    <?php echo form_close() ; ?>


    <br />


    <?php if ($encoded_url == true) : ?>
      <div class="alert alert-info">
        <strong><?php echo $this->lang->line('encode_encoded_url');
?> </strong>
        <?php echo anchor($encoded_url, $encoded_url) ; ?>
      </div>
    <?php endif ; ?>
```

Creating the view file–views/nav/top_nav.php

Each project in this book has its own navigation bar at the top of the page. This chapter is no exception although the actual navigation options for this project are limited — mostly because the app we're building only really does one thing. So create the nav/top_nav.php view file and add the following code to it:

```
<!-- Fixed navbar -->
<div class="navbarnavbar-inverse navbar-fixed-top" role="navigation">
<div class="container">
<div class="navbar-header">
<button type="button" class="navbar-toggle" data-toggle="collapse"
data-target=".navbar-collapse">
<span class="sr-only">Toggle navigation</span>
<span class="icon-bar"></span>
<span class="icon-bar"></span>
<span class="icon-bar"></span>
</button>
<a class="navbar-brand" href="#"><?php echo $this->lang->line('system_
system_name'); ?></a>
</div>
<div class="navbar-collapse collapse">
<ul class="navnavbar-nav">
<li class="active"><?php echo anchor('create', 'Create') ; ?></li>
</ul>
</div><!--/.navbar-collapse -->
</div>
</div>


<div class="container theme-showcase" role="main">
```

Creating controllers

There are two controllers in this project. The first one `create` is responsible for displaying the initial form to the user and validating the input. The second one `go` will redirect the user to the original URL.

Don't forget that the controllers extend the `core/MY_Controller.php` file and inherit the helpers loaded there.

Creating the controller file–controllers/create. php

The `create` controller in this project is responsible for the initial contact with the user; that is to say, it loads the view file `views/create.php` (that displays the form to the user) and processes the input—validation and more. We'll look at it in a second, but first let's create the controller:

Create the controller file `create.php` and add the following code to it:

```php
<?php if (!defined('BASEPATH')) exit('No direct script access
   allowed');

class Create extends MY_Controller {
function __construct() {
        parent::__construct();
            $this->load->helper('string');
            $this->load->library('form_validation');
            $this->form_validation->set_error_delimiters('<div
               class="alert alert-danger">', '</div>');
        }

public function index() {
        $this->form_validation->set_rules('url_address', $this->
           lang->line('create_url_address'),
           'required|min_length[1]|max_length[1000]|trim');

if ($this->form_validation->run() == FALSE) {
            // Set initial values for the view
            $page_data = array('success_fail'  => null,
                               'encoded_url'    => false);

            $this->load->view('common/header');
            $this->load->view('nav/top_nav');
            $this->load->view('create/create', $page_data);
```

```
            $this->load->view('common/footer');
        } else {
            // Begin to build data to be passed to database
            $data = array(
                'url_address' => $this->input->
                  post('url_address'),
            );

            $this->load->model('Urls_model');
    if ($res = $this->Urls_model->save_url($data)) {
            $page_data['success_fail'] = 'success';
            $page_data['encoded_url'] = $res;
        } else {
            // Some sort of error, set to display error
              message
            $page_data['success_fail'] = 'fail';
        }

            // Build link which will be displayed to the user
            $page_data['encoded_url'] = base_url() . '/' . $res;

            $this->load->view('common/header');
            $this->load->view('nav/top_nav');
            $this->load->view('create/create', $page_data);
            $this->load->view('common/footer');
        }
    }
}
```

So, the `create` controller does the following things for us:

- Form validation, where it checks to see if the input is what we expect
- Packaging up the `url_address` ready for the `Urls_model`
- Handling any error and success messages

Let's go through the controller by taking a look at what happens when the controller is loaded. As we're using CodeIgniter's form validation processes, you'll be aware that (`$this->form_validation->run() == FALSE`) will trigger the view files to be displayed, as shown here:

```
if ($this->form_validation->run() == FALSE) {
    // Set initial values for the view
$page_data = array('success_fail'   => null,
               'encoded_url'   => false);
```

```
        $this->load->view('common/header');
        $this->load->view('nav/top_nav');
        $this->load->view('create/create', $page_data);
        $this->load->view('common/footer');
    } else {
        ...
```

Before we display the view files, we set some variable values for the view file `create/create.php`. These values govern how the success and error messages are displayed. These are stored in the `$page_data` array (see the bold text in the preceding code).

Assuming there were no errors from the form validation, we grab the `url_address` from the post array and package it into an array, as follows:

```
$data = array(
    'url_address' => $this->input->post('url_address'),
);
```

We then load the `Urls_model` and send the `$data` array to the `save_url()` function of `Urls_model`:

```
$this->load->model('Urls_model');
if ($res = $this->Urls_model->save_url($data)) {
    $page_data['success_fail'] = 'success';
    $page_data['encoded_url'] = $res;
} else {
    $page_data['success_fail'] = 'fail';
}
```

 I have removed the comments to make it more legible for this explanation.

When successful, the model will return the `url_code` that we store in `$page_data['encoded_url']`.

This is then passed the `create/create.php` view file, which will display a success message to the user and their now shortened URL.

Creating the controller file–controllers/go.php

The `go` controller is the other end of the process. That is to say, the `create.php` controller creates the shortened URL and saves it to the database, and the `go.php` controller is responsible for taking a URL, finding the `$url_code` in the `uri` segments, looking in the database to see if it exists, and, if so, redirecting the user to the actual web address associated with it. Sounds simple, and in truth it is.

Create the go.php controller file and add the following code to it:

```php
<?php if (!defined('BASEPATH')) exit('No direct script access
allowed');

class Go extends MY_Controller {
function __construct() {
        parent::__construct();
            $this->load->helper('string');
        }

public function index() {
if (!$this->uri->segment(1)) {
redirect (base_url());
        } else {
            $url_code = $this->uri->segment(1);
            $this->load->model('Urls_model');
            $query = $this->Urls_model->fetch_url($url_code);

if ($query->num_rows() == 1) {
foreach ($query->result() as $row) {
                $url_address = $row->url_address;
            }

redirect (prep_url($url_address));
            } else {
                $page_data = array('success_fail'    => null,
                                   'encoded_url'     => false);

                $this->load->view('common/header');
                $this->load->view('nav/top_nav');
                $this->load->view('create/create', $page_data);
                $this->load->view('common/footer');
            }
        }
    }
}
```

The go controller really only gets going *after* the following lines:

```php
if (!$this->uri->segment(1)) {
redirect (base_url());
        } else {
            ...
```

The preceding lines check to see if there is a 1st segment in the URL. Normally, the first and second segments are taken up by the controller and function name (as the order in the URL usually goes controller/function/parameter). However, as we want the URL to be short (or at least that's the idea), we're taking our unique code from the first parameter. Think of it as shifting what would normally be in the third parameter to the left. So, two levels higher up means that what was in the third segment is now at the first.

How do we do this? How do we have a parameter (our unique code) as the 1st parameter instead of the controller name? Where did the controller and function names go and why does it still work when they're removed?

We alter the routes.php file, of course; this is explained earlier in this chapter.

Anyway, let's return to our code. If there is no item in the URL, then there isn't really anything for this controller to do. Thus, we'll redirect the user to the base_url() function, which will load the default controller (set as autoload.php); in this case, the default controller is the create.php file.

Now, assuming that there *was* a 1st parameter, we'll move on to the next part of the controller, the bit that works out the $url_code, as shown in the following code:

```
$url_code = $this->uri->segment(1);
$this->load->model('Urls_model');
$query = $this->Urls_model->fetch_url($url_code);

if ($query->num_rows() == 1) {
foreach ($query->result() as $row) {
  $url_address = $row->url_address;
     }

  redirect (prep_url($url_address));
} else {
 ...
```

Take a look at the preceding code. We grab the 1st uri segment and assign it to the $url_code variable. We need to check if this code exists in the database, so we load the Urls_model and call the fetch_url() function of Urls_model, passing to it $url_code.

The fetch_url() method will look in the database for a record corresponding to the value in $url_code. If nothing is found, it'll return false, causing the controller to load the create/create.php view.

However, if a record is found, `fetch_url()` returns the Active Record object. We now loop over the object, picking out the `url_address`, and storing it as the local variable `$url_address`, as shown here:

```
foreach ($query->result() as $row) {
$url_address = $row->url_address;
   }
```

Now, we have the original URL in the `$url_address` variable. We simply pass this directly to the `redirect()` CodeIgniter function, which will, as the name suggests, redirect the user to the original URL.

Notice the use of the `prep_url()` CodeIgniter function from within the `redirect()` function. This can be done as follows:

```
redirect (prep_url($url_address));
```

The `prep_url()` function will ensure that there is `http://` at the beginning of the URL, if it does not already have it

Creating the language file

Taking text out of the HTML or storing text in other files such as controllers can make maintaining applications or adding multiple languages a nightmare. Keeping languages in a separate dedicated file is always a good idea. With that in mind, we will create a language file for this app.

Create the language file `en_admin_lang.php` and add the following code to it:

```
<?php if (!defined('BASEPATH')) exit('No direct script access
allowed');

// General
$lang['system_system_name'] = "URLs a Swinger";

// Encode
$lang['encode_instruction_1']= "Enter a URL in the text box below and
we'll shorten it";
$lang['encode_encode_now']= "Shorten Now";
$lang['encode_encode_now_success']= "Your URL was successfully
shortened - check it out below";
$lang['encode_encode_now_error']= "We could not shorten your url, see
below for why";
$lang['encode_type_url_here']= "Write the URL here";
$lang['create_url_address'] = "Write the URL here";
$lang['encode_encoded_url']= "Hey look at this, your shortenedurl
is:";
```

Putting it all together

Now that we have made all the amendments to configuration files, created the database, and created all the files necessary for the app to work (controllers, models, views, and so on) let's run through a few scenarios briefly, just to make sure we know how the app functions.

Creating a shortened URL

Let's consider an example where Lucy visits the URL Shortener app and the `create` controller is called by CodeIgniter, displaying the `create/create.php` view file. The following is the sequence of events:

1. Lucy enters a URL in the text input and clicks on **Shorten Now**.
2. Upon submitting the form, the controller validates the URL. The URL is successfully validated and the validation returns no errors.
3. The URL entered by Lucy is then sent to the `save_url()` function of `Urls_model` that creates a unique code. The `save_url()` function uses the PHP construct `do while` and an Active Record database query to create a unique code that doesn't already exist in the database.
4. Once a code has been created that doesn't already exist, it is saved to the database along with a MySQL timestamp.
5. The app then displays a success message to Lucy, informing her that the URL was saved correctly. It also displays the URL for her to either click on or (more likely) copy-and-paste elsewhere.

Retrieving a URL

Let's consider an example where Jessica receives an e-mail from Lucy containing the shortened URL. The following is the sequence of events:

1. Jessica opens the e-mail and clicks on the URL in that e-mail.
2. Her computer opens a browser and takes her to our app. As the `create` controller is not the 1st `uri` segment, the `go` controller is run (we set this in the `routes.php` file).
3. The `go` controller loads the `Urls_model`, passing it the `url_code` (that was in the first segment of `uri`). The `fetch_url()` function of `Urls_model` looks in the database for the code and, if found, it returns the actual web address associated with that code to the `go` controller.
4. The `go` controller redirects the browser to the URL supplied by the model.
5. Jessica is happy as she can look at the cute cat video Lucy sent her! Awww!

Summary

So there you are! We've got ourselves a fairly good URL shortener application. It's certainly not feature-rich or the most advanced, but it works and is ready to be expanded upon should you wish. Perhaps you could add user accounts or payment for advanced features?

It currently uses Twitter Bootstrap for the frontend so it probably could do with an individual face-lift, a different style, look and feel, but it's currently user-friendly and responsive to mobile devices.

In the next chapter, we will create a discussion forum, allowing someone to create a discussion and then letting people comment and reply.

A simple admin moderation system will be provided to help prevent any untoward shenanigans such as naked pictures of celebrities or signals intelligence being posted up, or something like that—unless of course you're into that sort of thing, in which case I hear that the Ecuadorian embassy in London do a terribly good lunch; you might get fed up of it after a few months, though!

3
Discussion Forum

A discussion forum can be quite a useful resource to have on internal company projects or to allow clients to interact on projects, for example.

Discussion forums are a great way to create a community around a particular subject or topic, acting as a type of wiki. They are a store of knowledge of something or a record of a discussion, containing a history of changes of ideas and concepts and recording the evolution of thinking around a topic or subject. They can also be used to talk about cats.

To create this app, we'll create three controllers: one to handle discussions, one to handle comments, and one to handle any admin functionality that we might need, such as moderating comments and discussions.

We'll create a language file to store text, allowing you to have multiple language support, should that be required.

We will make amendments to the `config.php` file to allow for encryption support, which is necessary for sessions and password support.

We'll create all the necessary view files and even a `.css` file to help Bootstrap with some of the views.

This app, along with all the others in this book, relies on the basic setup we did in *Chapter 1*, *Introduction and Shared Project Resources*, although you can take large sections of the code and drop it into pretty much any app you might already have; please keep in mind that the setup done in the first chapter acts as the foundation for this chapter.

It is worth mentioning the limits of the application. This application contains the most basic discussion forum functionality. We create users on our way; however, there is no user management—to include that would be a large extension of the application code and slightly out of scope of a discussion forum.

Users are created when someone creates a comment or discussion using an e-mail address that is not currently stored in the `users` table. A password is generated for them and a hash is created based on that password.

As this application creates a password for them automatically, you might wish to tell them what that password is—perhaps by sending them an e-mail. However, you might not wish them to be able to log in at all. It's up to you—the functionality is there should you wish to expand upon it.

In this chapter, we will cover:

- Design and wireframes
- Creating the database
- Creating the models
- Creating the views
- Creating the controllers
- Putting it all together

So, without further ado, let's get on with it.

Design and wireframes

As always, before we start building, we should take a look at what we plan to build.

Firstly, we need to give a brief description of our intent; we plan to build an app that will let a user view any pre-existing discussion pages and then allow that user to comment on a page if they wish. The user can also create new discussions and other users can comment on them.

Let's take a look at a site map:

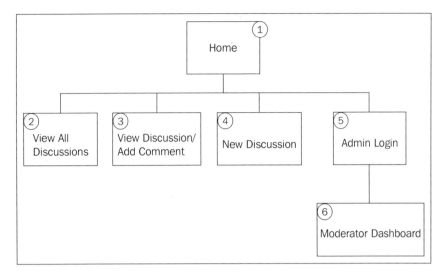

Now, let's go over each item and get a brief idea of what it does:

- **Home**: Imagine this as the index—the routing start point. The user will visit the Home page and will be redirected to point **2** (the View All Discussions page).

- **View All Discussions**: This will display all discussions in a list format. We'll have some filtering going on as well (the most recent first, most popular next, and so on). The user will be able to click on a discussion title and be redirected to the View Discussion page.

- **View Discussion/Add Comment**: This page displays the initial comment (written by the person who created the discussion) and all subsequent comments and contributions added by other users. A user is able to join in a discussion by filling in a form at the bottom of the View Discussion page.

- **New Discussion**: A user can create a new discussion. This discussion will then appear on the View All Discussions page as a new discussion.

We now begin to look at the admin-only functions (largely, discussion and comment moderation), which are as follows:

- **Admin Login**: This is just a simple login script. It is separate from the one used in *Chapter 6, Creating an Authentication System*.

- **Moderator Dashboard**: This displays all discussions and comments awaiting moderation and options in a list format, in order to allow or reject them.

Now that we have a fairly good idea of the structure and form of the site, let's take a look at some wireframes of each page.

The View All Discussions page

The following screenshot shows a wireframe of point **2** (the View All Discussions page) in the preceding diagram. The user is able to see all current discussions, the initial text written by the discussion creator (this acts as a brief introduction to the discussion subject), the total number of comments so far, the methods to sort the discussions into newest/oldest, and so on.

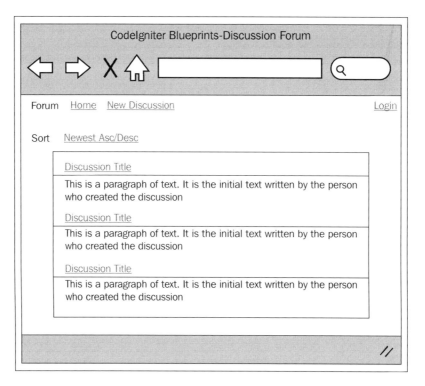

The View Discussion/Add Comment page

The following screenshot shows a wireframe from point **3** (the View Discussion/Add Comment page). You can see that this page displays the initial discussion text and all the replies. At the bottom of the list of replies, there is a form that allows the user to join the discussion. There is also a New Discussion link at the top; this will take the user to point **4** (the New Discussion page).

Notice the flag link next to each comment title. If a user clicks this, then the comment is immediately flagged for review by the admin. For example, let's say someone wrote something about a famous Hollywood actor or, something loony such as spaceships that might be considered potentially libelous; this comment can be flagged for review. If it is considered safe, it can be set as such; however, if it is not considered safe, it can be removed to prevent the writer of the comment from being followed everywhere by people in vans, turning up at their work, talking to their neighbors, and so on—a purely hypothetical, non-real-world, and completely made up example of something that has never happened ever, not even once.

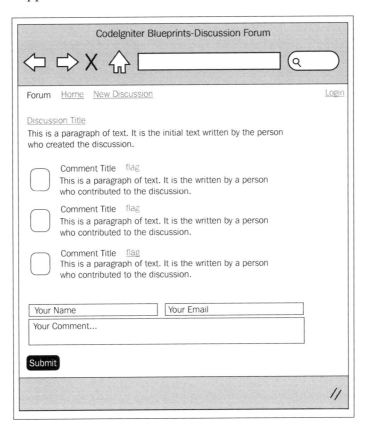

The New Discussion page

The following screenshot shows a wireframe from point **4** (the New Discussion page). You can see the form where the user can create a new discussion. The user is invited to enter the discussion title, their name, and the initial discussion text. Once the user has entered all relevant information into the form, they press the **Go** button, and the form is validated by the `create()` discussion controller function.

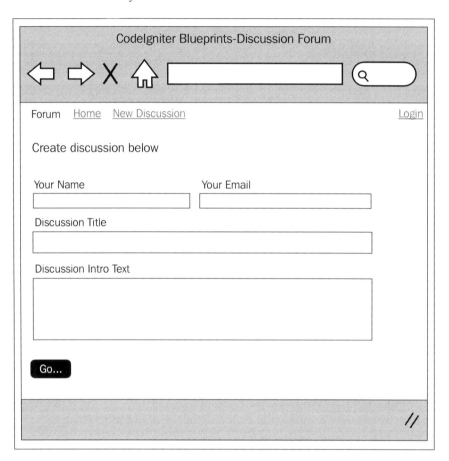

The admin Dashboard page

The following screenshot shows you the admin dashboard from point **6** (the Moderator Dashboard page). From this area, the admin can view any discussions and comments that have been flagged and moderate them, approving them or agreeing with the flag and deleting them.

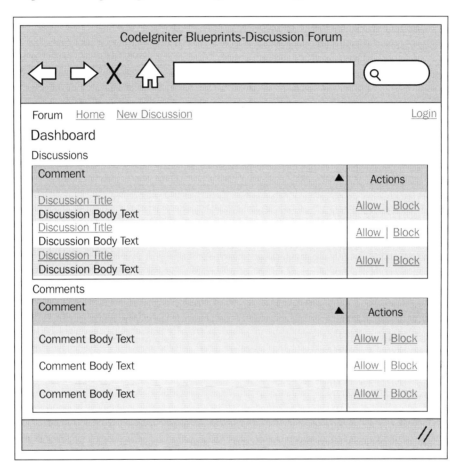

File overview

We're going to create 15 files for this application; these files are as follows:

- `/path/to/codeigniter/application/models/discussions_model.php`: This file provides read/write access to the database table `discussions`.

- `/path/to/codeigniter/application/models/comments_model.php`: This file provides read/write access to the database table `comments`.

- `/path/to/codeigniter/application/models/admin_model.php`: This file provides read/write access to the database, enabling an admin to moderate discussions and comments.

- `/path/to/codeigniter/application/views/discussions/new.php`: This file provides an interface to display a form, allowing the user to create a new discussion; it also displays any error or success messages to the user.

- `/path/to/codeigniter/application/views/discussions/view.php`: This file provides us with an interface, allowing the user to view all active discussions. It also provides filtering interface options (for example, sorting).

- `/path/to/codeigniter/application/views/comments/view.php`: This file provides us with an interface to display an individual discussion with all the comments other users have written to the user. There is also a form at the bottom of this view file that allows the user to join the discussion by creating a comment. Any validation or success messages related to adding a comment will be displayed in this view file as well.

- `/path/to/codeigniter/application/views/admin/dashboard.php`: This file displays a list of comments and/or discussions that require moderating.

- `/path/to/codeigniter/application/views/admin/login.php`: This file provides a login form for admins.

- `/path/to/codeigniter/application/views/nav/top_nav.php`: This file provides a navigation bar at the top of the page.

- `/path/to/codeigniter/application/controllers/discussions.php`: The `discussions` controller manages the creation of new discussions and displays a list of discussions to normal users.

- `/path/to/codeigniter/application/controllers/comments.php`: The `comments` controller manages the creation of new comments and links them to discussions. It also displays a list of comments to normal users.

- `/path/to/codeigniter/application/controllers/admin.php`: The `admin` controller handles the logging in of admins, the display of discussions and comments awaiting moderation, and the moderation of those discussions and comments.

- `/path/to/codeigniter/application/language/english/en_admin_lang.php`: This file provides language support for the application.

- `/path/to/codeigniter/application/views/common/login_header.php`: This file contains specific HTML markup to display the login form correctly.

- `/path/to/codeigniter/bootstrap/css/signin.css`: This is a css script containing specific css code to display the login form correctly.

The file structure of the preceding 15 files is as follows:

```
application/
├── controllers/
│   ├── discussions.php
│   ├── comments.php
│   ├── admin.php
├── models/
│   ├── comments_model.php
│   ├── discussions_model.php
│   ├── admin_model.php
├── views/discussions/        .
│   ├── view.php
│   ├── new.php
├── views/comments/
│   ├── view.php
├── views/admin/
│   ├── login.php
│   ├── dashboard.php
├── views/nav/
│   ├── top_nav.php
├── views/common/
│   ├── login_header.php
├── language/english/
│   ├── en_admin_lang.php
bootstrap/
├── css/
    ├── signin.css
```

Note the last item in the list: `signin.css`. This sits in the `bootstrap/css/` folder, which is at the same level as CodeIgniter's `application` folder. We installed Twitter Bootstrap in *Chapter 1, Introduction and Shared Project Resources*. In this chapter, we will go through placing the `bootstrap` folder at this folder level and location.

Creating the database

Okay, you should have already set up CodeIgniter and Bootstrap as described in *Chapter 1, Introduction and Shared Project Resources*. If not, then you should know that the code in this chapter is specifically built with the setup from the first chapter in mind. However, it's not the end of the world if you haven't—the code can easily be applied to other situations.

Firstly, we'll build the database. Copy the following MySQL code to your database:

```
CREATE DATABASE 'discuss_forum';
USE 'discuss_forum';

DROP TABLE IF EXISTS 'ci_sessions';
CREATE TABLE 'ci_sessions' (
  'session_id' varchar(40) COLLATE utf8_bin NOT NULL DEFAULT '0',
  'ip_address' varchar(16) COLLATE utf8_bin NOT NULL DEFAULT '0',
  'user_agent' varchar(120) COLLATE utf8_bin DEFAULT NULL,
  'last_activity' int(10) unsigned NOT NULL DEFAULT '0',
  'user_data' text COLLATE utf8_bin NOT NULL,
  PRIMARY KEY ('session_id'),
  KEY 'last_activity_idx' ('last_activity')
) ENGINE=MyISAM DEFAULT CHARSET=utf8 COLLATE=utf8_bin;

DROP TABLE IF EXISTS 'comments';
CREATE TABLE 'comments' (
  'cm_id' int(11) NOT NULL AUTO_INCREMENT,
  'ds_id' int(11) NOT NULL,
  'cm_body' text NOT NULL,
  'cm_created_at' timestamp NOT NULL DEFAULT CURRENT_TIMESTAMP,
  'usr_id' int(11) NOT NULL,
  'cm_is_active' int(1) NOT NULL,
  PRIMARY KEY ('cm_id')
) ENGINE=InnoDB DEFAULT CHARSET=utf8;

DROP TABLE IF EXISTS 'discussions';
CREATE TABLE 'discussions' (
  'ds_id' int(11) NOT NULL AUTO_INCREMENT,
  'usr_id' int(11) NOT NULL,
  'ds_title' varchar(255) NOT NULL,
  'ds_body' text NOT NULL,
  'ds_created_at' timestamp NOT NULL DEFAULT CURRENT_TIMESTAMP,
  'ds_is_active' int(1) NOT NULL,
  PRIMARY KEY ('ds_id')
) ENGINE=InnoDB AUTO_INCREMENT=1 DEFAULT CHARSET=utf8;

DROP TABLE IF EXISTS 'users';
```

```
CREATE TABLE 'users' (
  'usr_id' int(11) NOT NULL AUTO_INCREMENT,
  'usr_name' varchar(25) NOT NULL,
  'usr_hash' varchar(255) NOT NULL,
  'usr_email' varchar(125) NOT NULL,
  'usr_created_at' timestamp NOT NULL DEFAULT CURRENT_TIMESTAMP,
  'usr_is_active' int(1) NOT NULL,
  'usr_level' int(1) NOT NULL,
  PRIMARY KEY ('usr_id')
) ENGINE=InnoDB AUTO_INCREMENT=1 DEFAULT CHARSET=utf8;
```

 You don't have to call the database `discuss_forum` if you don't want to. Feel free to rename it to something else if you wish; just be sure to update `config/database.php` accordingly.

You'll see that the first table that we create is `ci_sessions`; we need this in order to allow CodeIgniter to manage sessions, specifically, logged-in users. However, this is just the standard session table that is available from *CodeIgniter User Guide*, so I'll not include a description of the table as it's not technically specific to this application. However if you're interested, there's a description at `http://ellislab.com/codeigniter/user-guide/libraries/sessions.html`.

Right, let's take a look at each item in each table and see what it means. The following table describes the `comments` table:

Table: comments	
Element	**Description**
cm_id	This is the primary key.
ds_id	This is the foreign key from the `discussions` table; it links the `comments` table to the `discussions` table. The link is `discussions.ds_id = comments.cm_id`.
cm_body	This is the body text of a comment.
cm_created_at	This is the MySQL timestamp that is created when the record is created.
usr_id	This is the foreign Key from the `users` table. A user is created when someone enters an e-mail address (when creating a discussion or comment) that doesn't already exist in the `users` table.
cm_is_active	This indicates whether the comment is active (1) or inactive (0); inactive means that a comment is not displayed in a forum but is displayed to an admin in the admin dashboard for moderation.

The following table describes the `discussions` table:

Table: discussions	
Element	**Description**
`ds_id`	This is the primary key.
`usr_id`	This is the foreign key from the `users` table. A user is created when someone enters an e-mail address (when creating a discussion or comment) that doesn't already exist in the users table.
`ds_title`	This is the title of a discussion forum.
`ds_body`	This is the body element of a discussion forum; it is the initial text—usually a question—that the creator of a discussion writes to entice people to comment.
`ds_created_at`	This is the MySQL timestamp that is created when the record is created.
`ds_is_active`	This indicates whether the discussion forum is active (1) or inactive (0); inactive means that a discussion is not displayed on the page but is displayed to an admin in the admin dashboard for moderation.

The following table describes the `users` table:

Table: users	
Element	**Description**
`usr_id`	This is the primary key.
`usr_name`	This is the username of an individual once they're in the database.
`usr_hash`	This is the hashed value of their password. The password is generated in the `new_comment()` function of `comments_model` and the `create()` function of `discussions_model` and is passed to the `$this->encrypt->sha1()` CodeIgniter function to create a hash. The hash is stored in the database in `users.usr_hash`; however, the password is not stored (as you would expect).

Table: users	
Element	**Description**
`usr_email`	This is the e-mail of the person writing a comment or creating a discussion forum. The application will look in the `users` table to see whether the e-mail already exists. If it does, the primary key (`usr_id`) for that record is assigned to a comment or discussion forum. If the e-mail does not already exist, then a row is created in the `users` table and the primary key is then assigned to the comment or discussion.
`usr_created_at`	This is the MySQL timestamp that is created when the record is created.
`usr_is_active`	This indicates whether the user is active (1) or inactive (0). Currently, there is no functionality to handle active or inactive users; this is something you can implement yourself should you wish.
`usr_level`	This indicates the permission level of the user. Standard users are given the integer value 1, and admins (that is, those who can log in) are given the integer value 2. There is no functionality to use this `usr_level` element; however, it is there should you wish to expand upon it.

At this early stage, it's important to discuss the concept of users in this application. We're not really going to employ any detailed user management, and users will only be created when someone enters their e-mail address when they add a comment or create a discussion. We're creating users here because it'll be easy for you to extend this functionality in your own time to manage users, should you wish.

We'll also need to make amendments to the `config/database.php` file—namely setting the database access details, username password, and so on. The steps are as follows:

1. Open the `config/database.php` file and find the following lines:

```
$db['default']['hostname'] = 'localhost';
$db['default']['username'] = 'your username';
$db['default']['password'] = 'your password';
$db['default']['database'] = 'urls';
```

2. Edit the values in the preceding lines, ensuring you replace these values with values that are more specific to your setup and situation. Enter your username, password, and so on.

Adjusting the config.php file

There are a few things in this file that we'll need to configure to support sessions and encryption. So, open the `config/config.php` file and make the changes described in this section.

We will need to set an encryption key. Both sessions as well as CodeIgniter's encryption functionality require an encryption key to be set in the `$config` array, so perform the following steps:

1. Find the following line:

   ```
   $config['encryption_key'] = '';
   ```

   Change it to the following:

   ```
   $config['encryption_key'] = 'a-random-string-of-alphanum-
   characters';
   ```

    Now, don't actually change this value to literally a-random-string-of-alphanum-characters obviously, but change it to, er, a random string of alphanum characters—if that makes sense. Yeah, you know what I mean.

2. Find the following lines:

   ```
   $config['sess_cookie_name'] = 'ci_session';
   $config['sess_expiration'] = 7200;
   $config['sess_expire_on_close'] = FALSE;
   $config['sess_encrypt_cookie'] = FALSE;
   $config['sess_use_database'] = FALSE;
   $config['sess_table_name'] = 'ci_sessions';
   $config['sess_match_ip'] = FALSE;
   $config['sess_match_useragent'] = TRUE;
   $config['sess_time_to_update'] = 300;
   ```

   Change them to the following:

   ```
   $config['sess_cookie_name'] = 'ci_session';
   $config['sess_expiration'] = 7200;
   $config['sess_expire_on_close'] = TRUE;
   $config['sess_encrypt_cookie'] = TRUE;
   $config['sess_use_database'] = TRUE;
   $config['sess_table_name'] = 'ci_sessions';
   $config['sess_match_ip'] = TRUE;
   $config['sess_match_useragent'] = TRUE;
   $config['sess_time_to_update'] = 300;
   ```

Adjusting the routes.php file

We want to redirect the user to the `discussions` controller rather than the default CodeIgniter `welcome` controller. To do this, we will need to amend the default controller setting in the `routes.php` file to reflect this, which can be done as follows:

1. Open the `config/routes.php` file for editing and find the following lines (near the bottom of the file):

   ```
   $route['default_controller'] = "welcome";
   $route['404_override'] = '';
   ```

2. Firstly, we need to change the default controller. Initially in a CodeIgniter application, the default controller is set to `welcome`; however, we don't need this. We want the default controller to be `discussions` instead. So, find the following line:

   ```
   $route['default_controller'] = "welcome";
   ```

   Change it to the following:

   ```
   $route['default_controller'] = "discussions";
   ```

Creating the models

We're going to create three models for this application; these are as follows:

- `discussions_model.php`: This helps in managing interactions with the `discussions` table
- `comments_model.php`: This helps in managing interactions with the `comments` table
- `admin_model.php`: This helps in managing interactions with the `users` table

Creating the model file – models/ discussions_model.php

The `discussions_model.php` model file has three functions; these are `fetch_discussions()`, `fetch_discussion()`, and `flag()`. The `fetch_discussions()` function fetches many discussions, the `fetch_discussion()` function fetches a single discussion, and the `flag()` function sets a discussion as one that requires moderation by an admin.

The steps to create this model file are as follows:

Create the `/path/to/codeigniter/application.models/discussion_model.php` file and add the following code to it:

```
<?php if ( ! defined('BASEPATH')) exit('No direct script access
allowed');

class Discussions_model extends CI_Model {
  function __construct() {
    parent::__construct();
  }
```

Let's first look at the `fetch_discussions()` function. The `fetch_discussions()` function will return the result of a database query to the `discussions` controller's `index()` function. It takes two arguments that are set to `null` by default. These are `$filter` and `$direction`, and they are used to add filtering and sorting to the query string.

The following query will only return active discussions—that is, any discussions whose `ds_is_active` value is not set to `0`. The `flag()` function of `discussions_model` (discussed later) sets a discussion to inactive:

```
function fetch_discussions($filter = null, $direction =
  null) {
  $query = "SELECT * FROM 'discussions', 'users'
            WHERE 'discussions'.'usr_id' =
              'users'.'usr_id'
            AND 'discussions'.'ds_is_active' != '0' ";
```

If the `filter` variable is initially null, then we will need to order the results to ascending. In the following code, we test whether `$filter` equals `null`; if not, `$dir = 'ASC'` sets the direction to ascending. If, however, `$filter` is not `null`, then we go into the PHP `if` statement and look at the value of `$direction`. We perform a PHP `switch case` procedure to quickly ascertain whether the value of `$direction` is `ASC` or `DESC`, writing the value of `$dir` to `ASC` or `DESC` accordingly:

```
if ($filter != null) {
  if ($filter == 'age') {
    $filter = 'ds_created_at';
    switch ($direction) {
      case 'ASC':
        $dir = 'ASC';
        break;
      case 'DESC':
```

```
            $dir = 'DESC';
            break;
        default:
            $dir = 'ASC';
    }
  }
} else {
  $dir = 'ASC';
}
```

Next, the query is executed and its return value is analyzed. If the query was successful, then $result is returned to the index() function of the discussions controller. The index() function of the discussions controller then stores this query result in the $page_data['query'] array item and passes it to the discussions/view.php view file. This is shown here:

```
$query .= "ORDER BY 'ds_created_at' " . $dir;
$result = $this->db->query($query, array($dir));

if ($result) {
  return $result;
} else {
  return false;
}
}

function fetch_discussion($ds_id) {
  $query = "SELECT * FROM 'discussions', 'users' WHERE
    'ds_id' = ?
         AND 'discussions'.'usr_id' = 'users'.'usr_id'";
  return $result = $this->db->query($query, array($ds_id));
}
```

Now, let's look at the create($data) function. The function takes an array (named $data) as its only argument. The $data array contains the following items:

*   usr_email: This is populated from the form in views/discussions/new.php
*   usr_id: This is populated by the model itself by looking in the database
*   usr_name: This is populated from the form in views/discussions/new.php
*   ds_title: This is populated from the form in views/discussions/new.php
*   ds_body: This is populated from the form in views/discussions/new.php

We want to associate this discussion forum with a user. Although we don't really manage users in this application, we still want to do this as it might be useful for us in the future. To associate a discussion with a user, we'll need to find an existing user ID (users.usr_id) or create a new user and assign that ID instead.

This function begins by looking at the users table to see whether the e-mail address in $data['usr_email'] already exists in the database. If it does, then usr_id is pulled out of the users table and written to $data['usr_id']; this will be stored until we update to the discussions table:

```
function create($data) {
    // Look and see if the email address already exists in the users
    // table, if it does return the primary key, if not create them
    // a user account and return the primary key.
    $usr_email = $data['usr_email'];
    $query = "SELECT * FROM 'users' WHERE 'usr_email' = ? ";
    $result = $this->db->query($query,array($usr_email));

    if ($result->num_rows() > 0) {
      foreach ($result->result() as $rows) {
        $data['usr_id'] = $rows->usr_id;
      }
    } else {
```

If the e-mail address doesn't exist in the users table, then a record is created. A password is generated using the random_string() CodeIgniter function. The password is stored in the $password variable and is passed to the sha1 CodeIgniter function to generate a hash string:

```
$password = random_string('alnum', 16);
$hash = $this->encrypt->sha1($password);
```

The $hash value along with usr_email and usr_name, submitted by the user, is added to the $user_data array. Also added to the $user_data array are some admin flags such as usr_is_active and usr_level.

The usr_is_active flag is set to 1 by default; this can be set to any other value you wish should you want to add user management functions. The usr_level flag is set to 1 by default; this can be set to any other value you wish should you want to add user management functions:

```
$user_data = array('usr_email' => $data['usr_email'],
                   'usr_name' => $data['usr_name'],
                   'usr_is_active' => '1',
                   'usr_level' => '1',
                   'usr_hash' => $hash);
```

The $user_data array is inserted to the database. Should you wish, you could send the user an e-mail containing their password; this will only be because you want to add user management functionality. The newly created user ID is returned by $this->db->insert_id() and stored in $data['usr_id']. This is shown here:

```
if ($this->db->insert('users',$user_data)) {
  $data['usr_id'] = $this->db->insert_id();
  // Send email with password???
}
}
```

Once the user ID is stored in the $data array, we create a new array, $discussion_data. The $discussion_data array contains all the data required for the creation of a discussion, as follows:

- ds_title: This is populated from the form in views/discussions/new.php
- ds_body: This is populated from the form in views/discussions/new.php
- usr_id: This is populated by a database lookup
- ds_is_active: This is set when we create the $discussion_data array

Once the $discussion_data array is created, we write the record to the discussion table:

```
$discussion_data = array('ds_title' => $data['ds_title'],
                         'ds_body' => $data['ds_body'],
                         'usr_id' => $data['usr_id'],
                         'ds_is_active' => '1');
```

If the insertion was successful, we return TRUE; if it wasn't successful, we return FALSE.

This model also contains the flag() function. The flag() function uses an UPDATE command to set the ds_is_active column to 0. This means that the discussion will not be displayed to users, as the fetch_discussions() function of discussions_model will only return discussions that have ds_is_active set to 1. This is shown here:

```
if ($this->db->insert('discussions',$discussion_data) ) {
  return $this->db->insert_id();
} else {
  return false;
}
}
```

The `flag()` function accepts one argument—that is, the primary key of the discussion passed by the `discussions` controller. When the user clicks on the **flag** link next to a discussion title in the `views/discussions/view.php` file, the `flag()` function of the `discussions` controller is called. The third `uri` segment in the **flag** link is the primary key of the discussion.

We use CodeIgniter's Active Record functionality to update the discussions record in the database, setting `ds_is_active` to 0. Setting `ds_is_active` to 0 will immediately prevent the discussion from being viewed in `views/discussions/view.php` and make it appear in the admin section for moderation:

```
function flag($ds_id) {
  $this->db->where('ds_id', $ds_id);
  if ($this->db->update('discussions', array('ds_is_active' =>
    '0'))) {
    return true;
  } else {
    return false;
  }
}
}
```

Creating the model file – comments_model. php

The `comments_model.php` model file contains three functions; these are `fetch_comments()`, `new_comment()`, and `flag()`. The `fetch_comments()` function fetches all comments that belong to a discussion forum and are active. The `new_comment()` function adds a comment to the database associated with a discussion forum by means of a foreign key. Finally, the `flag()` function will set a comment as one that requires moderation.

Create the `/path/to/codeigniter/application/models/comments_model.php` file and add the following code to it:

```
<?php if ( ! defined('BASEPATH')) exit('No direct script access
allowed');

class Comments_model extends CI_Model {
    function __construct() {
        parent::__construct();
    }
```

There are three functions in this model. These are as follows:

- `fetch_comments()`: This fetches all active comments that are associated with the current discussion from the `comments` table .

- `new_comments()`: This creates a new record in the `comments` table. The comment is associated with `users.usr_id` and `discussions.ds_id`.

- `flag()`: This sets a comment as being flagged for moderation by setting `comments.cm_is_active` to 0.

The `fetch_comments()` function accepts one argument—`$ds_id`—that is the primary key of the discussion in the database. We take this primary key and look in the database for comments belonging to that discussion, and users belonging to the comments, as shown here:

```
function fetch_comments($ds_id) {
    $query = "SELECT * FROM 'comments', 'discussions', 'users'
            WHERE 'discussions'.'ds_id' = ?
            AND 'comments'.'ds_id' = 'discussions'.'ds_id'
            AND 'comments'.'usr_id' = 'users'.'usr_id'
            AND 'comments'.'cm_is_active' = '1'
            ORDER BY 'comments'.'cm_created_at' DESC " ;


    $result = $this->db->query($query, array($ds_id));
```

These comments are then returned as an Active Record database result object. Or, the Boolean value `false` is returned if an error occurred, as shown here:

```
    if ($result) {
        return $result;
    } else {
        return false;
    }
}
```

The `new_comment()` function takes one argument, the `$data` array. This is populated in the `comments` controller, as shown here:

```
function new_comment($data) {
    // Look and see if the email address already exists in the
      users
    // table, if it does return the primary key, if not create
      them
    // a user account and return the primary key.
```

First off, we check whether the e-mail address used by the person who is commenting already exists in the database; we do this as we might want to add functionality to ban particular users later, delete posts from specific users, or even develop functionality to allow users to log in and view their previous posts:

```
$usr_email = $data['usr_email'];
$query = "SELECT * FROM 'users' WHERE 'usr_email' = ? ";
$result = $this->db->query($query,array($usr_email));

if ($result->num_rows() > 0) {
```

If we arrive here in the code, then the e-mail address is obviously already in the database, so we grab the users' primary key and store it in `$data['usr_id']`; later, we will save it to the comment:

```
foreach ($result->result() as $rows) {
    $data['usr_id'] = $rows->usr_id;
}
} else {
```

If we get here, then the user doesn't exist, so we create them in the `users` table, returning the primary key using the `$this->d->insert_id()` CodeIgniter function:

```
$password = random_string('alnum', 16);
$hash = $this->encrypt->sha1($password);

$user_data = array('usr_email' => $data['usr_email'],
                   'usr_name' => $data['usr_name'],
                   'usr_is_active' => '1',
                   'usr_level' => '1',
                   'usr_hash' => $hash);

if ($this->db->insert('users',$user_data)) {
    $data['usr_id'] = $this->db->insert_id();
}
}

$comment_data = array('cm_body' => $data['cm_body'],
                      'ds_id' => $data['ds_id'],
                      'cm_is_active' => '1',
                      'usr_id' => $data['usr_id']);
```

Now we save the comment to the `comments` table using the CodeIgniter Active Record function `$this->db->insert()`. This is shown here:

```
        if ($this->db->insert('comments',$comment_data) ) {
            return $this->db->insert_id();
        } else {
            return false;
        }
    }

  function flag($cm_id) {
    $this->db->where('cm_id', $cm_id);
    if ($this->db->update('comments', array('cm_is_active' =>
      '0'))) {
      return true;
    } else {
      return false;
    }
  }
}
```

Creating the model file – admin_model.php

There are four functions in the `admin_model.php` model, and these are as follows:

- `dashboard_fetch_comments()`: This fetches comments from the databases that have been flagged for moderation.

- `dashboard_fetch_discussions()`: This fetches discussions from the databases that have been flagged for moderation.

- `update_comments()`: This updates a comment based on the decision of the moderator, changing the value of `cm_is_active` to 1 if the comment is approved or deleting it if is unapproved.

- `update_discussions()`: This updates a discussion based on the decision of the moderator, changing the value of `cm_is_active` to 1 if approved or deleting it if is unapproved. If a discussion is deleted, then all comments associated with that discussion will also be deleted.

Create the `/path/to/codeigniter/application/models/admin_model.php`
file and add the following code to it:

```php
<?php if ( ! defined('BASEPATH')) exit('No direct script access
allowed');

class Admin_model extends CI_Model {
    function __construct() {
        parent::__construct();
    }
```

The following function will fetch all comments for moderation from the database.
Comments are for moderation if `comments.cm_is_active` is set to `0`. The database
is queried and all comments for moderation are returned to the `admin` controller.
This result will eventually be looped over in the `views/admin/dashboard.php` file:

```php
function dashboard_fetch_comments() {
    $query = "SELECT * FROM 'comments', 'users'
            WHERE 'comments'.'usr_id' = 'users'.'usr_id'
            AND 'cm_is_active' = '0' ";

    $result = $this->db->query($query);

    if ($result) {
        return $result;
    } else {
        return false;
    }
}
```

The following function will fetch all discussions for moderation from the
database. Discussions are for moderation if `discussions.ds_is_active` is set to `0`.
The database is queried and all discussions for moderation are returned to the
`admin` controller. This result will eventually be looped over in the `views/admin/
dashboard.php` file:

```php
function dashboard_fetch_discussions() {
    $query = "SELECT * FROM 'discussions', 'users'
            WHERE 'discussions'.'usr_id' = 'users'.'usr_id'
            AND 'ds_is_active' = '0' ";

    $result = $this->db->query($query);

    if ($result) {
```

```
        return $result;
    } else {
        return false;
    }
}

function does_user_exist($email) {
    $this->db->where('usr_email', $email);
    $query = $this->db->get('users');
    return $query;
}
```

The following function is called by the admin controller function when an admin is moderating comments. If a comment is deemed to be fine, then comments.cm_is_active is updated and set to 1. However, if it is not fine, then the comment is deleted from the comments table:

```
function update_comments($is_active, $id) {
    if ($is_active == 1) {
        $query = "UPDATE 'comments' SET 'cm_is_active' = ? WHERE
            'cm_id' = ? " ;
        if ($this->db->query($query,array($is_active,$id))) {
            return true;
        } else {
            return false;
        }
    } else {
        $query = "DELETE FROM 'comments' WHERE 'cm_id' = ?   " ;
        if ($this->db->query($query,array($id))) {
            return true;
        } else {
            return false;
        }
    }
}
```

The following function is called by the admin controller function when an admin is moderating discussions. If a discussion is deemed to be fine, then discussions.ds_is_active is updated and set to 1. However, if it is not fine, then the discussion is deleted from the discussions table. Any comments belonging to that discussion are also deleted from the comments table:

```
function update_discussions($is_active, $id) {
    if ($is_active == 1) {
```

```
            $query = "UPDATE 'discussions' SET 'ds_is_active' = ?
              WHERE 'ds_id' = ? " ;
            if ($this->db->query($query, array($is_active,$id))) {
                return true;
            } else {
                return false;
            }
        } else {
            $query = "DELETE FROM 'discussions' WHERE 'ds_id' = ?
              " ;
            if ($this->db->query($query,array($id))) {
                $query = "DELETE FROM 'comments' WHERE 'ds_id' = ?
                  " ;
                if ($this->db->query($query,array($id))) {
                    return true;
                }
            } else {
                return false;
            }
        }
    }
}
```

Creating views

There are six view files in this application, and these are as follows:

- `discussions/view.php`: This displays all active discussions

- `discussions/new.php`: This displays a form to the user, allowing them to create a discussion

- `comments/view.php`: This displays all active comments within a discussion

- `nav/top_nav.php`: This contains the top navigation links

- `admin/login.php`: This displays a login form for the user; don't forget to add the `signin.css` script, which you can find later in this chapter

- `common/login_header.php`: The `views/admin/login.php` view requires different resources from the rest of the application, which is supported by this header

Discussions

The `discussions/view.php` view file displays a list of all active discussions as well as sorting options.

Create the `/path/to/codeigniter/views/discussions/view.php` file and add the following code to it:

```
SORT: <?php echo anchor('discussions/index/sort/age/' . (($dir
  == 'ASC') ? 'DESC' : 'ASC'),'Newest '
            . (($dir == 'ASC') ? 'DESC' : 'ASC'));?>


<table class="table table-hover">
  <thead>
    <tr>
      <th><?php echo $this->lang->line('discussions_title') ;
        ?></th>
    </tr>
  </thead>
  <tbody>

    <?php foreach ($query->result() as $result) : ?>
      <tr>
        <td>
          <?php echo anchor('comments/index/'.$result-
            >ds_id,$result->ds_title) . ' '
              . $this->lang->line('comments_created_by') .
                $result->usr_name; ?>

          <?php echo anchor('discussions/flag/'.$result-
            >ds_id,
            $this->lang->line('discussion_flag')) ; ?>
          <br />
          <?php echo $result->ds_body ; ?>
        </td>
      </tr>
    <?php endforeach ; ?>

  </tbody>
</table>
```

Take a look at the first few lines. We open with a CodeIgniter `anchor()` statement. Let's take a closer look at the code for the link:

```
SORT: <?php echo anchor('discussions/index/sort/age/' . (($dir ==
  'ASC') ? 'DESC' : 'ASC'),'Newest ' . (($dir == 'ASC') ? 'DESC' :
  'ASC'));?>
```

Let's break this down into smaller sections:

- `anchor('discussions/index/age/sort/' .`: This sets the link for the `discussions` controller, `index()` function, and sorting by age (the created date—`discussions.ds_created_at`), but what is the direction? Well…

- `(($dir == 'ASC') ? 'DESC' : 'ASC'),`: The value of `$dir` comes from the `index()` function of the `discussions` controller. It is the current direction of the sort. We then use a PHP ternary operator to switch between the directions. It's a bit like an if/else statement but is more compact. It works like this: *if a variable is equal (or not equal) to a variable, then execute A, otherwise execute B.* For example, as an if/else statement, the code would be as follows:

```
if ($dir == 'ASC') {
  return 'DESC';
} else {
  return 'ASC';
}
```

  So, the second part of the link will flip-flop between ASC and DESC depending on the value held in `$dir`. Now, let's look at the rest.

- `'Newest ' . (($dir == 'ASC') ? 'DESC' : 'ASC'));?>`: This is the text that users will see as their link. You can see that we again make use of the ternary operator to display the text, flipping between Newest ASC and Newest DESC.

The rest of the view is fairly undramatic; all we do is loop over the database result from the discussions' `index()` function, displaying all active discussions as we go.

Comments

The comments view displays a list of all valid comments to the user for a selected discussion.

Create the `/path/to/codeigniter/application/views/comments/view.php` file and add the following code to it:

```
<!-- Discussion - initial comment -->
<?php foreach ($discussion_query->result() as $discussion_result)
  : ?>
  <h2>
      <?php echo $discussion_result->ds_title; ?><br />
```

```
          <small><?php echo $this->lang->line('comments_created_by') .
             $discussion_result->usr_name . $this->lang-
             >line('comments_created_at') . $discussion_result-
             >ds_created_at; ?></small>
      </h2>
      <p class="lead"><?php echo $discussion_result->ds_body; ?></p>
<?php endforeach ; ?>

<!-- Comment - list of comments -->
<?php foreach ($comment_query->result() as $comment_result) : ?>
   <li class="media">
     <a class="pull-left" href="#">
        <img class="media-object" src="<?php echo base_url() ;
           ?>img/profile.svg" />
     </a>
     <div class="media-body">
        <h4 class="media-heading"><?php echo $comment_result-
           >usr_name . anchor('comments/flag/'.$comment_result->ds_id
           . '/' . $comment_result->cm_id,$this->lang-
           >line('comments_flag')) ; ?></h4>
        <?php echo $comment_result->cm_body ; ?>
     </div>
   </li>
<?php endforeach ; ?>

<!-- Form - begin form section -->
<br /><br />
<p class="lead"><?php echo $this->lang-
   >line('comments_form_instruction');?></p>

<?php echo validation_errors(); ?>
<?php echo form_open('comments/index','role="form"') ; ?>
    <div class="form-group col-md-5">
      <label for="comment_name"><?php echo $this->lang-
         >line('comments_comment_name');?></label>
      <input type="text" name="comment_name" class="form-control"
         id="comment_name" value="<?php echo
         set_value('comment_name'); ?>">
    </div>
    <div class="form-group col-md-5">
      <label for="comment_email"><?php echo $this->lang-
         >line('comments_comment_email');?></label>
      <input type="email" name="comment_email" class="form-
         control" id="comment_email" value="<?php echo
         set_value('comment_email'); ?>">
```

```
    </div>
    <div class="form-group  col-md-10">
      <label for="comment_body"><?php echo $this->lang-
        >line('comments_comment_body');?></label>
      <textarea class="form-control" rows="3" name="comment_body"
        id="comment_body"><?php echo set_value('comment_body');
        ?></textarea>
    </div>
    <div class="form-group  col-md-11">
      <button type="submit" class="btn btn-success"><?php echo
        $this->lang->line('common_form_elements_go');?></button>
    </div>
  <?php echo form_hidden('ds_id',$ds_id) ; ?>
<?php echo form_close() ; ?>
```

Note the following line in the form:

```
<button type="submit" class="btn btn-success"><?php echo $this-
  >lang->line('common_form_elements_go');?></button>
```

You will see that we use a line from the `lang` file that is not in the code example;
this is because the `common_form_elements_go` line is to be found in *Chapter 1,
Introduction and Shared Project Resources*.

New discussion

The New Discussion view displays a form to the user and any validation error
messages that might need to be conveyed.

Create the `/path/to/codeigniter/application/views/discussions/new.php`
file and add the following code to it:

```
<!-- Form - begin form section -->
<br /><br />
<p class="lead"><?php echo $this->lang->line('discussion_form_
instruction');?></p>

<?php echo validation_errors(); ?>
<?php echo form_open('discussions/create','role="form"') ; ?>
    <div class="form-group col-md-5">
      <label for="usr_name"><?php echo $this->lang-
        >line('discussion_usr_name');?></label>
```

```
        <input type="text" name="usr_name" class="form-control"
          id="usr_name" value="<?php echo set_value('usr_name');
          ?>">
    </div>
    <div class="form-group col-md-5">
      <label for="usr_email"><?php echo $this->lang-
        >line('discussion_usr_email');?></label>
      <input type="email" name="usr_email" class="form-control"
        id="usr_email" value="<?php echo set_value('usr_email');
        ?>">
    </div>
    <div class="form-group col-md-10">
      <label for="ds_title"><?php echo $this->lang-
        >line('discussion_ds_title');?></label>
      <input type="text" name="ds_title" class="form-control"
        id="ds_title" value="<?php echo set_value('ds_title');
        ?>">
    </div>
    <div class="form-group  col-md-10">
      <label for="ds_body"><?php echo $this->lang-
        >line('discussion_ds_body');?></label>
      <textarea class="form-control" rows="3" name="ds_body"
        id="ds_body"><?php echo set_value('ds_body');
        ?></textarea>
    </div>
    <div class="form-group  col-md-11">
      <button type="submit" class="btn btn-success"><?php echo
        $this->lang->line('common_form_elements_go');?></button>
    </div>
  <?php echo form_close() ; ?>
```

Note the following line in the form:

```
<button type="submit" class="btn btn-success"><?php echo $this-
  >lang->line('common_form_elements_go');?></button>
```

You will see that we use a line from the `lang` file that is not in the code example; this is because the `common_form_elements_go` line is to be found in *Chapter 1, Introduction and Shared Project Resources*.

We provide options to the user to create a new discussion. We display form elements for them to enter their username, e-mail, discussion title, and the text of their discussion.

The form is submitted to the `create()` function of the `discussion` controller, where is it validated with any validation errors being displayed.

The top_nav file

Every project in this book has its own navigation file, and this is no exception. The top_nav file is standard Bootstrap navigation code; however, there are a few Codeigniter anchor() functions that provide the URL links and text.

Create the /path/to/codeigniter/application/views/common/top_nav.php file and add the following code to it:

```
<!-- Fixed navbar -->
<div class="navbar navbar-inverse navbar-fixed-top"
  role="navigation">
  <div class="container">
    <div class="navbar-header">
      <button type="button" class="navbar-toggle" data-
        toggle="collapse" data-target=".navbar-collapse">
        <span class="sr-only">Toggle navigation</span>
        <span class="icon-bar"></span>
        <span class="icon-bar"></span>
        <span class="icon-bar"></span>
      </button>
      <a class="navbar-brand" href="#"><?php echo $this->lang-
        >line('system_system_name'); ?></a>
    </div>
    <div class="navbar-collapse collapse">
      <ul class="nav navbar-nav">
        <li <?php if ($this->uri->segment(1) == '') {echo
          'class="active"';} ; ?>><?php echo anchor('/',
          $this->lang->line('top_nav_view_discussions')) ;
          ?></li>
        <li <?php if ($this->uri->segment(1) == 'discussions')
          {echo 'class="active"';} ; ?>><?php echo
          anchor('discussions/create', $this->lang-
          >line('top_nav_new_discussion')) ; ?></li>
      </ul>

      <ul class="nav navbar-nav navbar-right">
        <li><?php echo anchor('admin/login', $this->lang-
          >line('top_nav_login')) ; ?></li>
      </ul>
    </div><!--/.nav-collapse -->
  </div>
</div>

<div class="container theme-showcase" role="main">
```

The login view

The login view displays the form and any errors to the admin user when he/she wants to log in.

Create the `/path/to/codeigniter/application/views/admin/login.php` file and add the following code to it:

```php
<?php if (isset($login_fail)) : ?>
  <div class="alert alert-danger"><?php echo $this->lang-
    >line('admin_login_error') ; ?></div>
<?php endif ; ?>
<?php echo validation_errors(); ?>

<div class="container">
  <?php echo form_open('admin/login', 'class="form-signin"
    role="form"') ; ?>
    <h2 class="form-signin-heading"><?php echo $this->lang-
      >line('admin_login_header') ; ?></h2>
    <input type="email" name="usr_email" class="form-control"
      placeholder="<?php echo $this->lang-
      >line('admin_login_email') ; ?>" required autofocus>
    <input type="password" name="usr_password" class="form-
      control" placeholder="<?php echo $this->lang-
      >line('admin_login_password') ; ?>" required>
    <button class="btn btn-lg btn-primary btn-block"
      type="submit"><?php echo $this->lang-
      >line('admin_login_signin') ; ?></button>
  <?php echo form_close() ; ?>
</div>
```

There's not too much to get into here—everything is as you would expect. We display a form to the user, giving them text fields to enter their e-mail address and password, and errors are displayed above the form.

The form is submitted to the `login()` function of the `admin` controller, which will handle the technical process of logging the user in. If the login is successful, the user is directed to the `dashboard()` function of the `admin` controller.

The login_header file

The `admin/login.php` file requires different files and resources from the rest of the discussion forum application. For this reason, we're going to create a header file that's specific to the login page.

Create the `/path/to/codeigniter/application/common/login_header.php` file and add the following code to it:

```
<!DOCTYPE html>
<html lang="en">
  <head>
    <meta charset="utf-8">
    <meta http-equiv="X-UA-Compatible" content="IE=edge">
    <meta name="viewport" content="width=device-width, initial-
      scale=1">
    <meta name="description" content="">
    <meta name="author" content="">
    <link rel="shortcut icon" href="<?php echo
      base_url('bootstrap/ico/favicon.ico'); ?>">

    <title><?php echo $this->lang->line('system_system_name');
      ?></title>

    <!-- Bootstrap core CSS -->
    <link href="<?php echo base_url
      ('bootstrap/css/bootstrap.min.css'); ?>" rel="stylesheet">
    <!-- Bootstrap theme -->
    <link href="<?php echo base_url('bootstrap/css/bootstrap-
      theme.min.css'); ?>" rel="stylesheet">

    <!-- Custom styles for this template -->
    <link href="<?php echo base_url
      ('bootstrap/css/signin.css');?>" rel="stylesheet">


    <!-- Just for debugging purposes. Don't actually copy this
      line! -->
    <!--[if lt IE 9]><script src="../../assets/js/ie8-responsive-
      file-warning.js"></script><![endif]-->

    <!-- HTML5 shim and Respond.js IE8 support of HTML5 elements
      and media queries -->
    <!--[if lt IE 9]>
```

```
    <script src="https://oss.maxcdn.com/libs/html5shiv/
        3.7.0/html5shiv.js"></script>
    <script src="https://oss.maxcdn.com/libs/respond.js/
        1.4.2/respond.min.js"></script>
  <![endif]-->
</head>

<body>
```

Dashboard

The dashboard view is able to display to the admin user (in this case, a moderator) all discussion forums and comments that are awaiting moderation. These are displayed in a table in a list format, each item having two options for the moderator: Allow and Disallow.

Clicking on Allow will set the active status of the discussion (discussions.ds_is_active) or comment (comments.cm_is_active) to 1, making them appear once more for general users to see. However, Disallow will delete them from the database. If it is a discussion forum being disallowed, then all comments associated with that discussion will also be deleted.

Create the /path/to/codeigniter/application/views/admin/dashboard.php file and add the following code to it:

```
<h1 id="tables" class="page-header">Dashboard</h1>

<table class="table">
    <thead>
        <tr>
          <th>#</th>
          <th>Name</th>
          <th>Email</th>
          <td>Actions</td>
        </tr>
    </thead>
    <tbody>
        <?php if ($discussion_query->num_rows() > 0) : ?>
            <?php foreach ($discussion_query->result() as $row) :
              ?>
              <tr>
                <td><?php echo $row->ds_id ; ?></td>
                <td><?php echo $row->usr_name ; ?></td>
```

```
            <td><?php echo $row->usr_email ; ?></td>
            <td><?php echo anchor('admin/update_item/
                ds/allow/'.
                $row->ds_id,$this->lang->line('
                admin_dash_allow')) .
                ' ' . anchor('admin/update_item/ds/disallow/'.
                $row->ds_id,$this->lang->line('
                admin_dash_disallow')) ; ?>
            </td>
        </tr>
        <tr>
            <td colspan="3"><?php echo $row->ds_title;
                ?></td>
            <td></td>
        </tr>
        <tr>
            <td colspan="3"><?php echo $row->ds_body;
                ?></td>
            <td></td>
        </tr>
        <?php endforeach ; ?>
    <?php else : ?>
        <tr>
            <td colspan="4">No naughty forums here, horay!</td>
        </tr>
    <?php endif; ?>
    </tbody>
</table>

<table class="table">
    <thead>
        <tr>
            <th>#</th>
            <th>Name</th>
            <th>Email</th>
            <td>Actions</td>
        </tr>
    </thead>
    <tbody>
        <?php if ($comment_query->num_rows() > 0) : ?>
            <?php foreach ($comment_query->result() as $row) : ?>
                <tr>
                    <td><?php echo $row->cm_id ; ?></td>
```

```
            <td><?php echo $row->usr_name ; ?></td>
            <td><?php echo $row->usr_email ; ?></td>
            <td><?php echo anchor('admin/update_item/
                cm/allow/'.
                $row->cm_id,$this->lang->line('
                  admin_dash_allow')) .
                ' ' . anchor('admin/update_item/cm/disallow/'.
                $row->cm_id,$this->lang->line('
                  admin_dash_disallow')) ; ?>
            </td>
          </tr>
          <tr>
            <td colspan="3"><?php echo $row->cm_body;
               ?></td>
            <td></td>
          </tr>
        <?php endforeach ; ?>
    <?php else : ?>
          <tr>
            <td colspan="4">No naughty comments here,
               horay!</td>
          </tr>
    <?php endif; ?>
    </tbody>
</table>
```

The signin.css file

The signin.css file is required to display the login form correctly; this is the same signin.css file as the one that is available from the Twitter Bootstrap resource.

Create the /path/to/codeigniter/bootstrap/css/signin.css file and add the following code to it:

```
body {
  padding-top: 40px;
  padding-bottom: 40px;
  background-color: #eee;
}

.form-signin {
  max-width: 330px;
  padding: 15px;
```

```
  margin: 0 auto;
}
.form-signin .form-signin-heading,
.form-signin .checkbox {
  margin-bottom: 10px;
}
.form-signin .checkbox {
  font-weight: normal;
}
.form-signin .form-control {
  position: relative;
  height: auto;
  -webkit-box-sizing: border-box;
     -moz-box-sizing: border-box;
          box-sizing: border-box;
  padding: 10px;
  font-size: 16px;
}
.form-signin .form-control:focus {
  z-index: 2;
}
.form-signin input[type="email"] {
  margin-bottom: -1px;
  border-bottom-right-radius: 0;
  border-bottom-left-radius: 0;
}
.form-signin input[type="password"] {
  margin-bottom: 10px;
  border-top-left-radius: 0;
  border-top-right-radius: 0;
}
```

Creating the controllers

We're going to create three controllers for this application. These are as follows:

- `discussions.php`: This fetches discussions from the `discussions` table in the database and allows the user to create a new discussion

- `comments.php`: This fetches comments from the `comments` table in the database and allows the user to join a discussion by adding a comment to a discussion forum

- `admin.php`: This contains basic admin functions, login functionalities, and moderation options

The discussions controller

The `discussions.php` controller is responsible for the display of all valid discussions, processing the creation of new discussions and flagging any discussion for moderation. The `discussions` controller contains three functions, and these are as follows:

- `index()`: This displays all valid discussions
- `create()`: This creates a new discussion, handling any form validation
- `flag()`: This processes a discussion for moderation by calling the `flag()` function of `discussions_model.php`, setting `discussions.ds_is_active` to `0`

Create the `/path/to/codeigniter/application/controllers/discussions.php` file and add the following code to it:

```php
<?php if (!defined('BASEPATH')) exit('No direct script access
allowed');

class Discussions extends MY_Controller {
    function __construct() {
        parent::__construct();
        $this->load->helper('string');
        $this->load->library('encrypt');
        $this->load->model('Discussions_model');
        $this->load->library('form_validation');
        $this->form_validation->set_error_delimiters('<div
          class="alert alert-danger">', '</div>');
    }

    public function index() {
        if ($this->uri->segment(3)) {
            $filter = $this->uri->segment(4);
            $direction = $this->uri->segment(5);
            $page_data['dir'] = $this->uri->segment(5);
        } else {
            $filter = null;
            $direction = null;
            $page_data['dir'] = 'ASC';
        }

        $page_data['query'] = $this->Discussions_model
          ->fetch_discussions($filter,$direction);
```

```
        $this->load->view('common/header');
        $this->load->view('nav/top_nav');
        $this->load->view('discussions/view', $page_data);
        $this->load->view('common/footer');
    }


    public function create() {
    public function create() {
        $this->form_validation->set_rules('usr_name', $this->lang-
            >line('discussion_usr_name'),
            'required|min_length[1]|max_length[255]');
        $this->form_validation->set_rules('usr_email', $this-
            >lang->line('discussion_usr_email'),
            'required|min_length[1]|max_length[255]');
        $this->form_validation->set_rules('ds_title', $this->lang-
            >line('discussion_ds_title'),
            'required|min_length[1]|max_length[255]');
        $this->form_validation->set_rules('ds_body', $this->lang-
            >line('discussion_ds_body'),
            'required|min_length[1]|max_length[5000]');

        if ($this->form_validation->run() == FALSE) {
            $this->load->view('common/header');
            $this->load->view('nav/top_nav');
            $this->load->view('discussions/new');
            $this->load->view('common/footer');
        } else {
            $data = array('usr_name' => $this->input-
                >post('usr_name'),
                        'usr_email' => $this->input-
                            >post('usr_email'),
                        'ds_title' => $this->input-
                            >post('ds_title'),
                        'ds_body' =>  $this->input-
                            >post('ds_body')
                        );

            if ($ds_id = $this->Discussions_model->create($data)) {
                redirect('comments/index/'.$ds_id);
            } else {
                // error
                // load view and flash sess error
            }
        }
    }
}
```

```
    public function flag() {
        $ds_id = $this->uri->segment(3);
        if ($this->Discussions_model->flag($ds_id)) {
            redirect('discussions/');
        } else {
            // error
            // load view and flash sess error
        }
    }
}
```

Taking each function one by one, we'll begin with index(). The index() function is responsible for displaying all active discussions to the user.

The code begins by checking to see whether there is a value in the third uri segment or not.

If there is a value present, then this indicates that the user has pressed the sort's ascending or descending link; we'll discusses this in a moment but, for now, we'll assume that there is no value in the third segment.

As there is no value present, we set $filter and $direction to NULL, but we set $page_data['dir'] to ASC (short for ascending). This is set because, initially, the discussion forums are displayed in descending order of their created date; however, the sorting link needs to be written in the opposite direction from what is currently being displayed. Setting $page_data['dir'] to ASC (ascending) will enable the URL in the sort link to be ready for us should we need to click it.

We then ask the fetch_discussions() function of discussions_model.php to get all active discussions, passing to it two variables as arguments: $filter and $direction. These are set to null by default. The fetch_discussions() function will know not to apply these filters.

The direction of the sort link will flip-flop between ascending and descending—always being the opposite of what is currently displayed. This flip-flopping is done in the view file (this might not be the best place for it if you're being strict, but I thought that this was a location that you would find obvious, so there you go).

Check out the code and explanation for the discussions/view.php view file earlier in this chapter for a full explanation of how the flip-flopping functions.

Let's now look at the `create()` function; we initially set the validation rules and check to see whether the form has been submitted (or has been submitted with errors). Assuming that it has been submitted without errors, we save the post data in the `$data` array:

```
$data = array('usr_name' => $this->input->post('usr_name'),
              'usr_email' => $this->input->post('usr_email'),
              'ds_title' => $this->input->post('ds_title'),
              'ds_body' =>  $this->input->post('ds_body'));
```

Once all the form elements are packaged into the `$data` array, we send it off to the `create()` function of `discussions_model` to write to the database.

If the insert operation was successful, the model will return the primary key of the new discussion but will return `false` if there was an error.

We test the return value of the insert operation. If the insert was successful, we redirect the user to the `index()` function of the `comments` controller, passing to it the `$ds_id` value that was returned by the model. The user can then see their discussion, which is ready to be commented on:

```
if ($ds_id = $this->Discussions_model->create($data)) {
    redirect('comments/index/'.$ds_id);
} else {
    ...
```

If there was an error, then we have no new primary key, so we can't redirect the user. This has been left blank in this project; you can implement your own policy for this behavior; perhaps you can send them an e-mail informing them about this or write an error to the screen.

The comments controller

The `comments` controller manages all matters related to the flagging (for moderation) and creation of comments on discussions from users. The `comments` controller has two functions, and these are as follows:

- `index()`: This displays all comments for a specific discussion forum and handles the submission—that is, the validation of a user's comment.

- `flag()`: This allows a user to flag a comment for moderation by the admin. The `comments.cm_is_active` value in the database is set to `0` for the specific comment.

Create the `/path/to/codeigniter/application/controllers/comments.php` file and add the following code to it:

```php
<?php if (!defined('BASEPATH')) exit('No direct script access
  allowed');

class Comments extends MY_Controller {
    function __construct() {
        parent::__construct();
        $this->load->helper('string');
        $this->load->library('form_validation');
        $this->load->model('Discussions_model');
        $this->load->model('Comments_model');
        $this->form_validation->set_error_delimiters('<div
          class="alert alert-danger">', '</div>');
    }

    public function index() {
        if ($this->input->post()) {
            $ds_id = $this->input->post('ds_id');
        } else {
            $ds_id = $this->uri->segment(3);
        }

        $page_data['discussion_query'] = $this->Discussions_model-
          >fetch_discussion($ds_id);
        $page_data['comment_query'] = $this->Comments_model-
          >fetch_comments($ds_id);
        $page_data['ds_id'] = $ds_id;

        $this->form_validation->set_rules('ds_id', $this->lang-
          >line('comments_comment_hidden_id'),
          'required|min_length[1]|max_length[11]');
        $this->form_validation->set_rules('comment_name', $this-
          >lang->line('comments_comment_name'),
          'required|min_length[1]|max_length[25]');
        $this->form_validation->set_rules('comment_email', $this-
          >lang->line('comments_comment_email'),
          'required|min_length[1]|max_length[255]');
        $this->form_validation->set_rules('comment_body', $this-
          >lang->line('comments_comment_body'),
          'required|min_length[1]|max_length[5000]');
```

```
            if ($this->form_validation->run() == FALSE) {
                $this->load->view('common/header');
                $this->load->view('nav/top_nav');
                $this->load->view('comments/view', $page_data);
                $this->load->view('common/footer');
            } else {
                $data = array('cm_body' => $this->input-
                    >post('comment_body'),
                              'usr_email' => $this->input-
                                >post('comment_email'),
                              'usr_name' => $this->input-
                                >post('comment_name'),
                              'ds_id' =>  $this->input->post('ds_id')
                              );

                if ($this->Comments_model->new_comment($data)) {
                    redirect('comments/index/'.$ds_id);
                } else {
                    // error
                    // load view and flash sess error
                }
            }
        }

    public function flag() {
        $cm_id = $this->uri->segment(4);
        if ($this->Comments_model->flag($cm_id)) {
            redirect('comments/index/'.$this->uri->segment(3));
        } else {
            // error
            // load view and flash sess error
        }
    }
}
```

Let's start with the index() function. The index() function will begin by displaying all comments for a specific discussion. To do this, it needs to know what discussion to look at. So, let's go a step back. The discussions controller will display a list of active discussions.

The following is a section of code from discussions/view.php that we looked at in greater detail earlier. This code will loop through a set of database results, displaying each active discussion in table rows.

Check out the line highlighted in bold:

```
<!-- Comment - list of comments -->
<?php foreach ($comment_query->result() as $comment_result) : ?>
  <li class="media">
    <a class="pull-left" href="#">
      <img class="media-object" src="<?php echo base_url() ;
        ?>img/profile.svg" />
    </a>
    <div class="media-body">
      <h4 class="media-heading"><?php echo $comment_result->
      usr_name . anchor('comments/flag/'.$comment_result->ds_id .
        '/' . $comment_result->cm_id,$this->lang-
        >line('comments_flag')) ; ?></h4>
      <?php echo $comment_result->cm_body ; ?>
    </div>
  </li>
<?php endforeach ; ?>
```

This line displays the URL that enables the user to view the discussion and any comments associated with it by clicking on a discussion title link, which looks like the following:

```
comments/index/id-of-discussion
```

We can pass id-of-discussion as the third parameter of the link to the index() function of the comments controller. This is where we pick up the story. The index() function of the comments controller checks whether there is a third uri segment (if not, then it is possible that the form to create a comment has been submitted and would not exist in the uri segment).

It will grab the ID of the discussion and store it as the $ds_id variable:

```
if ($this->input->post()) {
    $ds_id = $this->input->post('ds_id');
} else {
    $ds_id = $this->uri->segment(3);
}
```

We then define some validation rules for CodeIgniter to apply to the Add A Comment form at the bottom of the comments/view.php file.

The comments/view.php file contains not only a foreach() loop to display the current comments on the selected discussion, but also a form with a name and e-mail text field and a body text area. This is where the user can enter their name, e-mail, and comment text and then submit the comment.

There is also a hidden field, named ds_id, that contains the primary key of the selected discussion. We need it in the form as a hidden element as, when the form is submitted, the third uri segment will disappear. Having the discussion ID as a hidden form element will allow index() to maintain a relationship between the comment and the discussion when the new comment form is submitted.

Assuming that there were no errors with the form and it is submitted without the need to report anything requiring the user's attention, the index() function attempts to write the comment to the comments table in the database.

Before we do that, however, we need to package all our data into an array that will be passed to Comments_model. Take a look at the following code:

```
$data = array('cm_body' => $this->input->post('comment_body'),
              'usr_email' => $this->input->post('comment_email'),
              'usr_name' => $this->input->post('comment_name'),
              'ds_id' =>  $this->input->post('ds_id')
    );
```

Here, you can see that we've got all the post elements including ds_id (highlighted in bold). This is now ready to be sent to the new_comment() model function for insertion into the database:

```
if ($this->Comments_model->new_comment($data)) {
    redirect('comments/index/'.$ds_id);
} else {
    // error
    // load view and flash sess error
}
```

The new_comment() model function will return true on a successful insertion and false otherwise. If it was successful, then we redirect the user to the comments controller's index() function and pass $ds_id as the third parameter where the index() function will begin, displaying all active comments associated with the selected discussion.

Now, let's move on to the flag() function. The flag() function will enable the user to indicate that a comment requires moderation by an admin.

Stepping back to the discussions controller, the discussions controller will display a list of active discussions.

The following is a section of code from `comments/view.php` that we looked at in greater detail earlier. This code will loop through a set of database results, displaying each active comment in a table of rows:

```
<!-- Comment - list of comments -->
<?php foreach ($comment_query->result() as $comment_result) : ?>
  <li class="media">
    <a class="pull-left" href="#">
      <img class="media-object" src="<?php echo base_url() ;
        ?>img/profile.svg" />
    </a>
    <div class="media-body">
      <h4 class="media-heading"><?php echo $comment_result->
        usr_name . anchor('comments/flag/'.$comment_result->ds_id
        . '/' . $comment_result->cm_id,$this->lang-
        >line('comments_flag')) ; ?></h4>
      <?php echo $comment_result->cm_body ; ?>
    </div>
  </li>
<?php endforeach ; ?>
```

Take a look at the line highlighted in bold:

```
anchor('comments/flag/'.$comment_result->ds_id . '/' .
  $comment_result->cm_id,$this->lang->line('comments_flag'))
```

This line contains a CodeIgniter `anchor()` statement with the `comments/flag/id-of-comment` URL. It is this line of code that creates the **flag** link next to each comment.

Look at the third and fourth parameters. The third parameter is the discussion ID (`discussions.ds_id`) and the fourth is the comment ID (`comments.cm_id`); both are used in the `flag()` function of `comments_model`. The code for this looks as follows:

```
public function flag() {
    $cm_id = $this->uri->segment(4);
    if ($this->Comments_model->flag($cm_id)) {
        redirect('comments/index/'.$this->uri->segment(3));
    } else {
        // error
        // load view and flash sess error
    }
}
```

If the insert operation returns `true`, then we redirect the user to the `comments` controller's `index()` function along with the discussion forum ID.

The admin controller

The `admin` controller contains all the functions required to run the moderation of comments and discussions and to log users in. It contains the following functions:

- `index()`: Every controller needs an index function and this is it. The `index()` function will check whether a user is logged in and redirect them elsewhere if not.

- `login()`: The `login()` function handles the process of logging a user into the system.

- `dashboard()`: This is responsible for displaying all comments and discussions that require moderation.

- `update_item()`: This is responsible for applying the decision of the moderator, whether to approve or delete a comment or discussion.

Create the `/path/to/codeigniter/application/controllers/admin.php` file and add the following code to it:

```php
<?php if (!defined('BASEPATH')) exit('No direct script access
  allowed');

class Admin extends MY_Controller {
    function __construct() {
        parent::__construct();
        $this->load->helper('string');
        $this->load->library('form_validation');
        $this->load->model('Admin_model');
        $this->form_validation->set_error_delimiters('<div
          class="alert alert-danger">', '</div>');
    }

    public function index() {
        if ($this->session->userdata('logged_in') == FALSE) {
            redirect('admin/login');
        }

        redirect('admin/dashboard');
    }

    public function login() {
        $this->form_validation->set_rules('usr_email', $this-
          >lang->line('admin_login_email'),
          'required|min_length[1]|max_length[255]');
```

```
$this->form_validation->set_rules('usr_password', $this-
   >lang->line('admin_login_password'),
   'required|min_length[1]|max_length[25]');

if ($this->form_validation->run() == FALSE) {
    $this->load->view('common/login_header');
    $this->load->view('nav/top_nav');
    $this->load->view('admin/login');
    $this->load->view('common/footer');
} else {
    $usr_email = $this->input->post('usr_email');
    $usr_password = $this->input->post('usr_password');

    $query = $this->Admin_model->
      does_user_exist($usr_email);

    if ($query->num_rows() == 1) { // One matching row
       found
         foreach ($query->result() as $row) {
             // Call Encrypt library
             $this->load->library('encrypt');

             // Generate hash from a their password
             $hash = $this->encrypt->sha1($usr_password);

             // Compare the generated hash with that in the
                database
             if ($hash != $row->usr_hash) {
                 // Didn't match so send back to login
                 $page_data['login_fail'] = true;
                 $this->load->view('common/login_header');
                 $this->load->view('nav/top_nav');
                 $this->load-
                    >view('admin/login',$page_data);
                 $this->load->view('common/footer');
             } else {
                 $data = array(
                     'usr_id' => $row->usr_id,
                     'usr_email' => $row->usr_email,
                     'logged_in' => TRUE
                 );

                 // Save data to session
```

```
                               $this->session->set_userdata($data);
                               redirect('admin/dashboard');
                        }
                  }
              }
          }
      }

      public function dashboard() {
          if ($this->session->userdata('logged_in') == FALSE) {
              redirect('admin/login');
          }

          $page_data['comment_query'] = $this->Admin_model-
              >dashboard_fetch_comments();
          $page_data['discussion_query'] = $this->Admin_model-
              >dashboard_fetch_discussions();

          $this->load->view('common/header');
          $this->load->view('nav/top_nav');
          $this->load->view('admin/dashboard',$page_data);
          $this->load->view('common/footer');
      }

      public function update_item() {
          if ($this->session->userdata('logged_in') == FALSE) {
              redirect('admin/login');
          }

          if ($this->uri->segment(4) == 'allow') {
              $is_active = 1;
          } else {
              $is_active = 0;
          }

          if ($this->uri->segment(3) == 'ds') {
              $result = $this->Admin_model->update_discussions
                  ($is_active, $this->uri->segment(5));
          } else {
              $result = $this->Admin_model->update_comments
                  ($is_active, $this->uri->segment(5));
          }

          redirect('admin');
      }
  }
```

Let's tackle this by first looking at the index() function. As the admin controller is only to be used by those logged in, the index() function will check to see whether an item called logged_in exists in the session. If logged_in is equal to FALSE, then it means that the user is not logged in, so they are redirected to the login() function.

This is very simple and we won't spend more time on it; however, a more complicated function is login(). The login() function is responsible for—as the name suggests—managing the login process for the admin moderator.

The first thing login() does is define form validation rules for the usr_email and usr_pwd form elements. These will govern how the data submitted by the user in the admin/login.php view file is validated.

We immediately test to see whether the form has been submitted:

```
if ($this->form_validation->run() == FALSE) {
    . . .
```

If the form hasn't been submitted, we'll load the view files to display the login form and wait for a response from the user.

However, if it has been submitted, then the form is validated against the validation criteria; if it passes validation, we try to work out whether the user exists in the database currently:

```
$query = $this->Admin_model->does_user_exist($usr_email);
    if ($query->num_rows() == 1) {
        . . .
```

If exactly one matching e-mail address has been found, then we will try to work out whether the users' password is correct. We load the CodeIgniter library using $this->load->library('encrypt') and generate a hash from the password that the user supplied in the login form:

```
$hash = $this->encrypt->sha1($usr_password);
```

We then compare that hash with the hash stored in the database belonging to the user:

```
if ($hash != $row->usr_hash) {
    . . .
```

If it does not match, then we load the login form and display an error message. However, if it does match, then the user must have typed the correct password; so we log them in by creating a CodeIgniter session for them:

```
$data = array(
    'usr_id' => $row->usr_id,
    'usr_email' => $row->usr_email,
    'logged_in' => TRUE
);

// Save data to session
$this->session->set_userdata($data);
redirect('admin/dashboard');
```

The user is then redirected to the dashboard. The dashboard will display any comments and discussions that are required for moderation.

Creating the language file

As with all the projects in this book, we're making use of the language file to serve text to users. This way, you can enable multiple region/multiple language support.

Create the /path/to/codeigniter/application/language/english/en_admin_lang.php file and add the following code to it:

```
<?php if (!defined('BASEPATH')) exit('No direct script access allowed');

// General
$lang['system_system_name'] = "Forum";

// Top Nav
$lang['top_nav_view_discussions'] = "Home";
$lang['top_nav_new_discussion'] = "New Discussion";
$lang['top_nav_login'] = "Login";

// Discussions
$lang['discussions_title'] = "Discussions";
$lang['discussions_num_comments'] = 'Comments';

// Comments
$lang['comments_form_instruction'] = "Join in, add your comment below.";
```

```
$lang['comments_flag'] = ' [Flag]';
$lang['comments_created_by'] = 'Created by ';
$lang['comments_created_at'] = ' at ';
$lang['comments_comment_name'] = 'Your name';
$lang['comments_comment_email'] = 'Your email';
$lang['comments_comment_body'] = 'Comment';


// Discussions
$lang['discussion_form_instruction'] = "Create your own discussion,
fill in the form below";
$lang['discussion_flag'] = ' [Flag]';
$lang['discussion_usr_name'] = 'Your name';
$lang['discussion_usr_email'] = 'Your email';
$lang['discussion_ds_title'] = 'Discussion title';
$lang['discussion_ds_body'] = 'Your question, point etc';


// Admin - login
$lang['admin_login_header'] = "Please sign in";
$lang['admin_login_email'] = "Email";
$lang['admin_login_password'] = "Password";
$lang['admin_login_signin'] = "Signin...";
$lang['admin_login_error'] = "Whoops!  Something went wrong - have
another go!";
$lang['admin_dash_allow'] = "Allow";
$lang['admin_dash_disallow'] = "Disallow";
```

Putting it all together

Now that we've created each file and resource necessary for the app, let's run through a few scenarios so that we can get a good idea of how it all works together.

A user creates a discussion forum

Let's consider an example where David visits the discussion forum in his browser. The following is the sequence of steps:

1. David clicks on the **New Discussion** link in the top navigation bar.

2. CodeIgniter loads the `create()` function in the `discussions` controller.

3. The `create()` function displays the `discussions/new.php` view file, which displays a form to users, enabling them to enter their name, e-mail, discussion title, and discussion body text.

4. David presses the **Go** button to submit the form. The form is submitted to the discussion controller's create() function.

5. The discussion controller's create() function validates the form. Assuming there were no errors, the create() function packages the post data into an array and sends it to the create() function of discussions_model.

6. The create() model function looks in the users database table to see whether the e-mail address already exists. If it does, the primary key of the user is returned and added to the Active Record insertion for the discussion. However, if the e-mail address doesn't exist, then the model function creates it. Instead, the primary key of this insertion is returned.

7. A password is created and a hash is generated from it. However, the password is not stored and David is not told what it is; this is perhaps a functionality you might not wish for, but you can easily add code to send David his password in an e-mail, should you wish.

A user comments on a discussion forum

Let's consider an example where Ed visits the discussion forum in his browser. The following is the sequence of events:

1. CodeIgniter loads the default controller—in this case, the discussion controller.

2. The discussion controller uses the fetch_discussions() function of discussions_model to get the latest discussions from the discussions database table and passes them to the discussions/view.php view file where they are displayed.

3. Ed likes the sound of one of the discussion forums and clicks on the name of the forum.

4. CodeIgniter loads the comments controller's index() function. The index() function takes the third uri segment (the discussion forum ID—discussions.ds_id) and passes it to the fetch_comments() function of comments_model.

5. The comments are displayed in the comments/view.php view file.

6. Ed reads the comment history and decides that the world would benefit from his opinion.

7. Ed scrolls to the bottom of the page where the form to add a comment is present. Ed enters his name, e-mail, and comment and clicks on **Go**.

8. The form is submitted to the `create()` function of `comments`. The `create()` function will validate the form. Assuming there were no errors, the `create()` function packages the post data into an array and sends it to the `create()` function of `comments_model`.

9. The `create()` model function looks in the `users` database table to see whether the e-mail address already exists. If it does, the primary key of the user is returned and added to the Active Record insertion for the comment. However, if the e-mail address doesn't exist, then the model function creates it. Instead, the primary key of this insertion is returned.

10. A password is created and a hash is generated from it. However, the password is not stored and Ed is not told what it is; this is perhaps a functionality you might not wish for, but you can easily add code to send Ed his password in an e-mail, should you wish.

11. Ed is redirected to the discussion forum where he can see his comment.

A user dislikes a comment and flags it for moderation

Let's consider an example where Nigel is looking through a discussion and sees a comment that he feels is necessary for moderation. The sequence of steps is as follows:

1. Outraged, he presses the **flag** link next to the comment.

2. CodeIgniter loads the `flag()` function of `comments`. The URL that is used to access this is `comments/flag/id-of-discussion/id-of-comment`.

3. CodeIgniter passes `id-of-comment` to the `flag()` function of `comments_model`, which will set `comments.cm_is_active` to `0`. This removes the comment from the discussion and places it in the moderation dashboard.

4. If the update of the comment was successful, CodeIgniter will redirect Nigel to the discussion he was looking at.

A moderator reviews comments awaiting moderation

Let's consider an example where Nick logs in to his admin account. The sequence of steps is as follows:

1. The `admin` controller loads the `dashboard()` function.

2. The `dashboard()` function loads a list of comments and discussions waiting for moderation.

3. Nick sees the full text of comments and discussions along with two options: **Allow** and **Disallow**.

4. Nick sees that there are two comments that require moderation.

5. Nick reads the first comment and decides that it is fine; he clicks on the **Allow** link. The structure of the link is `admin/update_item/cm/allow/id-or-comment`.

6. CodeIgniter loads the `update_item()` function of `admin`.

7. The `update_item()` function gets the type of thing that needs to be updated (comment: `cm` and discussion: `ds`); in this case, Nick is updating a comment to the first segment in `uri`, which is `cm`. The second `uri` segment is `allow` and the third `uri` segment is the ID of the comment (`comments.cm_id`).

8. The `update_comments()` function of `admin_model` is called, setting `comments.cm_is_active` to `1`. This allows the comment to be displayed once more.

9. Nick also notices the one remaining comment waiting for moderation. He reads the comment and decides that it's probably not the best comment and he wishes to remove it.

10. He clicks on the **Disallow** link. The structure of the link is `admin/update_item/cm/disallow/id-or-comment`.

11. CodeIgniter loads the `update_item()` function of `admin`.

12. The `update_item()` function gets the type of thing that needs to be updated (comment: `cm` and discussion: `ds`); in this case, Nick is updating a comment to the first segment in `uri`, which is `cm`. The second `uri` segment is `disallow` and the third `uri` segment is the ID of the comment (`comments.cm_id`).

13. The `update_comments()` function of `admin_model` is called. As `$is_active` is set to `0`, we will not allow the comment to be displayed but will delete it. A PHP if/else statement works out the value of `$is_active`, the else section is executed, and a MySQL DELETE command is called, deleting the comment from the database permanently.

Summary

We have done a lot in this chapter; we've created many files and there's a lot to take in. However, this project gives you the base system for a discussion forum. You might wish to add user management (particularly when it comes to sending the user their password), assuming you want people to log in? What would they do once they are logged in? These are for you to define, but you now have the base system; this allows you to build more.

4
Creating a Photo-sharing Application

There are quite a few image-sharing websites around at the moment. They all share roughly the same structure: the user uploads an image and that image can be shared, allowing others to view that image. Perhaps limits or constraints are placed on the viewing of an image, perhaps the image only remains viewable for a set period of time, or within set dates, but the general structure is the same. And I'm happy to announce that this project is exactly the same.

We'll create an application allowing users to share pictures; these pictures are accessible from a unique URL. To make this app, we will create two controllers: one to process image uploading and one to process the viewing and displaying of images stored.

We'll create a language file to store the text, allowing you to have support for multiple languages should it be needed.

We'll create all the necessary view files and a model to interface with the database.

However, this project along with all the others in this book relies on the basic setup we did in *Chapter 1*, *Introduction and Shared Project Resources*, although you can take large sections of the code and drop it into pretty much any project you may already have. Keep in mind that the setup done in the first chapter acts as a foundation for this chapter.

In this chapter, we will cover:

- Design and wireframes
- Creating the database
- Creating the models

- Creating the views
- Creating the controllers
- Putting it all together

So without further ado, let's get on with it.

Design and wireframes

As always, before we start building, we should take a look at what we plan to build.

First, a brief description of our intent: we plan to build an app to allow the user to upload an image. That image will be stored in a folder with a unique name. A URL will also be generated containing a unique code, and the URL and code will be assigned to that image. The image can be accessed via that URL.

The idea of using a unique URL to access that image is so that we can control access to that image, such as allowing an image to be viewed only a set number of times, or for a certain period of time only.

Anyway, to get a better idea of what's happening, let's take a look at the following site map:

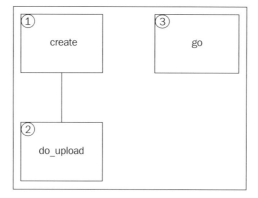

So that's the site map. The first thing to notice is how simple the site is. There are only three main areas to this project. Let's go over each item and get a brief idea of what they do:

- **create**: Imagine this as the start point. The user will be shown a simple form allowing them to upload an image. Once the user presses the Upload button, they are directed to `do_upload`.

- **do_upload**: The uploaded image is validated for size and file type. If it passes, then a unique eight-character string is generated. This string is then used as the name of a folder we will make. This folder is present in the main `upload` folder and the uploaded image is saved in it. The image details (image name, folder name, and so on) are then passed to the database model, where another unique code is generated for the image URL. This unique code, image name, and folder name are then saved to the database.

  The user is then presented with a message informing them that their image has been uploaded and that a URL has been created. The user is also presented with the image they have uploaded.

- **go**: This will take a URL provided by someone typing into a browser's address bar, or an `img src` tag, or some other method. The `go` item will look at the unique code in the URL, query the database to see if that code exists, and if so, fetch the folder name and image name and deliver the image back to the method that called it.

Now that we have a fairly good idea of the structure and form of the site, let's take a look at the wireframes of each page.

The create item

The following screenshot shows a wireframe for the `create` item discussed in the previous section. The user is shown a simple form allowing them to upload an image.

The do_upload item

The following screenshot shows a wireframe from the `do_upload` item discussed in the previous section. The user is shown the image they have uploaded and the URL that will direct other users to that image.

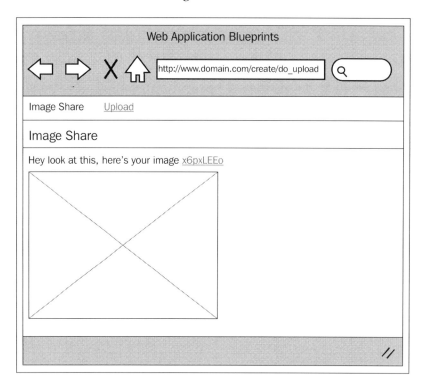

The go item

The following screenshot shows a wireframe from the go item described in the previous section. The `go` controller takes the unique code in a URL, attempts to find it in the database table images, and if found, supplies the image associated with it. Only the image is supplied, not the actual HTML markup.

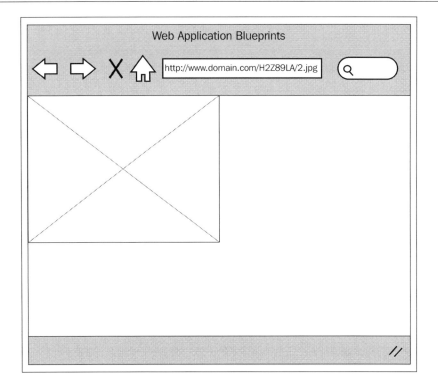

File overview

This is a relatively small project, and all in all we're only going to create seven files, which are as follows:

- /path/to/codeigniter/application/models/image_model.php: This provides read/write access to the images database table. This model also takes the upload information and unique folder name (which we store the uploaded image in) from the create controller and stores this to the database.

- /path/to/codeigniter/application/views/create/create.php: This provides us with an interface to display a form allowing the user to upload a file. This also displays any error messages to the user, such as wrong file type, file size too big, and so on.

- /path/to/codeigniter/application/views/create/result.php: This displays the image to the user after it has been successfully uploaded, as well as the URL required to view that image.

- /path/to/codeigniter/application/views/nav/top_nav.php: This provides a navigation bar at the top of the page.

- `/path/to/codeigniter/application/controllers/create.php`: This performs validation checks on the image uploaded by the user, creates a uniquely named folder to store the uploaded image, and passes this information to the model.

- `/path/to/codeigniter/application/controllers/go.php`: This performs validation checks on the URL input by the user, looks for the unique code in the URL and attempts to find this record in the database. If it is found, then it will display the image stored on disk.

- `/path/to/codeigniter/application/language/english/en_admin_lang.php`: This provides language support for the application.

The file structure of the preceding seven files is as follows:

```
application/
├── controllers/
│   ├── create.php
│   ├── go.php
├── models/
│   ├── image_model.php
├── views/create/
│   ├── create.php
│   ├── result.php
├── views/nav/
│   ├── top_nav.php
├── language/english/
│   ├── en_admin_lang.php
```

Creating the database

Okay, you should have already set up CodeIgniter and Bootstrap as described in *Chapter 1, Introduction and Shared Project Resources*; if you have not, then you should know that the code in this chapter is specifically built with the setup from *Chapter 1, Introduction and Shared Project Resources,* in mind. However, it's not the end of the world if you haven't. The code can easily be applied to other projects and applications you may have developed independently.

First, we'll build the database. Copy the following MySQL code into your database:

```
CREATE DATABASE `imagesdb`;
USE `imagesdb`;

DROP TABLE IF EXISTS `images`;
CREATE TABLE `images` (
  `img_id` int(11) NOT NULL AUTO_INCREMENT,
```

```
 `img_url_code` varchar(10) NOT NULL,
 `img_url_created_at` timestamp NOT NULL DEFAULT
   CURRENT_TIMESTAMP,
 `img_image_name` varchar(255) NOT NULL,
 `img_dir_name` varchar(8) NOT NULL,
 PRIMARY KEY (`img_id`)
) ENGINE=InnoDB AUTO_INCREMENT=1 DEFAULT CHARSET=utf8;
```

Right, let's take a look at each item in every table and see what they mean:

Table: images	
Element	**Description**
img_id	This is the primary key.
img_url_code	This stores the unique code that we use to identify the image in the database.
img_url_created_at	This is the MySQL timestamp for the record.
img_image_name	This is the filename provided by the CodeIgniter upload functionality.
img_dir_name	This is the name of the directory we store the image in.

We'll also need to make amends to the config/database.php file, namely setting the database access details, username, password, and so on.

Open the config/database.php file and find the following lines:

```
$db['default']['hostname'] = 'localhost';
$db['default']['username'] = 'your username';
$db['default']['password'] = 'your password';
$db['default']['database'] = 'imagesdb';
```

Edit the values in the preceding code ensuring you substitute those values for the ones more specific to your setup and situation—so enter your username, password, and so on.

Adjusting the config.php and autoload. php files

We don't actually need to adjust the config.php file in this project as we're not really using sessions or anything like that. So we don't need an encryption key or database information.

So just ensure that you are not autoloading the session in the `config/autoload.php` file or you will get an error, as we've not set any session variables in the `config/config.php` file.

Adjusting the routes.php file

We want to redirect the user to the `create` controller rather than the default CodeIgniter `welcome` controller. To do this, we will need to amend the default controller settings in the `routes.php` file to reflect this. The steps are as follows:

1. Open the `config/routes.php` file for editing and find the following lines (near the bottom of the file):

   ```
   $route['default_controller'] = "welcome";
   $route['404_override'] = '';
   ```

2. First, we need to change the default controller. Initially, in a CodeIgniter application, the default controller is set to `welcome`. However, we don't need that, instead we want the default controller to be `create`, so find the following line:

   ```
   $route['default_controller'] = "welcome";
   ```

   Replace it with the following lines:

   ```
   $route['default_controller'] = "create";
   $route['404_override'] = '';
   ```

3. Then we need to add some rules to govern how we handle URLs coming in and form submissions.

   Leave a few blank lines underneath the preceding two lines of code (default controller and 404 override) and add the following three lines of code:

   ```
   $route['create'] = "create/index";
   $route['(:any)'] = "go/index";
   $route['create/do_upload'] = "create/do_upload";
   ```

Creating the model

There is only one model in this project, `image_model.php`. It contains functions specific to creating and resetting passwords.

Create the `/path/to/codeigniter/application/models/image_model.php` file and add the following code to it:

```php
<?php if ( ! defined('BASEPATH')) exit('No direct script access
allowed');

class Image_model extends CI_Model {
  function __construct() {
    parent::__construct();
  }

  function save_image($data) {
    do {
      $img_url_code = random_string('alnum', 8);

      $this->db->where('img_url_code = ', $img_url_code);
      $this->db->from('images');
      $num = $this->db->count_all_results();
    } while ($num >= 1);

    $query = "INSERT INTO `images` (`img_url_code`,
      `img_image_name`, `img_dir_name`) VALUES (?,?,?) ";
    $result = $this->db->query($query, array($img_url_code,
      $data['image_name'], $data['img_dir_name']));

    if ($result) {
      return $img_url_code;
    } else {
      return flase;
    }
  }

  function fetch_image($img_url_code) {
    $query = "SELECT * FROM `images` WHERE `img_url_code` = ? ";
    $result = $this->db->query($query, array($img_url_code));

    if ($result) {
      return $result;
    } else {
      return false;
    }
  }
}
```

There are two main functions in this model, which are as follows:

- `save_image()`: This generates a unique code that is associated with the uploaded image and saves it, with the image name and folder name, to the database.

- `fetch_image()`: This fetches an image's details from the database according to the unique code provided.

Okay, let's take `save_image()` first. The `save_image()` function accepts an array from the `create` controller containing `image_name` (from the upload process) and `img_dir_name` (this is the folder that the image is stored in).

A unique code is generated using a `do...while` loop as shown here:

```
$img_url_code = random_string('alnum', 8);
```

First a string is created, eight characters in length, containing alpha-numeric characters. The `do...while` loop checks to see if this code already exists in the database, generating a new code if it is already present. If it does not already exist, this code is used:

```
do {
    $img_url_code = random_string('alnum', 8);

    $this->db->where('img_url_code = ', $img_url_code);
    $this->db->from('images');
    $num = $this->db->count_all_results();
} while ($num >= 1);
```

This code and the contents of the `$data` array are then saved to the database using the following code:

```
$query = "INSERT INTO `images` (`img_url_code`, `img_image_name`,
    `img_dir_name`) VALUES (?,?,?) ";
$result = $this->db->query($query, array($img_url_code,
    $data['image_name'], $data['img_dir_name']));
```

The `$img_url_code` is returned if the `INSERT` operation was successful, and `false` if it failed. The code to achieve this is as follows:

```
if ($result) {
    return $img_url_code;
} else {
    return false;
}
```

Creating the views

There are only three views in this project, which are as follows:

- `/path/to/codeigniter/application/views/create/create.php`: This displays a form to the user allowing them to upload an image.

- `/path/to/codeigniter/application/views/create/result.php`: This displays a link that the user can use to forward other people to the image, as well as the image itself.

- `/path/to/codeigniter/application/views/nav/top_nav.php`: This displays the top-level menu. In this project it's very simple, containing a project name and a link to go to the `create` controller.

So those are our views, as I said, there are only three of them as it's a simple project. Now, let's create each view file.

1. Create the `/path/to/codeigniter/application/views/create/create.php` file and add the following code to it:

```
<div class="page-header">
  <h1><?php echo $this->lang->line('system_system_name');
    ?></h1>
</div>

<p><?php echo $this->lang->line('encode_instruction_1');
  ?></p>

  <?php echo validation_errors(); ?>

<?php if (isset($success) && $success == true) : ?>
  <div class="alert alert-success">
    <strong><?php echo $this->lang->line('
      common_form_elements_success_notifty'); ?></strong>
      <?php echo $this->lang->
      line('encode_encode_now_success'); ?>
  </div>
<?php endif ; ?>

<?php if (isset($fail) && $fail == true) : ?>
  <div class="alert alert-danger">
    <strong><?php echo $this->lang->line('
      common_form_elements_error_notifty'); ?> </strong>
      <?php echo $this->lang->line('encode_encode_now_error
      '); ?>
    <?php echo $fail ; ?>
  </div>
```

```php
<?php endif ; ?>

<?php echo form_open_multipart('create/do_upload');?>
  <input type="file" name="userfile" size="20" />
  <br />
  <input type="submit" value="upload" />
<?php echo form_close() ; ?>
<br />
<?php if (isset($result) && $result == true) : ?>
  <div class="alert alert-info">
    <strong><?php echo $this->lang->line('
      encode_upload_url'); ?> </strong>
    <?php echo anchor($result, $result) ; ?>
  </div>
<?php endif ; ?>
```

This view file can be thought of as the main view file; it is here that the user can upload their image. Error messages are displayed here too.

2. Create the `/path/to/codeigniter/application/views/create/result.php` file and add the following code to it:

```php
<div class="page-header">
  <h1><?php echo $this->lang->line('system_system_name');
    ?></h1>
</div>

<?php if (isset($result) && $result == true) : ?>
    <strong><?php echo $this->lang->line('
      encode_encoded_url'); ?> </strong>
    <?php echo anchor($result, $result) ; ?>
    <br />
    <img src="<?php echo base_url() . 'upload/' .
      $img_dir_name . '/' . $file_name ;?>" />
<?php endif ; ?>
```

This view will display the encoded image resource URL to the user (so they can copy and share it) and the actual image itself.

3. Create the `/path/to/codeigniter/application/views/nav/top_nav.php` file and add the following code to it:

```html
<!-- Fixed navbar -->
<div class="navbar navbar-inverse navbar-fixed-top"
  role="navigation">
  <div class="container">
    <div class="navbar-header">
```

```
      <button type="button" class="navbar-toggle" data-
        toggle="collapse" data-target=".navbar-collapse">
        <span class="sr-only">Toggle navigation</span>
        <span class="icon-bar"></span>
        <span class="icon-bar"></span>
        <span class="icon-bar"></span>
      </button>
      <a class="navbar-brand" href="#"><?php echo $this-
        >lang->line('system_system_name'); ?></a>
    </div>
    <div class="navbar-collapse collapse">
      <ul class="nav navbar-nav">
        <li class="active"><?php echo anchor('create',
          'Create') ; ?></li>
      </ul>
    </div><!--/.nav-collapse -->
  </div>
</div>

<div class="container theme-showcase" role="main">
```

This view is quite basic but still serves an important role. It displays an option to return to the index() function of the create controller.

Creating the controllers

We're going to create two controllers in this project, which are as follows:

- /path/to/codeigniter/application/controllers/create.php: This handles the creation of unique folders to store images and performs the upload of a file.
- /path/to/codeigniter/application/controllers/go.php: This fetches the unique code from the database, and returns any image associated with that code.

These are two of our controllers for this project, let's now go ahead and create them.

Create the /path/to/codeigniter/application/controllers/create.php file and add the following code to it:

```
<?php if (!defined('BASEPATH')) exit('No direct script access
  allowed');

class Create extends MY_Controller {
  function __construct() {
```

```
      parent::__construct();
        $this->load->helper(array('string'));
        $this->load->library('form_validation');
        $this->load->library('image_lib');
        $this->load->model('Image_model');
        $this->form_validation->set_error_delimiters('<div
          class="alert alert-danger">', '</div>');
      }

  public function index() {
    $page_data = array('fail' => false,
                       'success' => false);
    $this->load->view('common/header');
    $this->load->view('nav/top_nav');
    $this->load->view('create/create', $page_data);
    $this->load->view('common/footer');
  }

  public function do_upload() {
    $upload_dir = '/filesystem/path/to/upload/folder/';
    do {
      // Make code
      $code = random_string('alnum', 8);

      // Scan upload dir for subdir with same name
      // name as the code
      $dirs = scandir($upload_dir);

      // Look to see if there is already a
      // directory with the name which we
      // store in $code
      if (in_array($code, $dirs)) { // Yes there is
        $img_dir_name = false; // Set to false to begin again
      } else { // No there isn't
        $img_dir_name = $code; // This is a new name
      }

    } while ($img_dir_name == false);

    if (!mkdir($upload_dir.$img_dir_name)) {
      $page_data = array('fail' => $this->lang->
        line('encode_upload_mkdir_error'),
                         'success' => false);
      $this->load->view('common/header');
```

```php
    $this->load->view('nav/top_nav');
    $this->load->view('create/create', $page_data);
    $this->load->view('common/footer');
  }

$config['upload_path'] = $upload_dir.$img_dir_name;
$config['allowed_types'] = 'gif|jpg|jpeg|png';
$config['max_size']   = '10000';
$config['max_width']  = '1024';
$config['max_height'] = '768';

$this->load->library('upload', $config);

if ( ! $this->upload->do_upload()) {
  $page_data = array('fail' => $this->upload->
    display_errors(),
                     'success' => false);
  $this->load->view('common/header');
  $this->load->view('nav/top_nav');
  $this->load->view('create/create', $page_data);
  $this->load->view('common/footer');
} else {
  $image_data = $this->upload->data();
  $page_data['result'] = $this->Image_model->save_image(
    array('image_name' => $image_data['file_name'],
    'img_dir_name' => $img_dir_name));
  $page_data['file_name'] = $image_data['file_name'];
  $page_data['img_dir_name'] = $img_dir_name;

  if ($page_data['result'] == false) {
    // success - display image and link
    $page_data = array('fail' => $this->lang->
      line('encode_upload_general_error'));
    $this->load->view('common/header');
    $this->load->view('nav/top_nav');
    $this->load->view('create/create', $page_data);
    $this->load->view('common/footer');
  } else {
    // success - display image and link
    $this->load->view('common/header');
    $this->load->view('nav/top_nav');
    $this->load->view('create/result', $page_data);
    $this->load->view('common/footer');
  }
}
  }
}
```

Let's start with the index() function. The index() function sets the fail and success elements of the $page_data array to false. This will suppress any initial messages from being displayed to the user. The views are loaded, specifically the create/create.php view, which contains the image upload form's HTML markup.

Once the user submits the form in create/create.php, the form will be submitted to the do_upload() function of the create controller. It is this function that will perform the task of uploading the image to the server.

First off, do_upload() defines an initial location for the upload folder. This is stored in the $upload_dir variable.

Next, we move into a do...while structure. It looks something like this:

```
do {
// something
} while ('...a condition is not met');
```

So that means *do something while a condition is not being met*. Now with that in mind, think about our problem—we have to save the image being uploaded in a folder. That folder must have a unique name. So what we will do is generate a random string of eight alpha-numeric characters and then look to see if a folder exists with that name. Keeping that in mind, let's look at the code in detail:

```
do {
  // Make code
  $code = random_string('alnum', 8);

  // Scan uplaod dir for subdir with same name
  // name as the code
  $dirs = scandir($upload_dir);

  // Look to see if there is already a
  // directory with the name which we
  // store in $code
  if (in_array($code, $dirs)) { // Yes there is
    $img_dir_name = false; // Set to false to begin again
  } else { // No there isn't
    $img_dir_name = $code; // This is a new name
  }
} while ($img_dir_name == false);
```

So we make a string of eight characters, containing only alphanumeric characters, using the following line of code:

```
$code = random_string('alnum', 8);
```

We then use the PHP function `scandir()` to look in `$upload_dir`. This will store all directory names in the `$dirs` variable, as follows:

```
$dirs = scandir($upload_dir);
```

We then use the PHP function `in_array()` to look for the value in `$code` in the list of directors from `scandir()`:

If we don't find a match, then the value in `$code` must not be taken, so we'll go with that. If the value is found, then we set `$img_dir_name` to `false`, which is picked up by the final line of the `do...while` loop:

```
...
} while ($img_dir_name == false);
```

Anyway, now that we have our unique folder name, we'll attempt to create it. We use the PHP function `mkdir()`, passing to it `$upload_dir` concatenated with `$img_dir_name`. If `mkdir()` returns `false`, the form is displayed again along with the `encode_upload_mkdir_error` message set in the language file, as shown here:

```
if (!mkdir($upload_dir.$img_dir_name)) {
  $page_data = array('fail' => $this->lang->
    line('encode_upload_mkdir_error'),
                      'success' => false);
  $this->load->view('common/header');
  $this->load->view('nav/top_nav');
  $this->load->view('create/create', $page_data);
  $this->load->view('common/footer');
}
```

Once the folder has been made, we then set the configuration variables for the upload process, as follows:

```
$config['upload_path'] = $upload_dir.$img_dir_name;
$config['allowed_types'] = 'gif|jpg|jpeg|png';
$config['max_size'] = '10000';
$config['max_width']  = '1024';
$config['max_height']  = '768';
```

Here we are specifying that we only want to upload `.gif`, `.jpg`, `.jpeg`, and `.png` files. We also specify that an image cannot be above 10,000 KB in size (although you can set this to any value you wish—remember to adjust the `upload_max_filesize` and `post_max_size` PHP settings in your `php.ini` file if you want to have a really big file).

We also set the minimum dimensions that an image must be. As with the file size, you can adjust this as you wish.

We then load the `upload` library, passing to it the configuration settings, as shown here:

```
$this->load->library('upload', $config);
```

Next we will attempt to do the upload. If unsuccessful, the CodeIgniter function `$this->upload->do_upload()` will return `false`. We will look for this and reload the upload page if it does return `false`. We will also pass the specific error as a reason why it failed. This error is stored in the `fail` item of the `$page_data` array. This can be done as follows:

```
if ( ! $this->upload->do_upload()) {
  $page_data = array('fail' => $this->upload-
    >display_errors(),
                      'success' => false);
  $this->load->view('common/header');
  $this->load->view('nav/top_nav');
  $this->load->view('create/create', $page_data);
  $this->load->view('common/footer');
} else {
...
```

If, however, it did not fail, we grab the information generated by CodeIgniter from the upload. We'll store this in the `$image_data` array, as follows:

```
$image_data = $this->upload->data();
```

Then we try to store a record of the upload in the database. We call the `save_image` function of `Image_model`, passing to it `file_name` from the `$image_data` array, as well as `$img_dir_name`, as shown here:

```
$page_data['result'] = $this->Image_model->
  save_image(array('image_name' => $image_data['file_name'],
  'img_dir_name' => $img_dir_name));
```

We then test for the return value of the `save_image()` function; if it is successful, then `Image_model` will return the unique URL code generated in the model. If it is unsuccessful, then `Image_model` will return the Boolean `false`.

If `false` is returned, then the form is loaded with a general error. If successful, then the `create/result.php` view file is loaded. We pass to it the unique URL code (for the link the user needs), and the folder name and image name, necessary to display the image correctly.

Create the `/path/to/codeigniter/application/controllers/go.php` file and add the following code to it:

```php
<?php if (!defined('BASEPATH')) exit('No direct script access
allowed');

class Go extends MY_Controller {
  function __construct() {
  parent::__construct();
    $this->load->helper('string');
  }

  public function index() {
    if (!$this->uri->segment(1)) {
      redirect (base_url());
    } else {
      $image_code = $this->uri->segment(1);
      $this->load->model('Image_model');
      $query = $this->Image_model->fetch_image($image_code);

      if ($query->num_rows() == 1) {
        foreach ($query->result() as $row) {
          $img_image_name = $row->img_image_name;
          $img_dir_name = $row->img_dir_name;
        }

        $url_address = base_url() . 'upload/' . $img_dir_name .'/' .
$img_image_name;
        redirect (prep_url($url_address));
      } else {
        redirect('create');
      }
    }
  }
}
```

The `go` controller has only one main function, `index()`. It is called when a user clicks on a URL or a URL is called (perhaps as the `src` value of an HTML `img` tag). Here we grab the unique code generated and assigned to an image when it was uploaded in the `create` controller.

This code is in the first value of the URI. Usually it would occupy the third parameter—with the first and second parameters normally being used to specify the controller and controller function respectively. However, we have changed this behavior using CodeIgniter routing. This is explained fully in the *Adjusting the routes. php file* section of this chapter.

Once we have the unique code, we pass it to the `fetch_image()` function of `Image_model`:

```
$image_code = $this->uri->segment(1);
$this->load->model('Image_model');
$query = $this->Image_model->fetch_image($image_code);
```

We test for what is returned. We ask if the number of rows returned equals exactly `1`. If not, we will then redirect to the `create` controller.

Perhaps you may not want to do this. Perhaps you may want to do nothing if the number of rows returned does not equal 1. For example, if the image requested is in an HTML `img` tag, then if an image is not found a redirect may send someone away from the site they're viewing to the upload page of this project—something you might not want to happen. If you want to remove this functionality, remove the following lines in bold from the code excerpt:

```
. . . .
            $img_dir_name = $row->img_dir_name;
            }

            $url_address = base_url() . 'upload/' . $img_dir_name .'/'
               . $img_image_name;
            redirect (prep_url($url_address));
        } else {
            redirect('create');
        }
      }
    }
  }
. . . .
```

Anyway, if the returned value is exactly `1`, then we'll loop over the returned database object and find `img_image_name` and `img_dir_name`, which we'll need to locate the image in the `upload` folder on the disk. This can be done as follows:

```
foreach ($query->result() as $row) {
  $img_image_name = $row->img_image_name;
  $img_dir_name = $row->img_dir_name;
}
```

We then build the address of the image file and redirect the browser to it, as follows:

```
$url_address = base_url() . 'upload/' . $img_dir_name .'/'
   . $img_image_name;
redirect (prep_url($url_address));
```

Creating the language file

As with all the projects in this book, we're making use of the language file to serve text to users. In this way, you can enable multiple region/multiple language support.

Create the `/path/to/codeigniter/application/language/english/en_admin_lang.php` file and add the following code to it:

```
<?php if (!defined('BASEPATH')) exit('No direct script access
   allowed');

// General
$lang['system_system_name'] = "Image Share";

// Upload
$lang['encode_instruction_1'] = "Upload your image to share it";
$lang['encode_upload_now'] = "Share Now";
$lang['encode_upload_now_success'] = "Your image was uploaded, you
   can share it with this URL";
$lang['encode_upload_url'] = "Hey look at this, here's your
   image:";
$lang['encode_upload_mkdir_error'] = "Cannot make temp folder";
$lang['encode_upload_general_error'] = "The Image cannot be saved
   at this time";
```

Putting it all together

Let's look at how the user uploads an image. The following is the sequence of events:

1. CodeIgniter looks in the `routes.php` config file and finds the following line:

   ```
   $route['create'] = "create/index";
   ```

   It directs the request to the `create` controller's `index()` function.

2. The `index()` function loads the `create/create.php` view file that displays the upload form to the user.

3. The user clicks on the Choose file button, navigates to the image file they wish to upload, and selects it.

4. The user presses the Upload button and the form is submitted to the `create` controller's `index()` function.

5. The `index()` function creates a folder in the main `upload` directory to store the image in, then does the actual upload.

6. On a successful upload, `index()` sends the details of the upload (the new folder name and image name) to the `save_image()` model function.

7. The `save_model()` function also creates a unique code and saves it in the `images` table along with the folder name and image name passed to it by the `create` controller.

8. The unique code generated during the database insert is then returned to the controller and passed to the result view, where it will form part of a success message to the user.

Now, let's see how an image is viewed (or fetched). The following is the sequence of events:

1. A URL with the syntax `www.domain.com/226KgfYH` comes into the application—either when someone clicks on a link or some other call (`<img src="">`).

2. CodeIgniter looks in the `routes.php` config file and finds the following line:

   `$route['(:any)'] = "go/index";`

3. As the incoming request does not match the other two routes, the preceding route is the one CodeIgniter applies to this request.

4. The `go` controller is called and the code of `226KgfYH` is passed to it as the 1st segment of `uri`.

5. The `go` controller passes this to the `fetch_image()` function of the `Image_model.php` file. The `fetch_image()` function will attempt to find a matching record in the database. If found, it returns the folder name marking the saved location of the image, and its filename.

6. This is returned and the path to that image is built. CodeIgniter then redirects the user to that image, that is, supplies that image resource to the user that requested it.

Summary

So here we have a basic image sharing application. It is capable of accepting a variety of images and assigning them to records in a database and unique folders in the filesystem. This is interesting as it leaves things open to you to improve on. For example, you can do the following:

- You can add limits on views. As the image record is stored in the database, you could adapt the database. Adding two columns called `img_count` and `img_count_limit`, you could allow a user to set a limit for the number of views per image and stop providing that image when that limit is met.

- You can limit views by date. Similar to the preceding point, but you could limit image views to set dates.

- You can have different URLs for different dimensions. You could add functionality to make several dimensions of image based on the initial upload, offering several different URLs for different image dimensions.

- You can report abuse. You could add an option allowing viewers of images to report unsavory images that might be uploaded.

- You can have terms of service. If you are planning on offering this type of application as an actual web service that members of the public could use, then I strongly recommend you add a terms of service document, perhaps even require that people agree to terms before they upload an image.

  In those terms, you'll want to mention that in order for someone to use the service, they first have to agree that they do not upload and share any images that could be considered illegal. You should also mention that you'll cooperate with any court if information is requested of you.

  You really don't want to get into trouble for owning or running a web service that stores unpleasant images; as much as possible you want to make your limits of liability clear and emphasize that it is the uploader who has provided the images.

In the next chapter, we will create a newsletter signup system. You'll be able to get people to sign up and have their details in a database. People will be allowed to unsubscribe and opt-in and opt-out of various settings.

5

Creating a Newsletter Signup

A newsletter signup is quite a handy application; you can adapt it quite easily to fit most applications without much fuss. It enables you to have a database of subscribers and manage them, editing their settings and removing them from the database should they choose to unsubscribe.

In this chapter, we will cover:

- Design and wireframes
- Creating a database
- Creating models
- Creating views
- Creating controllers
- Putting it all together

Introduction

In this project, we will create an application that will allow users to sign up for a newsletter. A form will be displayed, inviting a user to enter their e-mail address, and then it will define a couple of settings to submit that form. It will also let subscribers alter their settings and even unsubscribe entirely.

To create this app, we will create one controller. This will handle all parts of the project: subscribing, editing settings, and unsubscribing.

We'll create a language file to store text, allowing you to have multiple language support should that be required.

We'll create all the necessary view files and a model to interface with the database.

However, this app, along with all the others in this book, relies on the basic setup we did in *Chapter 1, Introduction and Shared Project Resources*. Although you can take large sections of the code and drop it into pretty much any app you might already have, please keep in mind that the setup done in the first chapter acts as a foundation for this chapter.

So, without further ado, let's get on with it.

Design and wireframes

As always, before we start building, we should take a look at what we plan to build.

First, let's look at a brief description of our intent: we plan to build an app that will allow people to sign up for a database of contacts that will be used as a newsletter signup database. We will enable users to subscribe by registering their e-mail address and some options. These will be saved in a database.

We will also enable people to amend their settings and even unsubscribe should they wish to.

Anyway, to get a better idea of what's happening, let's take a look at the following site map:

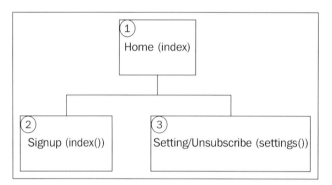

So, that's the site map; the first thing to notice is how simple the site is. There are only three main areas in this project. Let's go over each item and get a brief idea of what they do:

- **Home**: This is the initial landing area. The `index()` function is responsible for displaying a form to the user, inviting them to subscribe.
- **Signup**: This processes the validation of the form input and passes that data (if validated successfully) to the `add()` model function.

- **Settings/Unsubscribe**: This accepts the users' e-mail address as the third and fourth `uri` parameters and displays a form to the subscriber. This form contains the settings assigned to the e-mail address supplied. The user is able to amend these settings and unsubscribe should they wish to.

Now that we have a fairly good idea of the structure and form of the site, let's take a look at some wireframes of each page.

The Home – index() and Signup – index() items

The following screenshot shows you a wireframe from point **1** (the Home (`index()`) item) and point 2 (the Signup (`index()`) item) in the preceding diagram. The user is shown a textbox named `signup_email` in the HTML and two checkboxes named `signup_opt1` and `signup_opt2` in the HTML.

These options are just an example; they can be removed or amended should you wish. They are intended to act as a filter to the newsletters. For example, you could include frequency options giving weekly, monthly, or quarterly options. When you come to send your newsletters, you would only send the subscriber a newsletter based on those options – as I say, you can change them, add more, or have none if you wish.

The user can enter their e-mail address as shown in the following screenshot, apply any options they might wish to add, and submit the form. The form is submitted to the `signup` controller's `index()` function, which will then validate that data. On passing the validation, the `add()` function of `Signup_model` will create the record in the `signups` database table.

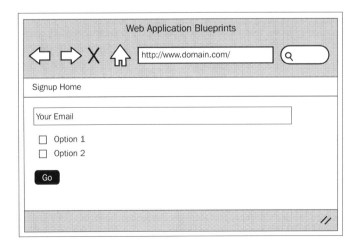

Settings/Unsubscribe – settings()

The following screenshot shows you a wireframe from point **3** (the Settings/ Unsubscribe (`settings()`) item) in the site map diagram. The user is presented with a form that is pre-populated with their settings.

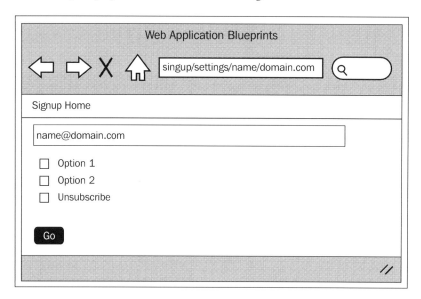

We were able to fetch the correct details because of the URL. The user's e-mail address is in the URL as the third and fourth segments.

The page is loaded when a user clicks on an unsubscribe link—perhaps in an e-mail. The URL for this link would take the `http://www.domain.com/signup/settings/name/domain.com` format.

You'll notice that we don't use the `http://www.domain.com/signup/settings/name@domain.com` format.

In the second URL, you can see the @ character; in the first, you can see that character replaced with a forward slash. In effect, we have turned the first part of the e-mail address (everything before @) into the third `uri` parameter, and the fourth parameter of the `uri` comes from the second part of the e-mail address (everything after @).

For security reasons, we are unable to use the @ character in the URL, so we cannot have `http://www.domain.com/signup/settings/name@domain.com` as the URL. This is default CodeIgniter behavior: certain characters are disallowed from URLs in an effort to reduce the chances of malicious scripts or commands being run.

File overview

This is a relatively small project, and all in all, we're only going to create six files. These are as follows:

- `/path/to/codeigniter/application/models/signup_model.php`: This provides read/write access to the database.

- `/path/to/codeigniter/application/views/signup/signup.php`: This displays a small form to the user, inviting them to enter their e-mail address and to check two checkboxes: **Option 1** and **Option 2**. You can amend these options, adding more or removing them completely. The options are there to help the person who is signing up define what information they want from the application.

- `/path/to/codeigniter/application/views/signup/settings.php`: This displays a small form to the user, showing their current settings with the application.

- `/path/to/codeigniter/application/views/nav/top_nav.php`: This provides a navigation bar at the top of the page.

- `/path/to/codeigniter/application/controllers/signup.php`: This contains all functions necessary to sign up new subscribers and amend their account details. This controller also handles any unsubscribe requests.

- `/path/to/codeigniter/application/language/english/en_admin_lang.php`: This provides language support for the application.

The file structure of the preceding six files is as follows:

```
application/
├── controllers/
│   ├── signup.php
├── models/
│   ├── signup_model.php
├── views/signup/
│   ├── signup.php
│   ├── settings.php
├── views/nav/
│   ├── top_nav.php
├── language/english/
│   ├── en_admin_lang.php
```

Creating the database

Okay, you should have already set up CodeIgniter and Bootstrap as described in *Chapter 1, Introduction and Shared Project Resources*. If not, then you should know that the code in this chapter is specifically built with the setup from *Chapter 1, Introduction and Shared Project Resources*, in mind. However it's not the end of the world if you haven't; the code can easily be applied to other situations.

First, we'll build the database. Copy the following MySQL code to your database:

```
CREATE DATABASE `signupdb`;
USE DATABASE `signupdb`;

CREATE TABLE `signups` (
    `signup_id` int(11) NOT NULL AUTO_INCREMENT,
    `signup_email` varchar(255) NOT NULL,
    `signup_opt1` int(1) NOT NULL,
    `signup_opt2` int(1) NOT NULL,
    `signup_active` int(1) NOT NULL,
    `signup_created_at` timestamp NOT NULL DEFAULT CURRENT_TIMESTAMP,
    PRIMARY KEY (`signup_id`)
) ENGINE=InnoDB AUTO_INCREMENT=1 DEFAULT CHARSET=utf8;
```

Right, let's take a look at each item in the table and see what it means:

Table: signups	
Element	Description
signup_id	This is the primary key.
signup_email	This shows you the users' e-mail addresses.
signup_opt1	This stores the users option for option 1 in the `views/signup/signup.php` file.
signup_opt2	This stores the users option for option 2 in the `views/signup/signup.php` file.
signup_active	This is a sort of soft delete. It's not currently supported in the application in this chapter, but is there should you wish to use it.
signup_created_at	This is a MySQL timestamp for the date on which the row was created in the table.

We'll also need to make amends to the `config/database.php` file, namely, setting the database access details, username password, and so on:

1. Open the `config/database.php` file and find the following lines:

```
$db['default']['hostname'] = 'localhost';
$db['default']['username'] = 'your username';
$db['default']['password'] = 'your password';
$db['default']['database'] = 'signupdb';
```

2. Edit the values in the preceding lines, ensuring you substitute these values with ones more specific to your setup and situation—so enter your username, password, and so on.

Adjusting the routes.php file

We want to redirect the user to the `signup` controller rather than the default CodeIgniter `welcome` controller. To do this, we will need to amend the default controller setting in the `routes.php` file.

Open the `config/routes.php` file to edit and find the following lines (near the bottom of the file):

```
$route['default_controller'] = "welcome";
$route['404_override'] = '';
```

First, we need to change the default controller. Initially, in a CodeIgniter application the default controller is set to `welcome`. However, we don't need this, instead we want the default controller to be `signup`. So, find the following line:

```
$route['default_controller'] = "welcome";
```

Replace the preceding line with the following:

```
$route['default_controller'] = "signup";
$route['404_override'] = '';
```

Creating the model

There is only one model in this project—`signup_model.php` that contains functions that are specific to adding a subscriber to the database, amending their settings and processing the removal of a subscriber should they unsubscribe.

This is our one and only model for this project. Let's briefly go over each function in it to give us a general idea of what it does, and then we will go into more details of the code.

There are four main functions in this model, which are as follows:

- `add()`: This accepts one argument: the `$data` array sent by the `signup` controller's `index()` function when a user successfully submits the form in `views/signup/signup.php`. The `add()` function takes the array and using the `$this->db->insert()` CodeIgniter Active Record function, it inserts the user's signup data in the `signups` table.

- `edit()`: This accepts one argument: the `$data` array sent by the `signup` controller's `settings()` function. This function is called only if the user is editing their settings rather than unsubscribing. The `edit()` function will update a user's profile.

- `delete()`: This accepts one argument: the `$data` array sent by the `signup` controller's `settings()` function. This function is called only if the user is unsubscribing rather than editing their settings. The function will return `true` if the delete was successful and `false` if not.

- `get_settings()`: This accepts one argument: the `$data` array sent by the `signup` controller's `settings()` function. The settings form needs to be populated with the correct data for the required e-mail address, and `get_settings()` supplies this information.

That's a quick overview, so let's create the model and discuss how it functions.

Create the `/path/to/codeigniter/application/models/signup_model.php` file and add the following code to it:

```php
<?php if ( ! defined('BASEPATH')) exit('No direct script access
   allowed');

class Signup_model extends CI_Model {
   function __construct() {
     parent::__construct();
   }
```

The following code snippet adds a subscriber to the database using the `$this->db->insert()` CodeIgniter Active Record function. This function is called by the `signup` controller's `index()` function. It accepts an array called `$data`; this array is the validated form input submitted by the user in the `views/signup/signup.php` form. On successfully writing to the database, it will return `true`; it will return `false` if an error occurs:

```php
public function add($data) {
   if ($this->db->insert('signups', $data)) {
     return true;
   } else {
```

```
        return false;
      }
    }
```

The following code snippet performs an update procedure on the `signups` database table using the `$this->db->update()` CodeIgniter Active Record function. It accepts an array called `$data`. This array is the validated form input submitted by the user in the `views/signup/settings.php` form. On a successful update, it will return `true`; it will return `false` if an error occurs:

```
public function edit($data) {
  $this->db->where('signup_email', $data['signup_email']);
  if ($this->db->update('signups', $data)) {
    return true;
  } else {
    return false;
  }
}
```

The following code snippet performs a delete procedure on the `signups` database table using the `$this->db->delete()` CodeIgniter Active Record function. It accepts an array called `$data`. This array is the validated form input submitted by the user in the `views/signup/settings.php` form and contains the subscribers' e-mail addresses only. On a successful deletion, it will return `true`; it will return `false` if an error occurs:

```
public function delete($data) {
  $this->db->where('signup_email', $data['signup_email']);
  if ($this->db->delete('signups')) {
    return true;
  } else {
    return false;
  }
}
```

The following code snippet performs a select procedure on the `signups` database table using the `$this->db->get()` CodeIgniter Active Record function. It accepts a variable called `$email`. This is the formatted e-mail address of the subscriber. This function returns a subscriber's database record. It is required by the `signup` controller's `settings()` function in order to pre-populate form items. On a successful selection, it will return a database result object; it will return `false` if an error occurs:

```
public function get_settings($email) {
  $this->db->where('signup_email', $email);
  $query = $this->db->get('signups');
```

```
    if ($query) {
      return $query;
    } else {
      return false;
    }
  }
 }
}
```

As you can see, the model is fairly straightforward and concise, so let's now take a look at the views.

Creating the views

There are three views in this project, and these are as follows:

- /path/to/codeigniter/application/views/signup/signup.php: This displays a form to the user, allowing them to sign up their e-mail address to the project.

- /path/to/codeigniter/application/views/signup/settings.php: This displays a form to the user, allowing them to amend their preferences and also unsubscribe should they wish.

- /path/to/codeigniter/application/views/nav/top_nav.php: This displays the top-level menu. In this project, this file is very simple, and as such it just contains a link to return to the index() function.

This is a good overview of the views. Now let's go over each one, build the code, and discuss how they function:

1. Create the /path/to/codeigniter/application/views/signup/signup. php file and add the following code to it:

```
<div class="row row-offcanvas row-offcanvas-right">
  <div class="col-xs-12 col-sm-9">
    <div class="row">
      <?php echo validation_errors(); ?>
      <?php echo form_open('/signup') ; ?>
      <?php echo form_input($signup_email); ?><br />
      <?php echo form_checkbox($signup_opt1) . $this->lang-
>line('signup_opt1'); ?><br />
      <?php echo form_checkbox($signup_opt2) . $this->lang-
>line('signup_opt2'); ?><br />
      <?php echo form_submit('', $this->lang->line('common_form_
elements_go'), 'class="btn btn-success"') ; ?><br />
      <?php echo form_close() ; ?>
    </div>
```

```
    </div>
</div>
```

The preceding HTML contains the form to enable a user to sign up to the application. The form also displays any validation errors.

2. Create the `/path/to/codeigniter/application/views/signup/settings.php` file and add the following code to it:

```
<div class="row row-offcanvas row-offcanvas-right">
  <div class="col-xs-12 col-sm-9">
    <div class="row">
      <?php echo validation_errors(); ?>
      <?php echo form_open('/signup/settings') ; ?>
      <?php echo form_input($signup_email); ?><br />
      <?php echo form_checkbox($signup_opt1) . $this->lang-
         >line('signup_opt1'); ?><br />
      <?php echo form_checkbox($signup_opt2) . $this->lang-
         >line('signup_opt2'); ?><br />
      <?php echo form_checkbox($signup_unsub) . $this-
         >lang->line('signup_unsub'); ?><br />
      <?php echo form_submit('', $this->lang->
         line('common_form_elements_go'), 'class="btn btn-
         success"') ; ?><br />
      <?php echo form_close() ; ?>
    </div>
  </div>
</div>
```

The preceding HTML contains the form to enable the subscriber to edit their settings or unsubscribe completely. The data for the form is fetched by the `get_settings()` function of `signup_model`.

3. Create the `/path/to/codeigniter/application/views/nav/top_nav.php` file and add the following code to it:

```
<!-- Fixed navbar -->
<div class="navbar navbar-inverse navbar-fixed-top"
  role="navigation">
  <div class="container">
    <div class="navbar-header">
      <button type="button" class="navbar-toggle" data-
        toggle="collapse" data-target=".navbar-collapse">
        <span class="sr-only">Toggle navigation</span>
        <span class="icon-bar"></span>
        <span class="icon-bar"></span>
        <span class="icon-bar"></span>
```

```
        </button>
        <a class="navbar-brand" href="<?php echo base_url() ;
          ?>"><?php echo $this->lang->line('
          system_system_name'); ?></a>
      </div>
      <div class="navbar-collapse collapse">
        <ul class="nav navbar-nav">
          <li class="active"><?php echo anchor('signup',
            $this->lang->line('nav_home')) ; ?></li>
        </ul>
      </div><!--/.nav-collapse -->
    </div>
  </div>
  <div class="container theme-showcase" role="main">
```

Creating the controllers

We're going to create only one controller in this project, which is /path/to/
codeigniter/application/controllers/signup.php.

Let's go over this controller now, look at the code, and discuss how it functions.

Create the /path/to/codeigniter/application/controllers/signup.php file
and add the following code to it:

```php
<?php if (!defined('BASEPATH')) exit('No direct script access
allowed');

class Signup extends MY_Controller {
  function __construct() {
    parent::__construct();
    $this->load->helper('form');
    $this->load->helper('url');
    $this->load->model('Signup_model');
    $this->load->library('form_validation');
    $this->form_validation->set_error_delimiters('<div
      class="alert alert-danger">', '</div>');
  }

  public function index() {
```

This function creates a subscriber in the database, so the first thing we need to do is set the form validation rules:

```
// Set validation rules
$this->form_validation->set_rules('signup_email', $this->lang-
   >line('signup_emailemail'), 'required|valid_email|
   min_length[1]|max_length[125]|is_unique[signups.signup_email]');
$this->form_validation->set_rules('signup_emailopt1', $this->lang-
   >line('signup_emailopt1'), 'min_length[1]|max_length[1]');
$this->form_validation->set_rules('signup_emailopt2', $this->lang-
   >line('signup_emailopt2'), 'min_length[1]|max_length[1]');


// Begin validation
if ($this->form_validation->run() == FALSE) {
```

If the form was submitted with errors, or if this is the first load instance of the function, then we will arrive at the following code. We define the following settings for the form elements in the `views/signup/signup.php` file:

```
$data['signup_email'] = array('name' => 'signup_email', 'class'
   => 'form-control', 'id' => 'signup_email', 'value' =>
   set_value('signup_email', ''), 'maxlength' => '100', 'size' =>
   '35', 'placeholder' => $this->lang->line('signup_email'));
$data['signup_opt1'] = array('name' => 'signup_opt1', 'id' =>
   'signup_opt1', 'value' => '1', 'checked' => FALSE, 'style' =>
   'margin:10px');
$data['signup_opt2'] = array('name' => 'signup_opt2', 'id' =>
   'signup_opt2', 'value' => '1', 'checked' => FALSE, 'style' =>
   'margin:10px');


$this->load->view('common/header');
$this->load->view('nav/top_nav', $data);
$this->load->view('signup/signup', $data);
$this->load->view('common/footer');
} else {
```

However, if there were no errors with the validation, we will arrive at the following code. We package the data from the form elements into an array called `$data` and send it to the `add()` function of `signup_model`. This will perform the task of writing the subscriber to the database:

```
$data = array('signup_email' => $this->input-
   >post('signup_email'),
               'signup_opt1' => $this->input-
                  >post('signup_opt1'),
               'signup_opt2' => $this->input-
                  >post('signup_opt2'),
```

```
                    'signup_active' => 1);

    if ($this->Signup_model->add($data)) {
      echo $this->lang->line('signup_success');
    } else {
      echo $this->lang->line('signup_error');
    }
  }
}
```

The following function is responsible for updating a subscriber's settings, or handling an unsubscribe request. Before it can do either of these things, it needs the users' e-mail address. The e-mail address is supplied when a subscriber clicks on a link (such as an unsubscribe link in an e-mail):

```
public function settings() {
    // Set validation rules
    $this->form_validation->set_rules('signup_email', $this->lang-
        >line('signup_email'), 'required|valid_email|min
        _length[1]|max_length[125]');
    $this->form_validation->set_rules('signup_opt1', $this->lang-
        >line('signup_opt1'), 'min_length[1]|max_length[1]');
    $this->form_validation->set_rules('signup_opt2', $this->lang-
        >line('signup_opt2'), 'min_length[1]|max_length[1]');
    $this->form_validation->set_rules('signup_unsub', $this->lang-
        >line('signup_unsub'), 'min_length[1]|max_length[1]');

    // Begin validation
    if ($this->form_validation->run() == FALSE) {
```

If validation was unsuccessful, or the form is being accessed for the first time, then we arrive at the following code. The first thing we try to do is get the details of the subscriber so that we can display the correct settings in the form. We pass the third and fourth parameters of the uri segment to the get_settings() function of signup_model. We join them by writing the @ symbol between the two uri segments, remembering that we cannot accept @ symbols in the URL for security reasons. This can be done as follows:

```
$query = $this->Signup_model->get_settings($this->uri->segment(3) .
'@' . $this->uri->segment(4));
if ($query->num_rows() == 1) {
  foreach ($query->result() as $row) {
    $signup_opt1 = $row->signup_opt1;
    $signup_opt2 = $row->signup_opt2;
  }
} else {
  redirect('signup');
}
```

The `get_settings()` function of `signup_model` will look in the `signups` table and return a result object.

First, we test to see whether the number of records found is exactly 1. Anything else and there's a problem: either more than one record exists in the database belonging to the same e-mail address, or no e-mail address was found at all, in which case we redirect the users to the `index()` function.

Anyway, if exactly one record was found, we then loop over the result object with a `foreach` loop and put the values that we will use to populate the form options into local variables: `$signup_opt1` and `$signup_opt2`.

We then define the settings for our form elements, passing `$signup_email`, `$signup_opt1` and `$signup_opt2` as well as settings for the unsubscribe checkbox to them:

```
$data['signup_email'] = array('name' => 'signup_email', 'class' =>
    'form-control', 'id' => 'signup_email', 'value' =>
    set_value('signup_email', $this->uri->segment(3) . '@' . $this-
    >uri->segment(4)), 'maxlength' => '100', 'size' => '35',
    'placeholder' => $this->lang->line('signup_email'));
$data['signup_opt1'] = array('name' => 'signup_opt1', 'id' =>
    'signup_opt1', 'value' => '1', 'checked' => ($signup_opt1 == 1)
    ? TRUE : FALSE, 'style' => 'margin:10px');
$data['signup_opt2'] = array('name' => 'signup_opt2', 'id' =>
    'signup_opt2', 'value' => '1', 'checked' => ($signup_opt2 == 1)
    ? TRUE : FALSE, 'style' => 'margin:10px');
$data['signup_unsub'] = array('name' => 'signup_unsub', 'id' =>
    'signup_unsub', 'value' => '1', 'checked' => FALSE, 'style' =>
    'margin:10px');
```

These form element settings are then sent to the `views/signup/settings.php` file:

```
$this->load->view('common/header');
$this->load->view('nav/top_nav', $data);
$this->load->view('signup/settings', $data);
$this->load->view('common/footer');
} else {
```

If the form is submitted without errors, then we arrive at the following code. The first thing we do is work out whether the user has indicated that they wish to unsubscribe. This is done by looking for the value of the `signup_unsub` form checkbox. If this has been checked by the user, then there is no need to update their settings. Instead, we delete the user by calling the `delete()` function of `signup_model`:

```
if ($this->input->post('signup_unsub') == 1) {
  $data = array('signup_email' => $this->input->
    post('signup_email'));
```

```
    if ($this->Signup_model->delete($data)) {
      echo $this->lang->line('unsub_success');
    } else {
      echo $this->lang->line('unsub_error');
    }
  } else {
```

However, if they haven't indicated that they want to unsubscribe by checking the form checkbox named `signup_unsub`, then we would want to update their details. We package up the values of the form inputs into an array called `$data` and make it ready to write to the database using the `edit()` function of `signup_model`:

```
$data = array('signup_email' => $this->input->
  post('signup_email'),
              'signup_opt1' => $this->input-
                >post('signup_opt1'),
              'signup_opt2' => $this->input-
                >post('signup_opt2'));
if ($this->Signup_model->edit($data)) {
  echo $this->lang->line('setting_success');
} else {
  echo $this->lang->line('setting_error');
}
      }
    }
  }
}
```

So, that was the `signup` controller. As you saw, it's a small, concise script that I'm sure you will be able to amend and extend as you wish.

Creating the language file

As with all the projects in this book, we're making use of the language file to serve text to users. This way, you can enable multiple region/multiple language support. Let's create the language file.

Create the `/path/to/codeigniter/application/language/english/en_admin_lang.php` file and add the following code to it:

```
<?php if (!defined('BASEPATH')) exit('No direct script access
  allowed');

s// General
$lang['system_system_name'] = "Signup";
```

```
// nav
$lang['nav_home'] = "Home";

// index()
$lang['singup_instruction'] = "";
$lang['signup_email'] = "Your Email";
$lang['signup_opt1'] = "Option 1";
$lang['signup_opt2'] = "Option 2";
$lang['signup_unsub'] = "Unsubscribe";
$lang['signup_success'] = "You have signed up";
$lang['signup_error'] = "There was an error in signing up";
$lang['setting_success'] = "Your settings have been amended";
$lang['setting_error'] = "There was an error in amending your
  settings";
$lang['unsub_success'] = "You have been unsubscribed";
$lang['unsub_error'] = "There was an error in unsubscribing you";
```

Putting it all together

Okay, here are a few examples that will help put everything together.

User subscribes

The sequence of events taking place when a user subscribes are as follows:

1. The user visits the application and CodeIgniter routes them to the `signup` controller.

2. The `index()` function in the `signup` controller displays the `views/signup/signup.php` view file.

3. The user views the form in the browser, enters their e-mail address, and submits the form with no validation errors.

4. The `index()` function packages the users' input into an array called `$data` and passes it to the `add()` function of `Signup_model`.

5. The `add()` function performs an Active Record insert to write the users' subscription to the `signups` database table.

User updates their settings

The following events take place when a user wants to update settings:

1. The user clicks on a link in an e-mail they have been sent.

2. The URL routes them to the `signup` controller's `settings()` function.

3. The `settings()` function takes the third and fourth parameters of the URL, joins the third and fourth segments with an @ character, and passes this "rebuilt" e-mail address to the `signup` controller's `get_settings()` function.

4. The `get_settings()` function looks in the database for a matching record, and if exactly one record is found, it returns it as a database result object to the `settings()` function.

5. Now that the `settings()` function has a matching record, it takes various items from the result object and assigns them to local variables.

6. These are then used to prepopulate the form items in the `views/signup/settings.php` file.

7. The user sees the form displayed with whichever settings the records are filled in.

8. The user wishes to check **Option 1** but leave **Option 2** unchecked. The user clicks on the checkbox of **Option 1**.

9. The user submits the form, the form is submitted to the `signup` controller's `settings()` function, and is validated successfully with no errors.

10. As there are no errors, the second part of the validation test (the rest) is run.

11. The value of the form element `signup_unsub` is checked. As the user is not unsubscribing, this will not equal `1`.

12. As `signup_unsub` does not equal `1`, the `edit()` function of `signup_model` is passed an array called `$data`. This `$data` array contains the contents of the posted form data.

13. The `edit()` function then performs a CodeIgniter Active Record update operation on the `$data` array.

User unsubscribes

When a user wants to unsubscribe, the following events take place:

1. The user clicks on a link in an e-mail they have been sent.

2. The URL routes them to the `signup` controller's `settings()` function.

3. The `settings()` function takes the third and fourth parameters of the URL, joins the third and fourth segments with an @ character, and passes this "rebuilt" e-mail address to the `signup` controller's `get_settings()` function.

4. The `get_settings()` function looks in the database for a matching record, and if exactly one record is found, it returns it as a database result object to the `settings()` function.

5. Now that the `settings()` function has a matching record, it takes various items from the result object and assigns them to local variables.

6. These are then used to pre-populate the form items in the `views/signup/settings.php` file.

7. The user sees the form displayed with whichever settings the records are filled in.

8. The user wishes to unsubscribe from the service.

9. The user checks Unsubscribe and submits the form. The form is submitted to the `signup` controller's `settings()` function and is validated successfully with no errors.

10. As there are no errors, the second part of the validation test (the rest) is run.

11. The value of the form element `signup_unsub` is checked. This equals 1 as the user is unsubscribing.

12. As `signup_unsub` equals 1, the `delete()` function of `signup_model` is passed an array called `$data`. This `$data` array contains the subscribers' e-mail address.

13. The `delete()` function then performs a CodeIgniter Active Record delete operation on the `$data` array.

Summary

In this project, you'll have the foundations of a useful signup application. As always, there are a few things you can do to expand upon the functionality, which do are as follows:

- Add more options that a user might apply to their subscription

- Add HTML/plaintext settings (and only send them what they've asked for)

- Add a signup sunset clause: allow someone to sign up for a certain time and once that time is arrived at, stop sending them newsletters.

6
Creating an Authentication System

CodeIgniter doesn't come with a user authentication system out of the box (urgh, that phrase), but nevertheless it doesn't. If you want to manage users and sessions, there are several options open to you. You can install an auth Spark, or you can develop your own solution—which is what we will do here.

One of the irritations I have with other "third-party" plugins (whatever their purpose) is that the code is almost always difficult, making maintenance and integration difficult. This authentication system is as simple as I can make it, and hopefully, it will be easy for you to adapt and extend it for your purposes.

The authentication system provided in this chapter will allow you to create and manage users, password resets, user e-mail notifications, user logins, and so on.

In this chapter, we will cover the following topics:

- Design and wireframes
- Creating the database
- Creating the models
- Creating the views
- Creating the controllers
- Putting it all together

Introduction

To create this app, we will create five controllers: one to handle signing in to sessions, one to handle admin functions (CRUD operations), one for user password management, one to allow a user to register, and one to offer functionality to a user once they are logged in.

We'll also create a language file to store text, allowing you to have multiple language support should that be required.

We will make amends to the `config.php` file to allow for encryption support necessary for sessions and password support.

We'll create all the necessary view files and even a CSS file to help Bootstrap with some of the views.

However, this app along with all the others in this book, relies on the basic setup we did in *Chapter 1*, *Introduction and Shared Project Resources*; although you can take large sections of the code and drop it into pretty much any app you might already have, please keep in mind that the setup done in the first chapter acts as a foundation for this chapter.

So without further ado, let's get on with it.

Design and wireframes

As always, before we start building, we should as always take a look at what we plan to build.

Firstly, a brief description of our intent: we plan to build an app that will provide the following functions:

- An admin can manage all users within the system and also allow individual users to edit and update their own data.

- Users can reset passwords if they have forgotten them; e-mails confirming this will be sent to these users

- New users are able to register and become part of the system; a password will be generated and sent to them in an e-mail

We will also look at how to implement code to check for a users' access level. You can use this code in your projects to limit users from specific controllers and controller functions.

To get a better idea of what's happening, let's take a look at the following site map:

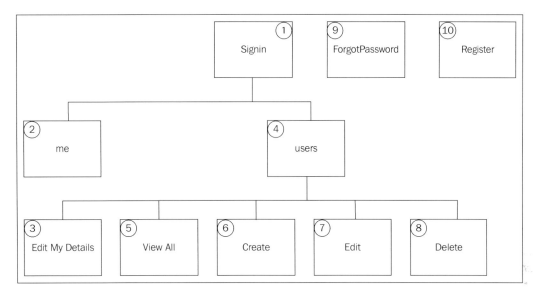

So, that's the site map; now, let's go over each item and get a brief idea of what it does:

- **Signin**: Imagine this as the start point. The user will be able to sign in at this point. Depending on the value in `users.usr_access_level`, they will either be directed to `me` or `users` controllers. The `me` controller is a place for normal users to edit and update their details, while the `users` controller offers a place for an admin to manage all users.

- **Me**: This currently displays a form to the user; however, consider this area a dashboard area for users who are not admins. Admins have their `users.usr_access_level` value set to 1. Currently, the `me` controller will load the `index` function, which will allow the user to edit their details—speaking of which, let's see the next block.

- **Edit My Details**: This will display a form to the current user. The form will allow the user to change and save their contact data.

- **Users**: The `users` controller handles admin functions such as all CRUD operations for users, password resets, and password scramble (for all users).

- **View All**: This lists all users and their current status in the database. The users are displayed in a table. Those users who are active (`users.usr_is_active = 1`) have no background color to their row, while users who are inactive (`users.usr_is_active = 0`) have an orange background color.

- **Create**: As the name suggests, this will display the `users/new_user` view that contains a form, allowing an admin to create a user within the system.

- **Edit**: This displays a form similar to the previous one, except that it is prepopulated with details of the current logged in user. This is loaded when the admin presses the Edit link in the View All page.

- **Delete**: This displays a confirmation page, asking the admin to confirm whether they wish to delete the user. This is loaded when the admin presses the Edit link in the View All page.

- **Forgot Password**: This displays a form to the user. The user is invited to enter their e-mail address in a form text field and press Submit. If the e-mail address exists in the database, then an e-mail is sent to the e-mail address with a URL in the body. This URL is the reset URL for this auth system. Appended to the URL is a unique code that is used by the system to verify that a password reset request is genuine.

- **Register**: This displays a form to the user, inviting them to enter their first name, last name, and e-mail address. Once successfully submitted (there were no validation errors), the new user is added to the system and an e-mail is sent to the new user informing them of their password; their password was generated automatically by the system on their registration.

Now that we have a fairly good idea of the structure and form of the site, let's take a look at some wireframes of each page.

Me – editing details

The following screenshot shows you a wireframe from the Edit My Details item discussed in the site map. The normal user (not an admin user) can view their details in an HTML form and by pressing Save, they can then update these details.

Viewing all users

The following screenshot shows you a wireframe from the View All item in the site map. The admin user is able to see all users within the system in a table grid. Users are listed and have Edit and Delete options, which the admin user can use.

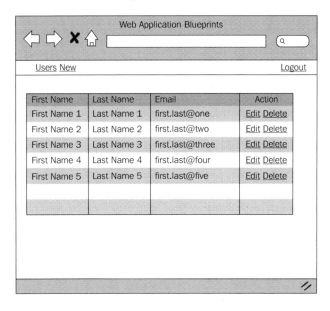

Creating users

The following screenshot shows you a wireframe from point **6** (the Create User item) in the site map. It displays a form that contains text fields, allowing an admin to enter a user's details. Notice that user access levels can be set here; level 1 is treated in the system as an admin, so the user will be able to have admin rights assigned to them, whereas higher numbers are normal users. Currently, only level 2 (as a normal user) is understood by the system; the dropdown has as many as five levels — you can apply these in your adaptation of this project as you see fit or even add more should you wish. Setting the user as active (`users.usr_is_active = 1`) or inactive (`users.usr_is_active = 0`) will restrict the user at login. An active user will have their login request processed by the `signin` script, whereas an inactive user won't.

Editing the user details

The form to edit user details is similar to the New User functionality discussed in the previous section. It is accessed through point **5** (the View Users functionality) of the site map when an admin user clicks on the Edit link (in the `/views/users/view_all_users.php` view file) next to a person's name. The interesting difference here is the Other Options panel with the Reset Password Email option. This will reset the user's password and send them an e-mail informing them of their new password.

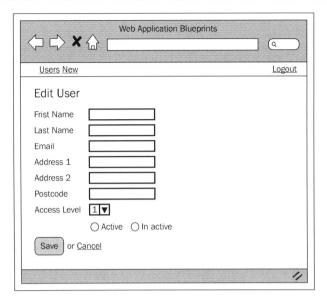

Deleting a user

This is a final confirmation page that asks for permission to delete a user. It is accessed through point **5** (the View Users functionality) in the site map. An admin clicks on the Edit link to view the Edit User page. Clicking on Delete will remove the user from the `users` table, whereas `Cancel` will return the admin to point **5** (the View Users item).

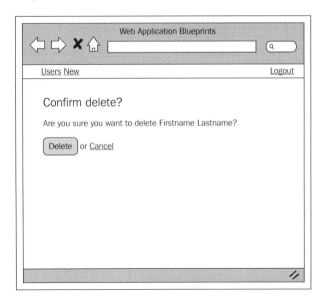

Sign in

The following screenshot shows you the plan for the signing-in page. The user can enter their username and password and press the Login button. Validation errors are displayed above the form (however, validation errors are not shown in the following screenshot). There is also a link for someone to initiate a process to reset password. The **Forgot Password** link will display a new form, allowing that person to enter an e-mail address.

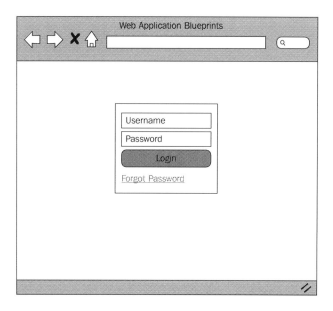

Register

The register functionality allows a nonuser to register with the system. The potential user is prompted to enter their first name, last name, and e-mail address. We use their first and last name in a welcome e-mail that will be sent to the e-mail address entered at this stage.

File overview

We're going to create quite a few files for this project, 23 files in all, and they are as follows:

- `/path/to/codeigniter/application/core/MY_Controller.php`: This acts as a parent class to child classes such as the `users.php` controller. It provides common resources such as commonly used helpers, libraries, and error delimiters.

- `/path/to/codeigniter/application/models/password_model.php`: This provides read/write access to the database—particularly around the `users` table—focusing on password specific operations.

- `/path/to/codeigniter/application/models/signin_model.php`: This provides methods that are specific to the sign-in process.

- `/path/to/codeigniter/application/models/users_model.php`: This provides methods that are specific to the `users` table.

- `/path/to/codeigniter/application/model/register_model.php`: This provides methods that assist in a user being added to the `users` table without an admin creating them first.

- `/path/to/codeigniter/application/views/nav/top_nav.php`: This provides a navigation bar at the top of the page.

- `/path/to/codeigniter/application/language/english/en_admin_lang.php`: This provides language support for the application.

- `/path/to/codeigniter/application/views/users/new_user.php`: This allows an admin to create a new user. The user is saved to the `users` table.

- `/path/to/codeigniter/application/views/users/view_all_users.php`: This allows an admin to view a list of all users in the `users` table.

- `/path/to/codeigniter/application/views/users/delete_user.php`: This allows an admin to delete a user.

- `/path/to/codeigniter/application/views/users/edit_user.php`: This allows an admin to edit the details of a user.

- `/path/to/codeigniter/application/views/users/forgot_password.php`: This allows someone who is not logged in to reset their password. This view contains a simple form that asks a user to enter their e-mail address. An e-mail is sent to this address with a unique code. This code is used to ensure that the change password request is genuine.

- `/path/to/codeigniter/application/views/users/me.php`: This allows a user who is not an admin to edit their details.

- `/path/to/codeigniter/application/views/users/new_password.php`: This allows a user who is not logged in to enter a new password.

- `/path/to/codeigniter/application/views/users/register.php`: This allows someone who is not already a user (a record in the `users` table) to sign in and generate a new row in the `users` table.

- `/path/to/codeigniter/application/views/users/signin.php`: This shows a simple login form.

- `/path/to/codeigniter/application/views/users/change_password.php`: This allows someone who is signed in to reset their password.

- `/path/to/codeigniter/application/views/email_scripts/welcome.txt`: This contains simple welcome text.

- `/path/to/codeigniter/application/views/email_scripts/new_password.txt`: This contains a simple instruction to click on a link to open the `password/new_password` controller function

- `/path/to/codeigniter/application/views/email_scripts/reset_password.txt`: This contains a simple message that informs a user that their password has been changed.

The file structure of the preceding 23 files is shown here:

```
application/
├── core/
│   ├── MY_Controller.php
├── controllers/
│   ├── me.php
│   ├── password.php
│   ├── register.php
│   ├── signin.php
│   ├── users.php
├── models/
│   ├── password_model.php
│   ├── register_model.php
│   ├── signin_model.php
│   ├── users_model.php
├── views/users/
│   ├── new_user.php
│   ├── view_all_users.php
│   ├── delete_user.php
│   ├── edit_user.php
│   ├── forgot_password.php
│   ├── me.php
│   ├── new_password.php
│   ├── register.php
│   ├── signin.php
│   ├── change_password.php
├── views/email_scripts/
│   ├── welcome.txt
│   ├── new_password.txt
│   ├── reset_password.txt
├── views/nav/
│   ├── top_nav.php
├── views/common/
│   ├── login_header.php
├── language/english/
│   ├── en_admin_lang.php
bootstrap/
├── css/
    ├── signin.css
```

Note the last item in the list, which is `signin.css`. This sits in the `bootstrap/css/` folder, which is at the same level as CodeIgniter's `application` folder. We installed Twitter Bootstrap in *Chapter 1, Introduction and Shared Project Resources*. In this chapter, we will go through how to place the `bootstrap` folder at the proper folder level and location.

Creating the database

Okay, you should have already set up CodeIgniter and Bootstrap as described in *Chapter 1, Introduction and Shared Project Resources*. If not, then you should know that the code in this chapter is specifically built with the setup from *Chapter 1, Introduction and Shared Project Resources*, in mind. However, it's not the end of the world if you haven't—the code can easily be applied to other situations.

Firstly, we'll build the database. Copy the following MySQL code into your database:

```
CREATE DATABASE `user_auth`;
USE `user_auth`;

CREATE TABLE `ci_sessions` (
  `session_id` varchar(40) COLLATE utf8_bin NOT NULL DEFAULT '0',
  `ip_address` varchar(16) COLLATE utf8_bin NOT NULL DEFAULT '0',
  `user_agent` varchar(120) COLLATE utf8_bin DEFAULT NULL,
  `last_activity` int(10) unsigned NOT NULL DEFAULT '0',
  `user_data` text COLLATE utf8_bin NOT NULL,
  PRIMARY KEY (`session_id`),
  KEY `last_activity_idx` (`last_activity`)
) ENGINE=MyISAM DEFAULT CHARSET=utf8 COLLATE=utf8_bin;

CREATE TABLE `users` (
  `usr_id` int(11) NOT NULL AUTO_INCREMENT,
  `acc_id` int(11) NOT NULL COMMENT 'account id',
  `usr_fname` varchar(125) NOT NULL,
  `usr_lname` varchar(125) NOT NULL,
  `usr_uname` varchar(50) NOT NULL,
  `usr_email` varchar(255) NOT NULL,
  `usr_hash` varchar(255) NOT NULL,
  `usr_add1` varchar(255) NOT NULL,
  `usr_add2` varchar(255) NOT NULL,
  `usr_add3` varchar(255) NOT NULL,
  `usr_town_city` varchar(255) NOT NULL,
  `usr_zip_pcode` varchar(10) NOT NULL,
  `usr_access_level` int(2) NOT NULL COMMENT 'up to 99',
```

```
`usr_is_active` int(1) NOT NULL COMMENT '1 (active) or 0
   (inactive)',
`usr_created_at` timestamp NOT NULL DEFAULT CURRENT_TIMESTAMP,
`usr_pwd_change_code` varchar(50) NOT NULL,
PRIMARY KEY (`usr_id`)
) ENGINE=InnoDB  DEFAULT CHARSET=utf8 AUTO_INCREMENT=1 ;
```

You'll see that the first table we create is `ci_sessions`. We need this to allow CodeIgniter to manage sessions, specifically logged in users. However, it is just the standard session table available from *CodeIgniter User Guide*, so I'll not include a description of that table as it's not technically specific to this application. However, if you're interested, there's a description at `http://ellislab.com/codeigniter/user-guide/libraries/sessions.html`.

Right, let's take a look at each item in each table and see what it means:

Table: users	
Element	**Description**
`usr_id`	This is the primary key.
`acc_id`	Should you wish to associate users with specific accounts (or group users together under a sort of umbrella), `acc_id` (for account ID) can be a hook that enables you to do that. You'll need to create an `accounts` table to do this, however.
`usr_fname`	This is the user's first name.
`usr_lname`	This is the user's last name.
`usr_uname`	This is the an option for a username.
`usr_email`	This is the user's e-mail address.

`usr_hash`	This is a hash of the user's password. The value in `users.usr_hash` is generated in two ways. The first is when someone manually changes their password (perhaps by the "forgot password" process). The `$this->encrypt->sha1($this->input->post('usr_password1'));` CodeIgniter function contains the new password from the user.
	
	The second way a password is created is when a password is generated by the system and is e-mailed to the user, for example, when an admin creates a new user manually. This way, the admin doesn't know what the password of the new user is.
	
	To achieve this, CodeIgniter uses the same `sha1()` encryption function; however, instead of a password being supplied from a user through `$POST`, it is made by creating a random string and passing it to `sha1()`, as shown here:
	
	`$password = random_string('alnum', 8);`
	`$hash = $this->encrypt->sha1($password);`

Table: users	
Element	**Description**
usr_add1	This is the first line of a person's address.
usr_add2	This is the second line of a person's address.
usr_add3	This is the third line of a person's address.
usr_town_city	This is the town or city of their address.
usr_zip_pcode	This is the postal code or zip code of the person's address.
usr_access_level	This is the indicates the permission level of the user. The permission level can govern what actions a user is allowed to perform.
usr_is_active	This is the indicates whether the user is active (1) or inactive (0)—inactive means that a user cannot log in.
usr_created_at	This is the MySQL timestamp that is created when the record is created.
usr_pwd_change_code	This is a unique code that's generated when a person wishes to change their password. This unique code is generated and sent in an e-mail to the user who wishes to change their password. The code is appended to a URL in the body of the e-mail. The user clicks on this link and is redirected to the auth system. The system looks at that code to check whether it is valid and matches the e-mail. If it matches, the user can follow onscreen instructions to create a new password for them.

We'll also need to make amends to the config/database.php file, namely setting the database access details, username password, and so on.

Open the config/database.php file and find the following lines:

```
$db['default']['hostname'] = 'localhost';
$db['default']['username'] = 'your username';
$db['default']['password'] = 'your password';
$db['default']['database'] = 'user_auth';
```

Edit the values in the preceding lines, ensuring you substitute these values with ones that are more specific to your setup and situation; so, enter your username, password, and so on.

Adjusting the config.php file

There are a few settings in this file that we'll need to configure to support sessions and encryption. So, open the `config/config.php` file and make the following changes:

1. We will need to set an encryption key; both sessions and CodeIgniter's encryption functionalities require an encryption key to be set in the `$config` array, so find the following line:

   ```
   $config['encryption_key'] = '';
   ```

   Then, change it to the following:

   ```
   $config['encryption_key'] = 'a-random-string-of-alphanum-
       characters';
   ```

   > Now, obviously don't actually change this value to literally a-random-string-of-alphanum-characters but change it to, er, a random string of alphanum characters instead — if that makes sense? Yeah, you know what I mean.

2. Next, find the following lines:

   ```
   $config['sess_cookie_name'] = 'ci_session';
   $config['sess_expiration'] = 7200;
   $config['sess_expire_on_close'] = FALSE;
   $config['sess_encrypt_cookie'] = FALSE;
   $config['sess_use_database'] = FALSE;
   $config['sess_table_name'] = 'ci_sessions';
   $config['sess_match_ip'] = FALSE;
   $config['sess_match_useragent'] = TRUE;
   $config['sess_time_to_update'] = 300;
   ```

   Then, change it to the following:

   ```
   $config['sess_cookie_name'] = 'ci_session';
   $config['sess_expiration'] = 7200;
   $config['sess_expire_on_close'] = TRUE;
   $config['sess_encrypt_cookie'] = TRUE;
   $config['sess_use_database'] = TRUE;
   $config['sess_table_name'] = 'ci_sessions';
   $config['sess_match_ip'] = TRUE;
   $config['sess_match_useragent'] = TRUE;
   $config['sess_time_to_update'] = 300;
   ```

Adjusting the routes.php file

We want to redirect the user to the `signin` controller rather than default CodeIgniter `welcome` controller. We will need to amend the default controller settings in the `routes.php` file to reflect this:

1. Open the `config/routes.php` file for editing and find the following lines (near the bottom of the file):

   ```
   $route['default_controller'] = "welcome";
   $route['404_override'] = '';
   ```

2. Firstly, we need to change the default controller. Initially in a CodeIgniter application, the default controller is set to `welcome`; however, we don't need this; instead, we want the default controller to be `signin`. So, find the following line:

   ```
   $route['default_controller'] = "welcome";
   ```

   Replace it with the following:

   ```
   $route['default_controller'] = "signin";
   ```

Creating the models

There are four models in this project, which are as follows:

- `models/password_model.php`: This contains functions that are specific to creating and resetting passwords.

- `models/register_model.php`: This contains functions that are specific to registering a user.

- `models/signin_model.php`: This contains functions that are specific to signing a user into the system.

- `models/users_model.php`: This contains the main bulk of the model functions for this project, specifically CRUD operations to be performed on users and various other admin functions.

So that's an overview of the models for this project; now, let's go and create each model.

Create the `/path/to/codeigniter/application/models/password_model.php` file and add the following code to it:

```php
<?php if ( ! defined('BASEPATH')) exit('No direct script access
   allowed');
```

```
class Password_model extends CI_Model {
  function __construct() {
     parent::__construct();
  }
```

The `does_code_match()` function will check whether the code supplied in the URL matches that in the database. If it does, it returns `true` or `false` if it doesn't. This is shown here:

```
function does_code_match($code, $email) {
  $query = "SELECT COUNT(*) AS `count`
            FROM `users`
            WHERE `usr_pwd_change_code` = ?
            AND `usr_email` = ? ";

      $res = $this->db->query($query, array($code, $email));
  foreach ($res->result() as $row) {
    $count = $row->count;
  }

  if ($count == 1) {
    return true;
  } else {
    return false;
  }
 }
}
```

Create the `/path/to/codeigniter/application/models/register_model.php` model file and add the following code to it:

```
<?php if ( ! defined('BASEPATH')) exit('No direct script access
  allowed');

class Register_model extends CI_Model {
  function __construct() {
    parent::__construct();
  }

  public function register_user($data) {
     if ($this->db->insert('users', $data)) {
       return true;
     } else {
       return false;
     }
  }
}
```

The `register` model contains just one function, which is `register_user()`. It simply uses the CodeIgniter Active Record `insert()` class to insert the contents of the `$data` array into the `users` table.

Create the `/path/to/codeigniter/application/models/users_model.php` model file and add the following code to it:

```php
<?php if ( ! defined('BASEPATH')) exit('No direct script access
  allowed');

class Users_model extends CI_Model {
  function __construct() {
    parent::__construct();
  }

  function get_all_users() {
    return $this->db->get('users');
  }

  function process_create_user($data) {
    if ($this->db->insert('users', $data)) {
      return $this->db->insert_id();
    } else {
      return false;
    }
  }

  function process_update_user($id, $data) {
    $this->db->where('usr_id', $id);
    if ($this->db->update('users', $data)) {
      return true;
    } else {
      return false;
    }
  }

  function get_user_details($id) {
    $this->db->where('usr_id', $id);
    $result = $this->db->get('users');

    if ($result) {
      return $result;
    } else {
      return false;
    }
```

```
    }

    function get_user_details_by_email($email) {
      $this->db->where('usr_email', $email);
      $result = $this->db->get('users');

      if ($result) {
        return $result;
      } else {
        return false;
      }
    }

    function delete_user($id) {
      if($this->db->delete('users', array('usr_id' => $id))) {
        return true;
      } else {
        return false;
      }
    }
  }
```

Let's look at the `make_code()` function. This function creates a unique code and saves it to the user's record. This code is sent out at the end of a URL in an e-mail to the user. If this code in the URL matches the code in the database, then chances are that it's a genuine password change as it is unlikely that someone would have accurately guessed the code.

Notice the PHP construct do...while—it looks something like this:

```
do {
// something
} while ('...a condition is met');
```

So, this means *do something while a condition is met*. With that in mind, think about our problem; we have to assign `users.usr_pwd_change_code` with a value that doesn't exist in the database already. The code should be a unique value to ensure that someone else doesn't have his or her password changed by mistake.

We use the do...while construct as a means to create code that is unique in the database by first creating the code and then looking through the `users` table for another occurrence of that code. If it is found, then the number of rows returned will be greater or equal to one. Then, another code is generated and another search for the `users` table happens.

This will repeat until a code that cannot be found in the `users` table is generated. This unique code is then returned as `$url_code`:

```
function make_code() {
  do {
    $url_code = random_string('alnum', 8);

    $this->db->where('usr_pwd_change_code = ', $url_code);
    $this->db->from('users');
    $num = $this->db->count_all_results();
  } while ($num >= 1);

  return $url_code;
}

function count_results($email) {
  $this->db->where('usr_email', $email);
  $this->db->from('users');
  return $this->db->count_all_results();
}
```

The following `update_user_password()` function accepts an array of data containing the user's primary key and a new password. The array is provided the `new_password()` function of `password_model`. The user's ID (`users.usr_id`) is from the session (as they're logged in) and the new password is from the form that `new_password()` loads (`views/users/new_password.php`):

```
function update_user_password($data) {
  $this->db->where('usr_id', $data['usr_id']);
  if ($this->db->update('users', $data)) {
      return true;
  } else {
      return false;
  }
}

function does_code_match($data, $email) {
  $query = "SELECT COUNT(*) AS `count`
              FROM `users`
              WHERE `usr_pwd_change_code` = ?
              AND `usr_email` = ? ";

  $res = $this->db->query($query, array($data['code'], $email));
  foreach ($res->result() as $row) {
    $count = $row->count;
```

```
        }

    if ($count == 1) {
        return true;
    } else {
        return false;

    }
  }

  function update_user_code($data) {
    $this->db->where('usr_email', $data['usr_email']);
    if ($this->db->update('users', $data)) {
        return true;
    } else {
        return false;

    }
  }
}
```

Create the /path/to/codeigniter/application/models/signin_model.php
model file and add the following code to it:

```
<?php if ( ! defined('BASEPATH')) exit('No direct script access
  allowed');

class Signin_model extends CI_Model {
    function __construct() {
        parent::__construct();
    }

    public function does_user_exist($email) {
        $this->db->where('usr_email', $email);
        $query = $this->db->get('users');
        return $query;
    }
}
```

This model contains only one function other than __construct(), that is,
does_user_exist($email). This function takes an e-mail address submitted
by the user from the sign-in view and returns the active record query.

The query is evaluated in the `signin` controller with the CodeIgniter database function `num_rows()`:

```
$query = $this->Signin_model->does_user_exist($usr_email);
if ($query->num_rows() == 1) {
...
```

If there is a single match, then the `signin` controller loops over the Active Record result and attempts to log the user in.

Creating the views

There are quite a few view files and e-mail template files in this project—in fact, we're going to create 10 view files, three e-mail scripts, and one header file each specific to logging in and amending a navigation file. Right, let's get to it.

The following are the standard view files used in this project:

- `path/to/codeigniter/application/views/users/new_user.php`: This displays a form to the admin user, allowing them to create a user. The new user is sent an e-mail that welcomes them to the system and informs them of their password. The e-mail script is `/views/email_scripts/welcome.txt`.

- `path/to/codeigniter/application/views/users/view_all_users.php`: This displays a list of users currently in the system. Admin users are able to edit or delete a user.

- `path/to/codeigniter/application/views/users/delete_user.php`: This displays a confirmation page to the admin user. This is displayed if the admin user presses Delete in the `view_all_users/php` view. The confirmation page asks whether the admin user really wishes to delete the selected user.

- `path/to/codeigniter/application/views/users/edit_user.php`: This displays a form to the admin user. This is displayed if the admin user presses Edit in the `view_all_users.php` view. The form is similar to the `new_user.php` file, except that there is a panel where the admin user can send an e-mail to the user to reset their password.

- `path/to/codeigniter/application/views/users/forgot_password.php`: This displays a form to anyone asking for an e-mail address. If this e-mail address is in the system, an e-mail will be sent to them with instructions on how to reset their password.

- `path/to/codeigniter/application/views/users/me.php`: This displays a form to the current logged in user. The form is similar to `edit_user.php`. It allows the current logged in user to edit and amend their account details.

- `path/to/codeigniter/application/views/users/new_password.php`: This displays a form to anyone, inviting then to enter their e-mail address—the code generated earlier from the forgotten password process is already a hidden form element. The code and e-mail address are compared, and if the code matches, a new password is generated for the user.

- `path/to/codeigniter/application/views/users/register.php`: This displays a form to the user, allowing them to enter their first and last names and e-mail addresses. They are then added to the database and a password is generated for them. This password is sent to them in an e-mail along with a welcome message. The text for this e-mail is in `/views/email_scripts/welcome.txt`.

- `path/to/codeigniter/application/views/users/signin.php`: This displays a form. The form allows a user (normal or admin) to sign in to the system with their username and password; remember that their password isn't stored in the `users` table, only a hash of that password is stored. To support this hashing, we'll need to alter the encryption key in the config file. We discussed this in the *Adjusting the config.php file* section of this chapter.

- `path/to/codeigniter/application/views/users/change_password.php`: This displays a form to anyone who is logged in. The form allows a user (normal or admin) to change their password.

The following are the e-mail scripts used in this application:

- `path/to/codeigniter/application/views/email_scripts/welcome.txt`: This contains the text for the welcome e-mail that is sent to a new user when they are either added by an admin from the `new_user.php` form or when they create an account themselves with the form in the `register.php` view.

- `path/to/codeigniter/application/views/email_scripts/new_password.txt`: This file contains the text informing the user of a password change.

- `path/to/codeigniter/application/views/email_scripts/reset_password.txt`: This contains a URL that a user can click on to begin the reset password process. The URL contains a unique code that the system uses to ensure that it is a genuine password change request.

The following are the login header and navigation views:

- `path/to/codeigniter/application/views/common/login_header.php`: The css requirements of the login form are different from that of the standard `/views/common/header.php` view. Specifically, it needs the `signin.css` file.

- `path/to/codeigniter/application/views/nav/top_nav.php`: This contains navigation options that allow admins and normal users to open various pages, and it also contains a logout link that allows a user to terminate their session.

Right, these were the view files, both standard HTML and TXT files for e-mails, and so on. Let's go over each file in turn and create them.

Create the `/path/to/codeigniter/application/views/users/register.php` file and add the following code to it:

```
<div class="container">
  <?php echo validation_errors(); ?>
  <?php echo form_open('register/index', 'role="form" class="form-
    signin"') ; ?>
    <h2 class="form-signin-heading"><?php echo $this->lang->
      line('register_page_title'); ?></h2>
    <input type="text" class="form-control" name="usr_fname"
      placeholder="<?php echo $this->lang->
      line('register_first_name'); ?>" autofocus>
    <input type="text" class="form-control" name="usr_lname"
      placeholder="<?php echo $this->lang->
      line('register_last_name'); ?>" >
    <input type="email" class="form-control" name="usr_email"
      placeholder="<?php echo $this->lang->line('register_email');
      ?>" >
    <?php echo form_submit('submit', 'Register', 'class="btn btn-
      lg btn-primary btn-block"'); ?>
  </form>
</div>
```

This displays a form to a potential user in the system. It requires the user to enter a first name, last name, and an e-mail address. The form is submitted to `register/index`, which will validate the data inputted by the user. If there were no errors, then the user is added to the `users` table, a password is generated for them, and a hash is generated and stored as `users.usr_hash` and e-mailed to them. The e-mail template is `welcome.txt`, which is given next.

Create the `/path/to/codeigniter/application/views/email_scripts/welcome.txt` file and add the following code to it:

```
Dear %usr_fname% %usr_lname%,

Welcome to the site.  Your password is:

%password%

Regards,
The Team
```

This is the text for the welcome e-mail sent to users when they register. Notice that there are three strings of text enclosed in a percent sign (%). These are strings of text that will be identified by the signup process and replaced using the `str_replace()` PHP function with their true values. For example, assume that I register with the site. My name is Robert Foster and my e-mail might be `rob-foster@domain.com`. The e-mail sent to `rob-foster@domain.com` would look like the following:

```
Dear Robert Foster,
Welcome to the site.  Your password is:


<this-is-the-password>


Regards,
The Team
```

Create the `/path/to/codeigniter/application/views/users/forgot_password.php` file and add the following code to it:

```php
<?php if (isset($login_fail)) : ?>
  <div class="alert alert-danger"><?php echo $this->lang->
    line('admin_login_error') ; ?></div>
<?php endif ; ?>
  <?php echo validation_errors(); ?>
  <?php echo form_open('password/forgot_password', 'class="form-
    signin" role="form"') ; ?>
    <h2 class="form-signin-heading"><?php echo $this->lang->
      line('forgot_pwd_header') ; ?></h2>
    <p class="lead"><?php echo $this->lang->
      line('forgot_pwd_instruction') ;?></p>
    <?php echo form_input(array('name' => 'usr_email', 'class' =>
      'form-control', 'placeholder' => $this->lang->
      line('admin_login_email'),'id' => 'email', 'value' =>
      set_value('email', ''), 'maxlength' => '100', 'size' =>
      '50', 'style' => 'width:100%')); ?>
    <br />
    <button class="btn btn-lg btn-primary btn-block"
      type="submit"><?php echo $this->lang->
      line('common_form_elements_go') ; ?></button>
    <br />
  <?php echo form_close() ; ?>
</div>
```

The `forgot_password.php` view file provides a short form to any user to begin the process of resetting their password. The user can enter their e-mail address and press the Go button. The form is submitted to the `password` controller's `forgot_password()` function, where it is validated.

If the e-mail address passes validation, then the `forgot_password()` function checks to see whether the e-mail address exists in the `users` table. If it exists, then a unique code is generated and stored in `users.usr_pwd_change_code`. If the code does not exist, then the user is just redirected to the `forgot_password()` function to try again.

This code is also appended to a URL and sent in the body of an e-mail to the user. The user is instructed to click on the link in the e-mail that will direct them to the `password` controller's `new_password()` function. The `new_password()` function will load the `users/new_password.php` view file, which will ask the user to enter their e-mail address.

This e-mail address is validated and `new_password()` will look in the `users` table to see whether the e-mail address exists. If it exists, it will check to see whether the value of the code in the URL matches the value stored in `users.usr_pwd_change_code`. If it does, then it is likely to be genuine and a new password is generated. This password is e-mailed to the user. A hash is created using the password and stored in `users.usr_hash`.

Create the `/path/to/codeigniter/application/views/users/signin.php` file and add the following code to it:

```php
<?php if (isset($login_fail)) : ?>
  <div class="alert alert-danger"><?php echo $this->lang->
    line('admin_login_error') ; ?></div>
<?php endif ; ?>
  <?php echo validation_errors(); ?>
  <?php echo form_open('signin/index', 'class="form-signin"
    role="form"') ; ?>
    <h2 class="form-signin-heading"><?php echo $this->lang->
      line('admin_login_header') ; ?></h2>
    <input type="email" name="usr_email" class="form-control"
      placeholder="<?php echo $this->lang->
      line('admin_login_email') ; ?>" required autofocus>
    <input type="password" name="usr_password" class="form-
      control" placeholder="<?php echo $this->lang->
      line('admin_login_password') ; ?>" required>
    <button class="btn btn-lg btn-primary btn-block"
      type="submit"><?php echo $this->lang->
      line('admin_login_signin') ; ?></button>
    <br />
    <?php echo anchor('password',$this->lang->
      line('signin_forgot_password')); ?>
  <?php echo form_close() ; ?>
</div>
```

The `signin` view is quite simple: a standard sign-in interface. The user can enter their e-mail address and password to sign in. Validation errors are echoed above the form if there were any errors, and a **Forgot Password** link allows the user to use a method to begin the process of resetting their password.

The error messages are contained in a `div` element with the `alert alert-danger` Bootstrap class; I prefer a big red error message rather than one of those limp-wristed orange jobbies; however, you can change it to something softer, such as `alert alert-warning`.

Create the `/path/to/codeigniter/application/views/users/view_all_users.php` file and add the following code to it:

```
<h2><?php echo $page_heading ; ?></h2>
<table class="table table-bordered">
    <thead>
        <tr>
          <th>#</th>
          <th>First Name</th>
          <th>Last Name</th>
          <th>Email</th>
          <td>Actions</td>
        </tr>
    </thead>
    <tbody>
    <?php if ($query->num_rows() > 0) : ?>
        <?php foreach ($query->result() as $row) : ?>
          <tr>
            <td><?php echo $row->usr_id ; ?></td>
            <td><?php echo $row->usr_fname ; ?></td>
            <td><?php echo $row->usr_lname ; ?></td>
            <td><?php echo $row->usr_email ; ?></td>
            <td><?php echo anchor('users/edit_user/'.
              $row->usr_id,$this->lang->
                line('common_form_elements_action_edit')) .
                ' ' . anchor('users/delete_user/'.
              $row->usr_id,$this->lang->
                line('common_form_elements_action_delete')) ; ?>
            </td>
          </tr>
        <?php endforeach ; ?>
        <?php else : ?>
          <tr>
            <td colspan="5" class="info">No users here!</td>
          </tr>
```

```
            <?php endif; ?>
        </tbody>
    </table>
```

The `view_all_users.php` view file displays all users within the system in a table at any one time. Only admin users are able to see this list.

The table has options for editing and deleting, allowing the user to edit a user (loading the `users` controller's `edit_user()` function) and delete a user (loading the `users` controller's `delete_user()` function).

Create the `/path/to/codeigniter/application/views/users/new_user.php` file and add the following code to it:

```php
<?php echo validation_errors() ; ?>
<div class="page-header">
  <h1><?php echo $page_heading ; ?></h1>
</div>
    <p class="lead"><?php echo $this->lang->
      line('usr_form_instruction_edit');?></p>
    <div class="span8">
<?php echo form_open('users/new_user','role="form" class="form"')
    ; ?>
      <div class="form-group">
        <?php echo form_error('usr_fname'); ?>
        <label for="usr_fname"><?php echo $this->lang->
          line('usr_fname');?></label>
        <?php echo form_input($usr_fname); ?>
      </div>
      <div class="form-group">
        <?php echo form_error('usr_lname'); ?>
        <label for="usr_lname"><?php echo $this->lang->
          line('usr_lname');?></label>
        <?php echo form_input($usr_lname); ?>
      </div>
      <div class="form-group">
        <?php echo form_error('usr_uname'); ?>
        <label for="usr_uname"><?php echo $this->lang->
          line('usr_uname');?></label>
        <?php echo form_input($usr_uname); ?>
      </div>

      <div class="form-group">
        <label for="usr_email"><?php echo $this->lang->
          line('usr_email');?></label>
        <?php echo form_input($usr_email); ?>
```

```
    </div>
    <div class="form-group">
      <label for="usr_confirm_email"><?php echo $this->lang->
        line('usr_confirm_email');?></label>
      <?php echo form_input($usr_confirm_email); ?>
    </div>

    <div class="form-group">
      <label for="usr_add1"><?php echo $this->lang->
        line('usr_add1');?></label>
      <?php echo form_input($usr_add1); ?>
    </div>

    <div class="form-group">
      <label for="usr_add2"><?php echo $this->lang->
        line('usr_add2');?></label>
      <?php echo form_input($usr_add2); ?>
    </div>

    <div class="form-group">
      <label for="usr_add3"><?php echo $this->lang->
        line('usr_add3');?></label>
      <?php echo form_input($usr_add3); ?>
    </div>

    <div class="form-group">
      <label for="usr_town_city"><?php echo $this->lang->
        line('usr_town_city');?></label>
      <?php echo form_input($usr_town_city); ?>
    </div>

    <div class="form-group">
      <label for="usr_zip_pcode"><?php echo $this->lang->
        line('usr_zip_pcode');?></label>
      <?php echo form_input($usr_zip_pcode); ?>
    </div>

    <div class="form-group">
      <label for="usr_access_level"><?php echo $this->lang->
        line('usr_access_level');?></label>
      <?php echo form_dropdown('usr_access_level',
        $usr_access_level, 'large'); ?>
    </div>

    <div class="form-group">
```

```
    <label for="usr_is_active"><?php echo $this->lang->
      line('usr_is_active');?></label>
    <input type="radio" name="usr_is_active" value="<?php echo
      set_value('usr_is_active') ; ?>" /> Active
    <input type="radio" name="usr_is_active" value="<?php echo
      set_value('usr_is_active') ; ?>" /> Inactive
    </div>

    <div class="form-group">
      <button type="submit" class="btn btn-success"><?php echo
        $this->lang->line('common_form_elements_go');?></button>
        or <? echo anchor('users',$this->lang->
        line('common_form_elements_cancel'));?>
      </div>
  <?php echo form_close() ; ?>
    </div>
  </div>
```

The `new_user.php` view file displays a form to an admin user, allowing them to create a user in the system. The form is submitted to the `users` controller's `new_user()` function. Validation errors are displayed above the form. On a successful submission (no validation errors), the `new_user()` function will create a password for the user and a hash value based on the password. The password will be sent to the user in an e-mail. The text of this e-mail is in the `/views/email_scripts/welcome.txt` file.

Create the `/path/to/codeigniter/application/views/users/edit_user.php` file and add the following code to it:

```
<div class="page-header">
  <h1><?php echo $page_heading ; ?></h1>
</div>
  <p class="lead"><?php echo $this->lang->
    line('usr_form_instruction_edit');?></p>

  <div class="span8">
    <?php echo form_open('users/edit_user','role="form"
      class="form"') ; ?>
      <div class="form-group">
        <?php echo form_error('usr_fname'); ?>
        <label for="usr_fname"><?php echo $this->lang->
          line('usr_fname');?></label>
        <?php echo form_input($usr_fname); ?>
      </div>
      <div class="form-group">
        <?php echo form_error('usr_lname'); ?>
```

```
    <label for="usr_lname"><?php echo $this->lang->
    line('usr_lname');?></label>
    <?php echo form_input($usr_lname); ?>
  </div>
  <div class="form-group">
    <?php echo form_error('usr_uname'); ?>
    <label for="usr_uname"><?php echo $this->lang->
      line('usr_uname');?></label>
    <?php echo form_input($usr_uname); ?>
  </div>
  <div class="form-group">
    <?php echo form_error('usr_email'); ?>
    <label for="usr_email"><?php echo $this->lang->
      line('usr_email');?></label>
    <?php echo form_input($usr_email); ?>
  </div>
  <div class="form-group">
    <?php echo form_error('usr_confirm_email'); ?>
    <label for="usr_confirm_email"><?php echo $this->lang->
      line('usr_confirm_email');?></label>
    <?php echo form_input($usr_confirm_email); ?>
  </div>
  <div class="form-group">
    <?php echo form_error('usr_add1'); ?>
    <label for="usr_add1"><?php echo $this->lang->
      line('usr_add1');?></label>
    <?php echo form_input($usr_add1); ?>
  </div>
  <div class="form-group">
    <?php echo form_error('usr_add2'); ?>
    <label for="usr_add2"><?php echo $this->lang->
      line('usr_add2');?></label>
    <?php echo form_input($usr_add2); ?>
  </div>
  <div class="form-group">
    <?php echo form_error('usr_add3'); ?>
    <label for="usr_add3"><?php echo $this->lang->
      line('usr_add3');?></label>
    <?php echo form_input($usr_add3); ?>
  </div>
  <div class="form-group">
    <?php echo form_error('usr_town_city'); ?>
    <label for="usr_town_city"><?php echo $this->lang->
      line('usr_town_city');?></label>
    <?php echo form_input($usr_town_city); ?>
```

```
        </div>
        <div class="form-group">
          <?php echo form_error('usr_zip_pcode'); ?>
          <label for="usr_zip_pcode"><?php echo $this->lang->
            line('usr_zip_pcode');?></label>
          <?php echo form_input($usr_zip_pcode); ?>
        </div>
        <div class="form-group">
          <?php echo form_error('usr_access_level'); ?>
          <label id="usr_access_level" for="usr_access_level"><?php
            echo $this->lang->line('usr_access_level');?></label>
          <?php echo form_dropdown('usr_access_level',
            $usr_access_level_options, $usr_access_level); ?>
        </div>
        <div class="form-group">
          <?php echo form_error('usr_is_active'); ?>
          <label for="usr_is_active"><?php echo $this->lang->
            line('usr_is_active');?></label>
          <input type="radio" name="usr_is_active" <?php if
            ($usr_is_active == 1) { echo 'checked' ;} ?> /> Active
          <input type="radio" name="usr_is_active" <?php if
            ($usr_is_active == 0) { echo 'checked' ;} ?> /> Inactive
        </div>

        <?php echo form_hidden($id); ?>

        <div class="form-group">
          <button type="submit" class="btn btn-success"><?php echo
            $this->lang->line('common_form_elements_go');?></button>
            or <? echo anchor('users',$this->lang->
            line('common_form_elements_cancel'));?>
        </div>
      <?php echo form_close() ; ?>
    </div>

    <?php echo anchor('users/pwd_email/'.$id['usr_id'],'Send
      Password Reset Email') ; ?>

  </div>
```

The edit_user.php view file displays a form to an admin user, allowing them to edit a user in the system. The form is accessed when an admin user clicks on Edit from the views/users/list_all_users.php view file. The form is submitted to the users controller's edit_user() function. Validation errors are displayed above the form.

Create the `/path/to/codeigniter/application/views/users/me.php` file and add the following code to it:

```php
<?php echo validation_errors() ; ?>
<div class="page-header">
  <h1><?php echo $page_heading ; ?></h1>
</div>
  <p class="lead"><?php echo $this->lang->
    line('usr_form_instruction');?></p>

  <div class="span8">
    <?php echo form_open('me/index','role="form"') ; ?>
      <div class="form-group">
        <?php echo form_error('usr_fname'); ?>
        <label for="usr_fname"><?php echo $this->lang->
          line('usr_fname');?></label>
        <?php echo form_input($usr_fname); ?>
      </div>
      <div class="form-group">
        <?php echo form_error('usr_lname'); ?>
        <label for="usr_lname"><?php echo $this->lang->
          line('usr_lname');?></label>
        <?php echo form_input($usr_lname); ?>
      </div>
      <div class="form-group">
        <?php echo form_error('usr_uname'); ?>
        <label for="usr_uname"><?php echo $this->lang->
          line('usr_uname');?></label>
        <?php echo form_input($usr_uname); ?>
      </div>

      <div class="form-group">
        <label for="usr_email"><?php echo $this->lang->
          line('usr_email');?></label>
        <?php echo form_input($usr_email); ?>
      </div>
      <div class="form-group">
        <label for="usr_confirm_email"><?php echo $this->lang->
          line('usr_confirm_email');?></label>
        <?php echo form_input($usr_confirm_email); ?>
      </div>

      <div class="form-group">
        <label for="usr_add1"><?php echo $this->lang->
          line('usr_add1');?></label>
```

```
      <?php echo form_input($usr_add1); ?>
    </div>
    <div class="form-group">
      <label for="usr_add2"><?php echo $this->lang->
        line('usr_add2');?></label>
      <?php echo form_input($usr_add2); ?>
    </div>
    <div class="form-group">
      <label for="usr_add3"><?php echo $this->lang->
        line('usr_add3');?></label>
      <?php echo form_input($usr_add3); ?>
    </div>
    <div class="form-group">
      <label for="usr_town_city"><?php echo $this->lang->
        line('usr_town_city');?></label>
      <?php echo form_input($usr_town_city); ?>
    </div>
    <div class="form-group">
      <label for="usr_zip_pcode"><?php echo $this->lang->
        line('usr_zip_pcode');?></label>
      <?php echo form_input($usr_zip_pcode); ?>
    </div>

    <?php echo form_hidden($id); ?>

    <div class="form-group">
      <button type="submit" class="btn btn-success"><?php echo
        $this->lang->line('common_form_elements_go');?></button>
        or <? echo anchor('users',$this->lang->
        line('common_form_elements_cancel'));?>
    </div>
  <?php echo form_close() ; ?>
</div>

<?php echo anchor('me/pwd_email/'.$id,'Reset Email') ; ?>
```

Again, like the forms in `new_user` and `edit_user` views, this form is similar; however, it includes a Reset Email link, which will run the `me` controller's `pwd_email()` function to create a new password and e-mail it to the current user. The password isn't stored in the database; only a hash value is stored (`users.usr_hash`).

Create the `/path/to/codeigniter/application/views/users/register.php` file and add the following code to it:

```
<div class="container">
  <?php echo validation_errors(); ?>
```

```
<?php echo form_open('register/index', 'role="form" class="form-
    signin"') ; ?>
    <h2 class="form-signin-heading"><?php echo $this->lang->
        line('register_page_title'); ?></h2>
    <input type="text" class="form-control" name="usr_fname"
        placeholder="<?php echo $this->lang->
        line('register_first_name'); ?>" required autofocus>
    <input type="text" class="form-control" name="usr_lname"
        placeholder="<?php echo $this->lang->
        line('register_last_name'); ?>" required>
    <input type="email" class="form-control" name="usr_email"
        placeholder="<?php echo $this->lang->line('register_email');
        ?>" required>
    <?php echo form_submit('submit', 'Register', 'class="btn btn-
        lg btn-primary btn-block"'); ?>
    </form>
</div>
```

The `register.php` view file displays a form to a person wishing to become a user within the system. The user is invited to enter a first name and last name as well as their e-mail address. They then press the Register button.

The form is submitted to the `register` controller's `index()` function. The `index()` function will perform validation, and any errors are displayed above the form.

Assuming that there were no errors and the form was submitted without problems, the `index()` function will attempt to write them to the `users` table. A password is generated and sent to the user in the form of an e-mail. The contents of the e-mail are stored in the `views/email_scripts/welcome.txt` view file.

Create the `/path/to/codeigniter/application/views/users/signin.php` file and add the following code to it:

```
<?php if (isset($login_fail)) : ?>
    <div class="alert alert-danger"><?php echo $this->lang->
        line('admin_login_error') ; ?></div>
<?php endif ; ?>
    <?php echo validation_errors(); ?>
    <?php echo form_open('signin/index', 'class="form-signin"
        role="form"') ; ?>
    <h2 class="form-signin-heading"><?php echo $this->lang->
        line('admin_login_header') ; ?></h2>
    <input type="email" name="usr_email" class="form-control"
        placeholder="<?php echo $this->lang->
        line('admin_login_email') ; ?>" required autofocus>
```

```
<input type="password" name="usr_password" class="form-
   control" placeholder="<?php echo $this->lang->
   line('admin_login_password') ; ?>" required>
<button class="btn btn-lg btn-primary btn-block"
   type="submit"><?php echo $this->lang->
   line('admin_login_signin') ; ?></button>
<br />
<?php echo anchor('password',$this->lang->
   line('signin_forgot_password')); ?>
<?php echo form_close() ; ?>
</div>
```

The `signin.php` view file displays a form to a user. The user is invited to enter their e-mail address and password. The form is submitted to the `signin` controller's `index()` function, which will validate the input, and assuming there were no errors, attempt to process the sign-in request.

Only users who are active can sign in (`users.usr_is_active = 1`) and admin users (`users.usr_accss_level = 1`) will see options that are only available to admins. The normal users (`users.usr_access_level = 2`) will be directed to the `me` controller.

 You can, of course, adapt this behavior to any other controller. Instructions on how to do this are discussed in the *Ensuring correct access* section.

Create the `/path/to/codeigniter/application/views/users/change_password.php` file and add the following code to it:

```
<?php if (isset($login_fail)) : ?>
   <div class="alert alert-danger"><?php echo $this->lang->
      line('admin_login_error') ; ?></div>
<?php endif ; ?>
   <?php echo validation_errors(); ?>
   <?php echo form_open('me/change_password', 'class="form-signin"
      role="form"') ; ?>
      <h2 class="form-signin-heading"><?php echo $this->lang->
         line('forgot_pwd_header') ; ?></h2>
      <p class="lead"><?php echo $this->lang->
         line('forgot_pwd_instruction') ;?></p>
      <table border="0">
         <tr>
            <td><?php $this->lang->line('signin_new_pwd_email') ;
               ?></td>
         </tr>
         <tr>
```

```
        <td><?php echo form_input($usr_new_pwd_1); ?></td>
    </tr>
    <tr>
        <td><?php echo form_input($usr_new_pwd_2); ?></td>
    </tr>
  </table>
  <button class="btn btn-lg btn-primary btn-block"
    type="submit"><?php echo $this->lang->
    line('common_form_elements_go') ; ?></button>
  <br />
<?php echo form_close() ; ?>
</div>
```

This view file displays an HTML form to the user, allowing them to enter two new passwords for their account. The form is submitted to the `me` controller's `change_password()` function, which validates the two passwords supplied and checks whether they match each other, apart from various other validation checks. If validation is passed, then a hash is created from the supplied passwords and that hash is saved to the user's record in the database.

Creating the controllers

In this project, there are six controllers, which are as follows:

- `/core/MY_Controller.php`: This is the parent controller class that contains common resources.

- `/controllers/password.php`: This contains functions that allow the user to request a new password.

- `/controllers/me.php`: This provides a location for a normal (that is, not an admin) user to alter their account settings: name, e-mail, and so on.

- `/controllers/register.php`: This contains functions that allow a new user to sign up and have their details recorded in the `users` table.

- `/controllers/signin.php`: This provides a method for users to log in to their account and to start a session.

- `/controllers/users.php`: This provides functions for an admin to manage users who have signed up and whose records are in the `users` table.

These are our six controllers (one to extend and five that are extended); let's go over each one and create them.

Create the `/path/to/codeigniter/application/core/MY_Controller.php` controller file and add the following code to it:

```php
<?php if ( ! defined('BASEPATH')) exit('No direct script access
  allowed');
class MY_Controller extends CI_Controller {
  function __construct() {
    parent::__construct();
    $this->load->helper('form');
    $this->load->helper('url');
    $this->load->helper('security');
    $this->load->helper('language');
    $this->load->library('session');
    $this->load->library('form_validation');
    $this->form_validation->set_error_delimiters('<div
      class="alert alert-warning" role="alert">', '</div>');
    $this->lang->load('en_admin', 'english');
  }
}
```

The `core/MY_Controller.php` controller acts as an overarching parent controller for all controllers that require the user to be logged in before they're accessed.

Create the `/path/to/codeigniter/application/controllers/password.php` controller file and add the following code to it. As this controller need not be accessed by a logged-in user, we're not extending it with the `MY_Controller`, but only the default `CI_Controller`:

```php
<?php if (!defined('BASEPATH')) exit('No direct script access
  allowed');
class Password extends CI_Controller {
  function __construct() {
    parent::__construct();
    $this->load->library('session');
    $this->load->helper('form');
    $this->load->helper('file');
    $this->load->helper('url');
    $this->load->helper('security');
    $this->load->model('Users_model');
    $this->lang->load('en_admin', 'english');
    $this->load->library('form_validation');
    $this->form_validation->set_error_delimiters('<div class="bs-
      callout bs-callout-error">', '</div>');
  }

  public function index() {
    redirect('password/forgot_password');
  }
```

The **Reset Password page** provides a form to the user, allowing them to enter their e-mail address. Once the user has submitted the form, a code is generated and prepended to a URL link. This link is sent in an e-mail to the e-mail address provided. The unique code in the URL is used by the `password` controller's next function, which is `new_password()`, but we'll go into that later.

First, we define the validation rules for the form in the `users/forgot_password.php` view file, as shown here:

```
public function forgot_password() {
  $this->form_validation->set_rules('usr_email', $this->lang->
    line('signin_new_pwd_email'),
    'required|min_length[5]|max_length[125]|valid_email');
```

If the form is being viewed for the first time or has failed the preceding validation rules, then the `$this->form_validation()` CodeIgniter function returns `FALSE`, loading the `users/forgot_password.php` view file:

```
if ($this->form_validation->run() == FALSE) {
  $this->load->view('common/login_header');
  $this->load->view('users/forgot_password');
  $this->load->view('common/footer');
```

If the user's e-mail passes validation, then we will try to generate a unique code and send them an e-mail:

```
} else {
  $email = $this->input->post('usr_email');
  $num_res = $this->Users_model->count_results($email);
```

First, we look to see whether the e-mail address supplied in the form actually exists in the database. If not, then `$num_res` will not equal 1. If this is the case, then we redirect the user to the `forgot_password()` function. If, however, it exists, then we continue to process the request with an if statement:

```
if ($num_res == 1) {
```

We call the `make_code()` function of `Users_model`, which will generate a unique code for us and return it as the `$code` variable. This `$code` variable is added to the `$data` array and sent to the `update_user_code()` function of `Users_model`, which will write the unique code that was just generated to `users.usr_pwd_change_code` in preparation for the `new_password()` function shown here (`new_password()` is run when the user clicks on the URL in the e-mail we will soon send them):

```
$code = $this->Users_model->make_code();
$data = array(
  'usr_pwd_change_code' => $code,
```

```
        'usr_email' => $email
   );

   if ($this->Users_model->update_user_code($data)) { // Update okay,
     so send email
     $result = $this->Users_model->get_user_details_by_email($email);

     foreach ($result->result() as $row) {
       $usr_fname = $row->usr_fname;
       $usr_lname = $row->usr_lname;
     }
```

Right, the code has been created and saved to the correct account in the database, and we're now ready to start with the e-mail. Let's define the link that will go in the e-mail. For this example, it is `http://www.domain.com/password/new_password/` `UNIQUE-CODE-HERE`; however, you'll need to change this to reflect the path and domain on your servers:

```
   $link = "http://www.domain.com/password/new_password/".$code;
```

Now we need to load the `reset_password.txt` file. This file contains the template text for the body of the e-mail we'll send. Again, you'll need to change the file path of this file to that on your system. We pass the filename to the `read_file()` CodeIgniter function that will open the file and return its contents. The contents of this file, that is, the text in the file, is stored as a string in the `$file` variable:

```
        $path = '/path/to/codeigniter/application/views/
          email_scripts/reset_password.txt';
   $file = read_file($path);
```

Using the `str_replace()` PHP function, we'll replace the variables in the `$file` variable with the correct values:

```
   $file = str_replace('%usr_fname%', $usr_fname, $file);
   $file = str_replace('%usr_lname%', $usr_lname, $file);
   echo $file = str_replace('%link%', $link, $file);
```

Now we're ready to send the e-mail to the user. We're using PHP's `mail()` function to send the e-mail for us. If the e-mail was sent, then we will redirect the user to the sign-in page. If not, then we just reload the function:

```
        if (mail ($email, $this->lang->
          line('email_subject_reset_password'),$file, 'From:
          me@domain.com')) {
          redirect('signin');
        }
      } else {
```

```
        // Some sort of error happened, redirect user back to form
        redirect('password/forgot_password');
      }
    } else { // Some sort of error happened, redirect user back to
      form
      redirect('password/forgot_password');
    }
  }
}
```

The `new_password()` function is accessed when a user clicks on the URL in the e-mail they were sent during the execution of the previous function—`forgot_password()`. It displays a form to the user, allowing them to enter their new password.

First we define the validation rules for the form in the `users/new_password.php` view file:

```
public function new_password() {
  $this->form_validation->set_rules('code', $this->lang->
    line('signin_new_pwd_code'),
    'required|min_length[4]|max_length[8]');
  $this->form_validation->set_rules('usr_email', $this->lang->
    line('signin_new_pwd_email'),
    'required|min_length[5]|max_length[125]');
  $this->form_validation->set_rules('usr_password1', $this->
    lang->line('signin_new_pwd_email'),
    'required|min_length[5]|max_length[125]');
  $this->form_validation->set_rules('usr_password2', $this->
    lang->line('signin_new_pwd_email'),
    'required|min_length[5]|max_length[125]|
    matches[usr_password1]');

  if ($this->input->post()) {
    $data['code'] = xss_clean($this->input->post('code'));
  } else {
    $data['code'] = xss_clean($this->uri->segment(3));
  }
```

If the form is being viewed for the first time or has failed the preceding validation rules, then the `$this->form_validation()` CodeIgniter function returns `FALSE`, loading the `users/new_password.php` view file. The view file contains three form elements: one for a user's email and two for their new password:

```
if ($this->form_validation->run() == FALSE) {
  $data['usr_email']     = array('name' => 'usr_email',
    'class' => 'form-control', 'id' => 'usr_email',      'type'
    => 'text',      'value' => set_value('usr_email', ''),
    'maxlength'    => '100', 'size' => '35', 'placeholder' =>
    $this->lang->line('signin_new_pwd_email'));
```

```
    $data['usr_password1'] = array('name' => 'usr_password1',
        'class' => 'form-control', 'id' => 'usr_password1', 'type'
        => 'password', 'value' => set_value('usr_password1', ''),
        'maxlength'   => '100', 'size' => '35', 'placeholder' =>
        $this->lang->line('signin_new_pwd_pwd'));
    $data['usr_password2'] = array('name' => 'usr_password2',
        'class' => 'form-control', 'id' => 'usr_password2', 'type'
        => 'password', 'value' => set_value('usr_password2', ''),
        'maxlength'   => '100', 'size' => '35', 'placeholder' =>
        $this->lang->line('signin_new_pwd_confirm'));

    $this->load->view('common/login_header', $data);
    $this->load->view('users/new_password', $data);
    $this->load->view('common/footer', $data);
} else {
```

If the form has passed validation, then we will try to match the code in the URL with an account using the e-mail address as a search term:

```
// Does code from input match the code against the email
$email = xss_clean($this->input->post('usr_email'));
```

If the `does_code_match()` function of `Users_model` returns a false value, then there is no record in the database that has the e-mail address and code that matches the e-mail address supplied in the form and the code in the URL. If that's the case, we redirect them to the `forgot_password()` function to start the process again. If, however, it matches, then this is obviously a genuine request:

```
if (!$this->Users_model->does_code_match($data, $email)) { //
  Code doesn't match
      redirect ('users/forgot_password');
    } else {   // Code does match
```

As this is most likely a genuine request and the e-mail and unique code have matched, let's create a hash value from the supplied password:

```
$hash = $this->encrypt->sha1($this->input->post('usr_password1'));
```

We can store this hash in the `$data` array along with the supplied e-mail:

```
$data = array(
  'usr_hash' => $hash,
  'usr_email' => $email
);
```

Now let's take this e-mail and hash and pass to the `update_user_password()` function of `Users_model`:

```
if ($this->Users_model->update_user_password($data)) {
```

Now that the user has updated their password, let's send them an e-mail confirming this:

```
$link = 'http://www.domain.com/signin';
$result = $this->Users_model->get_user_details_by_email($email);

foreach ($result->result() as $row) {
  $usr_fname = $row->usr_fname;
  $usr_lname = $row->usr_lname;
}
```

We need to load the `new_password.txt` file. This file contains the template text for the body of the e-mail we'll send. Again, you'll need to change the file path of this file to that on your system. We pass the filename to the `read_file()` CodeIgniter function that will open the file and return its contents. The contents of this file, that is, the text in the file, is stored as a string in the `$file` variable:

```
$path = '/ path/to/codeigniter/application/views/email_scripts/
  new_password.txt';
$file = read_file($path);
```

Using the `str_replace()` PHP function, we'll replace the variables in the `$file` variable with the correct values. Once this e-mail is sent, we redirect them to the `signin` controller where they can log in using their new password:

```
$file = str_replace('%usr_fname%', $usr_fname, $file);
$file = str_replace('%usr_lname%', $usr_lname, $file);
$file = str_replace('%password%', $password, $file);
$file = str_replace('%link%', $link, $file);
if (mail ($email, $this->lang->line('
  email_subject_new_password'),$file, 'From:
  me@domain.com') ) {
  redirect ('signin');
  }
 }
 }
 }
 }
}
```

Create the `/path/to/codeigniter/application/controllers/me.php` controller file and add the following code to it:

```
<?php if ( ! defined('BASEPATH')) exit('No direct script access
allowed');

class Me extends CI_Controller {
```

The me controller is to be used by users who are not admins—in other words, users whose value of `users.usr_access_level` is set to 2 or above.

This project allows the user to change their details, name, e-mail address, and so on. However, you can adapt the me controller to display any number of things. Or, using the following code in the `__construct()` function of another controller, you can provide functions for specific levels of users:

```
if ( ($this->session->userdata('logged_in') == FALSE) ||
    (!$this->session->userdata('usr_access_level') >= 2) ) {
        redirect('signin');
}
```

We will go through this in more detail later on in the *Putting it all together* section of this chapter; however, let's quickly mention it here anyway. The preceding code checks to see whether the user is logged in and then checks the users' access level (`users.usr_access_level`).

If the `users.usr_access_level` value is not greater than or equal to 2 (which is the level of a normal user), then it will redirect them to `signin` or `signout`—in other words, it will log them out and terminate their session.

By adjusting the value that is compared (for example 1, 2, 3, and so on), you can ensure that users with a specific value can only access this controller:

```
function __construct() {
  parent::__construct();
  $this->load->helper('form');
  $this->load->helper('url');
  $this->load->helper('security');
  $this->load->helper('file'); // for html emails
  $this->load->helper('language');
  $this->load->model('Users_model');
  $this->load->library('session');

  // Load language file
  $this->lang->load('en_admin', 'english');
  $this->load->library('form_validation');
  $this->form_validation->set_error_delimiters('<div class="alert
    alert-warning" role="alert">', '</div>');

  if ( ($this->session->userdata('logged_in') == FALSE) ||
      (!$this->session->userdata('usr_access_level') >= 2) ) {
          redirect('signin/signout');
  }
}
```

The `index()` function allows a normal user to update their details in the database. First, we set our validation rules for the form:

```
public function index() {
  // Set validation rules
  $this->form_validation->set_rules('usr_fname', $this->lang->
    line('usr_fname'), 'required|min_length[1]|max_length[125]');
  $this->form_validation->set_rules('usr_lname', $this->lang->
    line('usr_lname'), 'required|min_length[1]|max_length[125]');
  $this->form_validation->set_rules('usr_uname', $this->lang->
    line('usr_uname'), 'required|min_length[1]|max_length[125]');
  $this->form_validation->set_rules('usr_email', $this->lang->
    line('usr_email'), 'required|min_length[1]|max_length[255]|
    valid_email');
  $this->form_validation->set_rules('usr_confirm_email', $this->
    lang->line('usr_confirm_email'), 'required|min_length[1]|
    max_length[255]|valid_email|matches[usr_email]');
  $this->form_validation->set_rules('usr_add1', $this->lang->
    line('usr_add1'), 'required|min_length[1]|max_length[125]');
  $this->form_validation->set_rules('usr_add2', $this->lang->
    line('usr_add2'), 'required|min_length[1]|max_length[125]');
  $this->form_validation->set_rules('usr_add3', $this->lang->
    line('usr_add3'), 'required|min_length[1]|max_length[125]');
  $this->form_validation->set_rules('usr_town_city', $this->lang->
    line('usr_town_city'), 'required|min_length[1]
    |max_length[125]');
  $this->form_validation->set_rules('usr_zip_pcode', $this->lang->
    line('usr_zip_pcode'), 'required|min_length[1]|
    max_length[125]');

  $data['id'] = $this->session->userdata('usr_id');

  $data['page_heading'] = 'Edit my details';
  // Begin validation
```

If the form is being viewed for the first time or has failed the preceding validation rules, then the `$this->form_validation()` CodeIgniter function returns FALSE, loading the `users/me.php` view file:

```
if ($this->form_validation->run() == FALSE) { // First load, or
  problem with form
```

Here, we define the setting for the HTML form items to be displayed in the `users/me.php` view file. As we are editing a user who is already logged in, we'll need to grab their details from the database in order to prepopulate the form elements.

We call the `get_user_details()` function of `Users_model`, passing to it the user ID fetched from the session:

```
$query = $this->Users_model->get_user_details($data['id']);
foreach ($query->result() as $row) {
  $usr_fname = $row->usr_fname;
  $usr_lname = $row->usr_lname;
  $usr_uname = $row->usr_uname;
  $usr_email = $row->usr_email;
  $usr_add1 = $row->usr_add1;
  $usr_add2 = $row->usr_add2;
  $usr_add3 = $row->usr_add3;
  $usr_town_city = $row->usr_town_city;
  $usr_zip_pcode = $row->usr_zip_pcode;
}
```

Once we have fetched the users details and saved them to local variables, we apply them to the form items. To do this, we use the `set_value()` CodeIgniter function, the first parameter being the name of the form element (for example, `<input type="text" name="this-is-the-name" />`) and the second parameter being the actual value of the form element:

```
$data['usr_fname'] = array('name' => 'usr_fname', 'class' =>
  'form-control', 'id' => 'usr_fname', 'value' =>
  set_value('usr_fname', $usr_fname), 'maxlength'   => '100',
  'size' => '35');
$data['usr_lname'] = array('name' => 'usr_lname', 'class' =>
  'form-control', 'id' => 'usr_lname', 'value' =>
  set_value('usr_lname', $usr_lname), 'maxlength'   => '100',
  'size' => '35');
$data['usr_uname'] = array('name' => 'usr_uname', 'class' =>
  'form-control', 'id' => 'usr_uname', 'value' =>
  set_value('usr_uname', $usr_uname), 'maxlength'   => '100',
  'size' => '35');
$data['usr_email'] = array('name' => 'usr_email', 'class' =>
  'form-control', 'id' => 'usr_email', 'value' =>
  set_value('usr_email', $usr_email), 'maxlength'   => '100',
  'size' => '35');
$data['usr_confirm_email'] = array('name' =>
  'usr_confirm_email', 'class' => 'form-control', 'id' =>
  'usr_confirm_email', 'value' => set_value('usr_confirm_email',
  $usr_email), 'maxlength'   => '100', 'size' => '35');
$data['usr_add1'] = array('name' => 'usr_add1', 'class' =>
  'form-control', 'id' => 'usr_add1', 'value' =>
  set_value('usr_add1', $usr_add1), 'maxlength'   => '100',
  'size' => '35');
```

```
$data['usr_add2'] = array('name' => 'usr_add2', 'class' =>
    'form-control', 'id' => 'usr_add2', 'value' =>
    set_value('usr_add2', $usr_add2), 'maxlength'   => '100',
    'size' => '35');
$data['usr_add3'] = array('name' => 'usr_add3', 'class' =>
    'form-control', 'id' => 'usr_add3', 'value' =>
    set_value('usr_add3', $usr_add3), 'maxlength'   => '100',
    'size' => '35');
$data['usr_town_city'] = array('name' => 'usr_town_city',
    'class' => 'form-control', 'id' => 'usr_town_city', 'value' =>
    set_value('usr_town_city', $usr_town_city), 'maxlength'   =>
    '100', 'size' => '35');
$data['usr_zip_pcode'] = array('name' => 'usr_zip_pcode',
    'class' => 'form-control', 'id' => 'usr_zip_pcode', 'value' =>
    set_value('usr_zip_pcode', $usr_zip_pcode), 'maxlength'   =>
    '100', 'size' => '35');

$this->load->view('common/header', $data);
$this->load->view('nav/top_nav', $data);
$this->load->view('users/me', $data);
$this->load->view('common/footer', $data);
} else { // Validation passed, now escape the data
```

Now that validation has passed, we'll save the posted data to the $data array in preparation to save it to the process_update_user() function of Users_model:

```
$data = array(
    'usr_fname' => $this->input->post('usr_fname'),
    'usr_lname' => $this->input->post('usr_lname'),
    'usr_uname' => $this->input->post('usr_uname'),
    'usr_email' => $this->input->post('usr_email'),
    'usr_add1' => $this->input->post('usr_add1'),
    'usr_add2' => $this->input->post('usr_add2'),
    'usr_add3' => $this->input->post('usr_add3'),
    'usr_town_city' => $this->input->post('usr_town_city'),
    'usr_zip_pcode' => $this->input->post('usr_zip_pcode')
);

if ($this->Users_model->process_update_user($id, $data)) {
    redirect('users');
}
}
}
```

The me controller also contains the change_password() function. This allows the user who is accessing the controller to change their password. Once accessed, the / views/users/change_password.php view file displays a simple form that asks for a new password. Once the form is submitted and validated successfully, a hash is created using the new password provided and saved to the logged-in user's record:

```php
public function change_password() {
  $this->load->library('form_validation');
  $this->form_validation->set_rules('usr_new_pwd_1', $this->
    lang->line('signin_new_pwd_pwd'),
    'required|min_length[5]|max_length[125]');
  $this->form_validation->set_rules('usr_new_pwd_2', $this->
    lang->line('signin_new_pwd_confirm'), 'required|
    min_length[5]|max_length[125]|matches[usr_new_pwd_1]');

  if ($this->form_validation->run() == FALSE) {
    $data['usr_new_pwd_1'] = array('name' => 'usr_new_pwd_1',
      'class' => 'form-control', 'type' => 'password', 'id' =>
      'usr_new_pwd_1', 'value' => set_value('usr_new_pwd_1',
      ''), 'maxlength'   => '100', 'size' => '35', 'placeholder'
      => $this->lang->line('signin_new_pwd_pwd'));
    $data['usr_new_pwd_2'] = array('name' => 'usr_new_pwd_2',
      'class' => 'form-control', 'type' => 'password', 'id' =>
      'usr_new_pwd_2', 'value' => set_value('usr_new_pwd_2',
      ''), 'maxlength'   => '100', 'size' => '35', 'placeholder'
      => $this->lang->line('signin_new_pwd_confirm'));
    $data['submit_path'] = 'me/change_password';

    $this->load->view('common/login_header', $data);
    $this->load->view('users/change_password', $data);
    $this->load->view('common/footer', $data);
  } else {
    $hash = $this->encrypt->sha1($this->input->
      post('usr_new_pwd_1'));

    $data = array(
      'usr_hash' => $hash,
      'usr_id' => $this->session->userdata('usr_id')
    );

    if ($this->Users_model->update_user_password($data)) {
      redirect('signin/signout');
    }
  }
}
```

Create the `/path/to/codeigniter/application/controllers/register.php` controller file and add the following code to it:

```
<?php if (!defined('BASEPATH')) exit('No direct script access
allowed');

class Register extends CI_Controller {
  function __construct() {
  parent::__construct();
  $this->load->helper('form');
  $this->load->helper('url');
  $this->load->helper('security');
  $this->load->model('Register_model');
  $this->load->library('encrypt');
  $this->lang->load('en_admin', 'english');
  $this->load->library('form_validation');
  $this->form_validation->set_error_delimiters('<div class="alert
    alert-warning" role="alert">', '</div>');
  }
```

The `index()` function displays a small form to a new user. This form allows them to enter basic information such as the e-mail address and name. Once the user presses the Register button and for form is successfully validated, the user is sent a welcome e-mail and is added to the database.

First, we set the validation rules for the form in `views/users/register.php`:

```
public function index() {
  // Set validation rules
  $this->form_validation->set_rules('usr_fname', $this->lang->
    line('first_name'), 'required|min_length[1]|max_length[125]');
  $this->form_validation->set_rules('usr_lname', $this->lang->
    line('last_name'), 'required|min_length[1]|max_length[125]');
  $this->form_validation->set_rules('usr_email', $this->lang->
    line('email'), 'required|min_length[1]|max_length[255]|
    valid_email|is_unique[users.usr_email]');

  // Begin validation
  if ($this->form_validation->run() == FALSE) { // First load, or
    problem with form
    $this->load->view('common/login_header');
    $this->load->view('users/register');
    $this->load->view('common/footer');
  } else {
```

Once the form is successfully validated, we create an e-mail for them. This is done by using the `random_string()` CodeIgniter function. We generate an eight-character string of alphanumeric digits. This is stored in the `$password` variable—we'll need this to create the hash (which will be stored in `users.usr_hash`) and to send it to the user in an e-mail (otherwise they won't know what their password is):

```
// Create hash from user password
$password = random_string('alnum', 8);
```

After we create their password, we create a hash value of it. This is done by passing `$password` to `$this->encrypt->sha1()`:

```
$hash = $this->encrypt->sha1($password);
```

Now, we save everything to the `$data` array in preparation of writing to the database. This is done by calling the `register_user()` function of `Register_model` and passing it the `$data` array:

```
$data = array(
    'usr_fname' => $this->input->post('usr_fname'),
    'usr_lname' => $this->input->post('usr_lname'),
    'usr_email' => $this->input->post('usr_email'),
    'usr_is_active' => 1,
    'usr_access_level' => 2,
    'usr_hash' => $hash
);
```

If the `register_user()` function returns `true`, then we send the user an e-mail, otherwise we send them back to the `register` controller:

```
        if ($this->Register_model->register_user($data)) {
            $file = read_file('../views/email_scripts/welcome.txt');
            $file = str_replace('%usr_fname%', $data['usr_fname'],
              $file);
            $file = str_replace('%usr_lname%', $data['usr_lname'],
              $file);
            $file = str_replace('%password%', $password, $file);
            redirect('signin');
        } else {
            redirect('register');
        }
    }
  }
}
```

Create the `/path/to/codeigniter/application/controllers/signin.php` controller file and add the following code to it:

```php
<?php if (!defined('BASEPATH')) exit('No direct script access
  allowed');

class Signin extends CI_Controller {
  function __construct() {
    parent::__construct();
    $this->load->library('session');
    $this->load->helper('form');
    $this->load->helper('url');
    $this->load->helper('security');
    $this->lang->load('en_admin', 'english');
    $this->load->library('form_validation');
    $this->form_validation->set_error_delimiters('<div
      class="alert alert-warning" role="alert">', '</div>');
  }
```

The `index()` function displays a form to the user, allowing them to enter their e-mail address and password. It also handles any validation from the sign-in form.

First off, the `index()` function checks to see whether the user is already logged in—after all, there's no point in someone trying to log in when they're already logged in. So, we check for the value of the `logged_in` userdata item. If this exists and equals `TRUE`, then they must already be logged in. If this is the case, then we work out their user level to see whether they are a normal user or an admin. If they are an admin, they're redirected to the admin area, that is, the `users` controller; if they are not an admin user, they are redirected to the `me` controller:

```php
public function index() {
  if ($this->session->userdata('logged_in') == TRUE) {
    if ($this->session->userdata('usr_access_level') == 1) {
      redirect('users');
    } else {
      redirect('me');
    }
  } else {
```

If they get to this point in the code, then they are not logged in, which means that we have to display a form so they can log in. Now, we define the validation rules for the sign-in form:

```php
// Set validation rules for view filters
$this->form_validation->set_rules('usr_email', $this->lang->
  line('signin_email'), 'required|valid_email|
  min_length[5]|max_length[125]');
```

```
$this->form_validation->set_rules('usr_password', $this->
    lang->line('signin_password'), 'required|
    min_length[5]|max_length[30]');

if ($this->form_validation->run() == FALSE) {
    $this->load->view('common/login_header');
    $this->load->view('users/signin');
    $this->load->view('common/footer');
} else {
```

Assuming that the validation has passed, we store their e-mail and password in local variables, load `Signin_model`, and call the `does_user_exist()` function, passing to it the e-mail address supplied by the user. If anything other than one record is found, then the form redirects to the `signin` controller for the user to try again:

```
$usr_email = $this->input->post('usr_email');
$password = $this->input->post('usr_password');

$this->load->model('Signin_model');
$query = $this->Signin_model->does_user_exist($usr_email);
```

If, however, exactly one record is found, then we will try to log them in:

```
if ($query->num_rows() == 1) { // One matching row found
    foreach ($query->result() as $row) {
        // Call Encrypt library
        $this->load->library('encrypt');
```

We generate a hash from the password supplied by the user and compare it to the hash value in the database result object returned by the `does_user_exist()` call:

```
// Generate hash from a their password
$hash = $this->encrypt->sha1($password);

if ($row->usr_is_active != 0) { // See if the user is active or not
    // Compare the generated hash with that in the database
    if ($hash != $row->usr_hash) {
```

If the user gets to this part in the code, then it means that the hash values didn't match, so we'll display the sign-in view with an error message:

```
// Didn't match so send back to login
$data['login_fail'] = true;
$this->load->view('common/login_header');
$this->load->view('users/signin', $data);
$this->load->view('common/footer');
} else {
```

However, if the user gets here then the hash values match, the password supplied by the user must be correct. So, we package a few items into the $data array, which they will find useful once they are logged in:

```
$data = array(
    'usr_id' => $row->usr_id,
    'acc_id' => $row->acc_id,
    'usr_email' => $row->usr_email,
    'usr_access_level' => $row->usr_access_level,
    'logged_in' => TRUE
);
```

Then, create a session for them with $this->session->set_userdata():

```
// Save data to session
$this->session->set_userdata($data);
```

Finally, we work out what controller to redirect them to. If they are an admin user (users.usr_access_level = 1), they will be directed to users; if they are a normal user (users.usr_access_level = 2), they will be directed to the me controller; however, if users.usr_access_level is anything other than 1 or 2, then they are also directed to the me controller by default:

```
if ($data['usr_access_level'] == 2) {
                redirect('me');
            } elseif ($data['usr_access_level'] == 1) {
                redirect('users');
            } else {
                redirect('me');
            }
        }
    } else {
        // User currently inactive
        redirect('signin');
    }
        }
    }
        }
    }
```

What comes up must come down, or something like that; anyway. what's logged in must be logged out (dreadful!) anyway — signout() is a quick function that destroys the session and redirects the user to the signin controller.

The `signin` controller is called when a user (admin or otherwise) clicks on the Logout link in the `top_nav.php` view. Once redirected, the `signin` controller will recognize they are no longer logged in and display the sign-in form:

```
public function signout() {
  $this->session->sess_destroy();
  redirect ('signin');
  }
}
```

Create the `/path/to/codeigniter/application/controllers/users.php` controller file and add the following code to it:

```
<?php if ( ! defined('BASEPATH')) exit('No direct script access allowed');

class Users extends MY_Controller {
  function __construct() {
    parent::__construct();
    $this->load->helper('file'); // for html emails
    $this->load->model('Users_model');
    $this->load->model('Password_model');

    if ( ($this->session->userdata('logged_in') == FALSE) ||
       ($this->session->userdata('usr_access_level') != 1) ) {
       redirect('signin');
    }
  }
}
```

Okay, the first thing to notice is the `__construct()` function. We test the user's access level (`users.usr_access_level`)—if it is not equal to 1 at least, then they are not an admin user—so, we redirect them out of the controller:

```
public function index() {
  $data['page_heading'] = 'Viewing users';
  $data['query'] = $this->Users_model->get_all_users();
  $this->load->view('common/header', $data);
  $this->load->view('nav/top_nav', $data);
  $this->load->view('users/view_all_users', $data);
  $this->load->view('common/footer', $data);
}
```

Now, let's take a look at the preceding function. The `index()` function loads the `get_all_users()` function of `Users_model` that, as the name suggests, gets all users in the `users` table. The result of this is stored in the `$data` array's `query` item and is then passed to the `views/users/view_all_users.php` view file. This view file will display all users in a table format with two options for editing and deleting.

The `new_user()` function handles the creation of users within the system. Initially, the `new_user()` function sets the validation rules:

```
public function new_user() {
  // Set validation rules
  $this->form_validation->set_rules('usr_fname', $this->lang->
    line('usr_fname'), 'required|min_length[1]|max_length[125]');
  $this->form_validation->set_rules('usr_lname', $this->lang->
    line('usr_lname'), 'required|min_length[1]|max_length[125]');
  $this->form_validation->set_rules('usr_uname', $this->lang->
    line('usr_uname'), 'required|min_length[1]|max_length[125]');
  $this->form_validation->set_rules('usr_email', $this->lang->
    line('usr_email'), 'required|min_length[1]|max_length[255]|
    valid_email|is_unique[users.usr_email]');
  $this->form_validation->set_rules('usr_confirm_email', $this->
    lang->line('usr_confirm_email'), 'required|min_length[1]|
    max_length[255]|valid_email|matches[usr_email]');
  $this->form_validation->set_rules('usr_add1', $this->lang->
    line('usr_add1'), 'required|min_length[1]|max_length[125]');
  $this->form_validation->set_rules('usr_add2', $this->lang->
    line('usr_add2'), 'required|min_length[1]|max_length[125]');
  $this->form_validation->set_rules('usr_add3', $this->lang->
    line('usr_add3'), 'required|min_length[1]|max_length[125]');
  $this->form_validation->set_rules('usr_town_city', $this->lang->
    line('usr_town_city'), 'required|min_length[1]|
    max_length[125]');
  $this->form_validation->set_rules('usr_zip_pcode', $this->lang->
    line('usr_zip_pcode'), 'required|min_length[1]|
    max_length[125]');
  $this->form_validation->set_rules('usr_access_level', $this->
    lang->line('usr_access_level'), 'min_length[1]|
    max_length[125]');
  $this->form_validation->set_rules('usr_is_active', $this->lang->
    line('usr_is_active'), 'min_length[1]|max_length[1]|
    integer|is_natural');

  $data['page_heading'] = 'New user';
  // Begin validation
```

After we set the validation rules (shown in the preceding code), we then test for the return value of `$this->form_validation()`. If it's the first time the page is accessed or any form item fails validation, then FALSE is returned, and the following code is run. Here, we define the settings for the HTML form elements displayed in the `views/users/new_user.php` view:

```
if ($this->form_validation->run() == FALSE) { // First load, or
problem with form
```

```
$data['usr_fname'] = array('name' => 'usr_fname', 'class' =>
  'form-control', 'id' => 'usr_fname', 'value' =>
  set_value('usr_fname', ''), 'maxlength'  => '100', 'size' =>
  '35');
$data['usr_lname'] = array('name' => 'usr_lname', 'class' =>
  'form-control', 'id' => 'usr_lname', 'value' =>
  set_value('usr_lname', ''), 'maxlength'  => '100', 'size' =>
  '35');
$data['usr_uname'] = array('name' => 'usr_uname', 'class' =>
  'form-control', 'id' => 'usr_uname', 'value' =>
  set_value('usr_uname', ''), 'maxlength'  => '100', 'size' =>
  '35');
$data['usr_email'] = array('name' => 'usr_email', 'class' =>
  'form-control', 'id' => 'usr_email', 'value' =>
  set_value('usr_email', ''), 'maxlength'  => '100', 'size' =>
  '35');
$data['usr_confirm_email'] = array('name' =>
  'usr_confirm_email', 'class' => 'form-control', 'id' =>
  'usr_confirm_email', 'value' => set_value('usr_confirm_email',
  ''), 'maxlength'  => '100', 'size' => '35');
$data['usr_add1'] = array('name' => 'usr_add1', 'class' =>
  'form-control', 'id' => 'usr_add1', 'value' =>
  set_value('usr_add1', ''), 'maxlength'  => '100', 'size' =>
  '35');
$data['usr_add2'] = array('name' => 'usr_add2', 'class' =>
  'form-control', 'id' => 'usr_add2', 'value' =>
  set_value('usr_add2', ''), 'maxlength'  => '100', 'size' =>
  '35');
$data['usr_add3'] = array('name' => 'usr_add3', 'class' =>
  'form-control', 'id' => 'usr_add3', 'value' =>
  set_value('usr_add3', ''), 'maxlength'  => '100', 'size' =>
  '35');
$data['usr_town_city'] = array('name' => 'usr_town_city',
  'class' => 'form-control', 'id' => 'usr_town_city', 'value' =>
  set_value('usr_town_city', ''), 'maxlength'  => '100', 'size'
  => '35');
$data['usr_zip_pcode'] = array('name' => 'usr_zip_pcode',
  'class' => 'form-control', 'id' => 'usr_zip_pcode', 'value' =>
  set_value('usr_zip_pcode', ''), 'maxlength'  => '100', 'size'
  => '35');
$data['usr_access_level'] = array(1=>1, 2=>2, 3=>3, 4=>4, 5=>5);

$this->load->view('common/header', $data);
$this->load->view('nav/top_nav', $data);
$this->load->view('users/new_user',$data);
$this->load->view('common/footer', $data);
} else { // Validation passed, now escape the data
```

Assuming that the form data has passed validation, we begin to create a password for the user. We use the random_string() CodeIgniter function to generate an alphanumeric string of characters 8 digits in length.

We then generate a hash from this password using the $this->encrypt->sha1() CodeIgniter function, as shown in the following snippet. Later on in the code, we send the password to the user in an e-mail:

```
$password = random_string('alnum', 8);
$hash = $this->encrypt->sha1($password);
```

We save the form input and $hash to the $data arrays:

```
$data = array(
  'usr_fname' => $this->input->post('usr_fname'),
  'usr_lname' => $this->input->post('usr_lname'),
  'usr_uname' => $this->input->post('usr_uname'),
  'usr_email' => $this->input->post('usr_email'),
  'usr_hash' => $hash,
  'usr_add1' => $this->input->post('usr_add1'),
  'usr_add2' => $this->input->post('usr_add2'),
  'usr_add3' => $this->input->post('usr_add3'),
  'usr_town_city' => $this->input->post('usr_town_city'),
  'usr_zip_pcode' => $this->input->post('usr_zip_pcode'),
  'usr_access_level' => $this->input->post('usr_access_level'),
  'usr_is_active' => $this->input->post('usr_is_active')
);
```

Once it is stored in the $data array, we attempt to save the hash to the database with the process_create_user() function of Users_model:

```
if ($this->Users_model->process_create_user($data)) {
  $file = read_file('../views/email_scripts/welcome.txt');
  $file = str_replace('%usr_fname%', $data['usr_fname'],
    $file);
  $file = str_replace('%usr_lname%', $data['usr_lname'],
    $file);
  $file = str_replace('%password%', $password, $file);
  redirect('users');
} else {

  }
 }
}
```

Should the admin user choose to edit a user's details, they can click on Edit against the user's name when they're viewing the full user list, as described earlier for the `index()` function. If they do press Edit, then the `edit_user()` function is called—this is a basic function that uses the form validation functionality to validate the user's details should the form be submitted.

Initially, we begin by defining the form validation rules:

```
public function edit_user() {
  // Set validation rules
  $this->form_validation->set_rules('usr_id', $this->lang->
    line('usr_id'), 'required|min_length[1]|max_length[125]');
  $this->form_validation->set_rules('usr_fname', $this->lang->
    line('usr_fname'), 'required|min_length[1]|max_length[125]');
  $this->form_validation->set_rules('usr_lname', $this->lang->
    line('usr_lname'), 'required|min_length[1]|max_length[125]');
  $this->form_validation->set_rules('usr_uname', $this->lang->
    line('usr_uname'), 'required|min_length[1]|max_length[125]');
  $this->form_validation->set_rules('usr_email', $this->lang->
    line('usr_email'), 'required|min_length[1]|max_length[255]|
    valid_email');
  $this->form_validation->set_rules('usr_confirm_email', $this->
    lang->line('usr_confirm_email'), 'required|min_length[1]|
    max_length[255]|valid_email|matches[usr_email]');
  $this->form_validation->set_rules('usr_add1', $this->lang->
    line('usr_add1'), 'required|min_length[1]|max_length[125]');
  $this->form_validation->set_rules('usr_add2', $this->lang->
    line('usr_add2'), 'required|min_length[1]|max_length[125]');
  $this->form_validation->set_rules('usr_add3', $this->lang->
    line('usr_add3'), 'required|min_length[1]|max_length[125]');
  $this->form_validation->set_rules('usr_town_city', $this->lang->
    line('usr_town_city'), 'required|min_length[1]|
    max_length[125]');
  $this->form_validation->set_rules('usr_zip_pcode', $this->lang->
    line('usr_zip_pcode'), 'required|min_length[1]|
    max_length[125]');
  $this->form_validation->set_rules('usr_access_level', $this->
    lang->line('usr_access_level'), 'min_length[1]|
    max_length[125]');
  $this->form_validation->set_rules('usr_is_active', $this->lang->
    line('usr_is_active'), 'min_length[1]|max_length[1]|
    integer|is_natural');
```

The user's primary key (`users.usr_id`) is appended to the Edit link and passed to the `edit_user()` function. This is used to look up the user in the `users` table. The `get_user_details($id)` function of `Users_model` takes one parameter—the value of `$id` (as passed in the Edit link or posted using `$_POST` if the form is submitted)—and looks for the user. Once found, the details of the query are written to local variables and saved to the `$data` array. This, in turn, is passed to the `edit_user.php` view where it is used to populate the form items with the correct data:

```php
if ($this->input->post()) {
  $id = $this->input->post('usr_id');
} else {
  $id = $this->uri->segment(3);
}

$data['page_heading'] = 'Edit user';
// Begin validation
```

After we set the validation rules, we test for the return value of `$this->form_validation()`. If it's the first time the page is accessed or any form item fails validation, then `FALSE` is returned, and the following code is run. Here, we define the settings for the HTML form elements displayed in the `views/users/edit_user.php` view:

```php
if ($this->form_validation->run() == FALSE) { // First load, or
  problem with form
    $query = $this->Users_model->get_user_details($id);
    foreach ($query->result() as $row) {
      $usr_id = $row->usr_id;
      $usr_fname = $row->usr_fname;
      $usr_lname = $row->usr_lname;
      $usr_uname = $row->usr_uname;
      $usr_email = $row->usr_email;
      $usr_add1 = $row->usr_add1;
      $usr_add2 = $row->usr_add2;
      $usr_add3 = $row->usr_add3;
      $usr_town_city = $row->usr_town_city;
      $usr_zip_pcode = $row->usr_zip_pcode;
      $usr_access_level = $row->usr_access_level;
      $usr_is_active = $row->usr_is_active;
    }
```

We build the HTML form elements here, defining their settings in the `$data` array, as shown in the following code:

```
$data['usr_fname'] = array('name' => 'usr_fname', 'class' =>
    'form-control', 'id' => 'usr_fname', 'value' =>
    set_value('usr_fname', $usr_fname), 'maxlength'  => '100',
    'size' => '35');
$data['usr_lname'] = array('name' => 'usr_lname', 'class' =>
    'form-control', 'id' => 'usr_lname', 'value' =>
    set_value('usr_lname', $usr_lname), 'maxlength'  => '100',
    'size' => '35');
$data['usr_uname'] = array('name' => 'usr_uname', 'class' =>
    'form-control', 'id' => 'usr_uname', 'value' =>
    set_value('usr_uname', $usr_uname), 'maxlength'  => '100',
    'size' => '35');
$data['usr_email'] = array('name' => 'usr_email', 'class' =>
    'form-control', 'id' => 'usr_email', 'value' =>
    set_value('usr_email', $usr_email), 'maxlength'  => '100',
    'size' => '35');
$data['usr_confirm_email'] = array('name' =>
    'usr_confirm_email', 'class' => 'form-control', 'id' =>
    'usr_confirm_email', 'value' => set_value('usr_confirm_email',
    $usr_email), 'maxlength'  => '100', 'size' => '35');
$data['usr_add1'] = array('name' => 'usr_add1', 'class' =>
    'form-control', 'id' => 'usr_add1', 'value' =>
    set_value('usr_add1', $usr_add1), 'maxlength'  => '100',
    'size' => '35');
$data['usr_add2'] = array('name' => 'usr_add2', 'class' =>
    'form-control', 'id' => 'usr_add2', 'value' =>
    set_value('usr_add2', $usr_add2), 'maxlength'  => '100',
    'size' => '35');
$data['usr_add3'] = array('name' => 'usr_add3', 'class' =>
    'form-control', 'id' => 'usr_add3', 'value' =>
    set_value('usr_add3', $usr_add3), 'maxlength'  => '100',
    'size' => '35');
$data['usr_town_city'] = array('name' => 'usr_town_city',
    'class' => 'form-control', 'id' => 'usr_town_city', 'value' =>
    set_value('usr_town_city', $usr_town_city), 'maxlength'  =>
    '100', 'size' => '35');
$data['usr_zip_pcode'] = array('name' => 'usr_zip_pcode',
    'class' => 'form-control', 'id' => 'usr_zip_pcode', 'value' =>
    set_value('usr_zip_pcode', $usr_zip_pcode), 'maxlength'  =>
    '100', 'size' => '35');
$data['usr_access_level_options'] = array(1=>1, 2=>2, 3=>3,
    4=>4, 5=>5);
$data['usr_access_level'] = array('value' =>
    set_value('usr_access_level', ''));
$data['usr_is_active'] = $usr_is_active;
```

```
$data['id'] = array('usr_id' => set_value('usr_id', $usr_id));

$this->load->view('common/header', $data);
$this->load->view('nav/top_nav', $data);
$this->load->view('users/edit_user', $data);
$this->load->view('common/footer', $data);
} else { // Validation passed, now escape the data
```

Assuming that the form input passed validation, we save the new user information to the `$data` array:

```
$data = array(
  'usr_fname' => $this->input->post('usr_fname'),
  'usr_lname' => $this->input->post('usr_lname'),
  'usr_uname' => $this->input->post('usr_uname'),
  'usr_email' => $this->input->post('usr_email'),
  'usr_add1' => $this->input->post('usr_add1'),
  'usr_add2' => $this->input->post('usr_add2'),
  'usr_add3' => $this->input->post('usr_add3'),
  'usr_town_city' => $this->input->post('usr_town_city'),
  'usr_zip_pcode' => $this->input->post('usr_zip_pcode'),
  'usr_access_level' => $this->input->post('usr_access_level'),
  'usr_is_active' => $this->input->post('usr_is_active')
);
```

Once everything is added to the `$data` array, we try to update the user's details using the `process_update_user()` function of `Users_model`:

```
if ($this->Users_model->process_update_user($id, $data)) {
  redirect('users');
}
}
}
```

By pressing the Delete link in the `views/users/view_all_users.php` file, the users controller's `delete_user()` function is called. Like the `edit_user()` function, `delete_user()` uses the `users_usr_id` primary key appended to the end of the Delete link URL and passes it to the `delete_user($id)` function of `Users_model`. This model function takes one parameter—the `$id` (as passed in the Delete link or posted using `$_POST` if the form is submitted)—and deletes the user from the `users` table:

```
public function delete_user() {
  // Set validation rules
  $this->form_validation->set_rules('id', $this->lang->
    line('usr_id'), 'required|min_length[1]|max_length[11]|
    integer|is_natural');
```

```php
    if ($this->input->post()) {
      $id = $this->input->post('id');
    } else {
      $id = $this->uri->segment(3);
    }

    $data['page_heading'] = 'Confirm delete?';
    if ($this->form_validation->run() == FALSE) { // First load,
      or problem with form
      $data['query'] = $this->Users_model->get_user_details($id);
      $this->load->view('common/header', $data);
      $this->load->view('nav/top_nav', $data);
      $this->load->view('users/delete_user', $data);
      $this->load->view('common/footer', $data);
    } else {
      if ($this->Users_model->delete_user($id)) {
        redirect('users');
      }
    }
  }

  public function pwd_email() {
    $id = $this->uri->segment(3);
    send_email($data, 'reset');
    redirect('users');
  }
}
```

Creating the language file

As with all the projects in this book, we're making use of the language file to serve text to users. This way, you can enable multiple region/multiple language support.

Create the `/path/to/codeigniter/application/language/english/en_admin_lang.php` file and add the following code to it:

```php
<?php if (!defined('BASEPATH')) exit('No direct script access
  allowed');

// General
$lang['system_system_name'] = "Auth System";

// Top Nav
$lang['top_nav_users'] = "Users";
```

```
$lang['top_nav_new'] = 'New';
$lang['top_nav_signin'] = "Login";
$lang['top_nav_signout'] = "Logout";

// Login
$lang['signin_email'] = "Email";
$lang['signin_password'] = "Password";
$lang['admin_login_header'] = "Please sign in";
$lang['admin_login_email'] = "Email";
$lang['admin_login_password'] = "Password";
$lang['admin_login_signin'] = "Signin...";
$lang['admin_login_error'] = "Whoops!  Something went wrong - have
  another go!";
$lang['forgot_pwd_header'] = 'Reset Password...';
$lang['forgot_pwd_instruction'] = 'Enter your email in the box
  below and if your email is in the database we will send you a
  new password' ;

$lang['signin_forgot_password'] = "Forgot Password?";

// Register
$lang['register_page_title'] = "Register...";
$lang['register_first_name'] = "First Name";
$lang['register_last_name'] = "Last Name";
$lang['register_email'] = "Email";

// Emails
$lang['email_subject_new_password'] = "Your new password.";
$lang['email_subject_reset_password'] = "Reset your password.";

// New/Edit User
$lang['usr_form_instruction_new'] = "New User Details";
$lang['usr_form_instruction_edit'] = "Edit User Details";
$lang['usr_id'] = "ID";
$lang['usr_fname'] = "First name";
$lang['usr_lname'] = "Last Name";
$lang['usr_uname'] = "Username";
$lang['usr_email'] = "Email";
$lang['usr_confirm_email'] = "Confirm Email";
$lang['usr_add1'] = "Address 1";
$lang['usr_add2'] = "Address 2";
$lang['usr_add3'] = "Address 3";
$lang['usr_town_city'] = "Town/City";
$lang['usr_zip_pcode'] = "Zip/Postal Code";
```

```
$lang['usr_access_level'] = "User Access Level";
$lang['is_active'] = "User is active?";

// Forgot password
$lang['forgot_pwd_success_heading'] = "Email Sent:";
$lang['forgot_pwd_success_msg'] = "An email has been sent to the
  address provided.";

// New password
$lang['signin_new_pwd_instruction'] = "Reset your password";
$lang['signin_new_pwd_email'] = "Your email";
$lang['signin_new_pwd_pwd'] = "Password";
$lang['signin_new_pwd_confirm'] = "Confirm password";
$lang['signin_new_pwd_code'] = "Code";

// Delete
$lang['delete_confirm_message'] = "Are you sure you want to delete
  the user: ";
```

Putting it all together

Okay, so that's the code. Now, let's take a look at some ways in which it can be used—this will help us get a good idea about how it all interacts with each other.

User registration

The following is the sequence of steps:

- A user opens the `register` controller in their browser and is prompted to enter their first name, last name, and e-mail address
- The user submits the form and the form is posted to the `index()` register function
- The `register` controller saves the user's details to the `users` table and generates a password for them
- This is sent to them in an e-mail and is sent to the email address submitted earlier
- The user can then log back in to the system and amend their details as they wish

Ensuring correct access

It is possible to allocate controllers and even certain functions to be accessed by users with a specific access level only. We touched on this earlier in the chapter; however, we're going to discuss it here as well.

Look at the following code snippet, specifically, the parts in bold:

```
if ( ($this->session->userdata('logged_in') == FALSE) ||
  ($this->session->userdata('usr_access_level') != 1) ) {
    redirect('signin');
}
```

This function can be placed into any controller or function as you wish; doing so will protect this code block from access to users without the correct access level. The first part checks whether a user is logged in (that is, if a session exists), but the second comparison looks at the user access level set at the sign-in. By adjusting the value checked for, you can tailor access to specific users, user groups, or access levels.

Summary

So there you are—a simple auth system using Twitter Bootstrap as a frontend. It should be simple to adapt and amend to suit your needs but still enable you to do the basics.

In the next chapter we will look at creating a simple e-commerce site that will allow you to have a simple shop and a look at options on how you can extend it.

7
Creating an E-Commerce Site

This is a small, concise e-commerce application. There's no admin CMS to manage products (it would have been too much to write about in this chapter), but there is an easy-to-use (and importantly for you easy to adapt) process to display products and let customers order them.

In this chapter, we will cover:

- Design and wireframes
- Creating the database
- Creating models
- Creating views
- Creating controllers
- Putting it all together

Introduction

In this project, we will create a simple shopping cart. This application will allow customers to view products, filter products by category, and add products to their cart.

It will also let customers alter their shopping cart by removing items or changing the quantity of these items.

Finally, there is a customer details form that allows their personal details to be saved against an order for processing.

To create the web application for this project, we will create one controller; this will handle the display of products, amend the quantities of products in the cart, and also handle the processing of orders.

We'll create a language file to store text, which will allow you to have multiple language support should that be required.

We'll create all the necessary view files and a model to interface with the database.

However, this app along with all the others in this book relies on the basic setup we did in *Chapter 1*, *Introduction and Shared Project Resources*; although you can take large sections of the code and drop it into pretty much any app you might already have, please keep in mind that the setup done in the first chapter acts as a foundation for this chapter.

So without further ado, let's get on with it.

Design and wireframes

As always, before we start building, we should take a look at what we plan to build.

Firstly, we will provide a brief description of our intent. We plan to build an app that will allow people to view products as an online shop. They can sort these products by category. Add products to a cart and enter their details to create an order. A special code called `order_fulfilment_code` is generated (saved in the database in `orders.order_fulfilment_code`). This code will allow you to track any order through a payment system.

Anyway, to get a better idea of what's happening, let's take a look at the following site map:

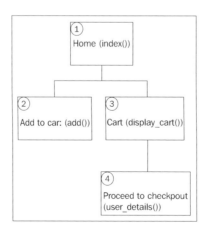

So that's the site map—the first thing to notice is how simple the site is. There are only four main areas to this project. Let's go over each item and get a brief idea of what it does:

- **Home**: This is the initial landing area. The `index()` function displays products to view and also displays categories with which a user can filter the products to see items related to that category. So, by clicking on the Books category, they will see only products that are assigned the category as books.

- **Add to cart**: This processes the addition of a product to the user's cart. The number of items in a cart is presented in the navigation bar at all times.

- **Cart**: This displays a list of items in the cart as well as an option to increase or decrease the number of each items in that cart.

- **Proceed to checkout**: This displays a form to the users, inviting them to enter their information. Once they press Go, their order and details are added to the database for processing.

Now that we have a fairly good idea of the structure and form of the site, let's take a look at some wireframes of each page.

Home – index()

The following screenshot shows you a wireframe from point **1** (the Home (`index()`) item) in the site map. Initially, the user is shown a list of products. This list is not filtered. On the right-hand side of the wireframe is a list of categories (as found in the `categories` table). The user is able to click on these categories to filter the results they view on the left-hand side, and clicking on All Categories clears the filter once more.

Beneath each product is the **Add to cart** button, which allows the user to add a particular product to their cart.

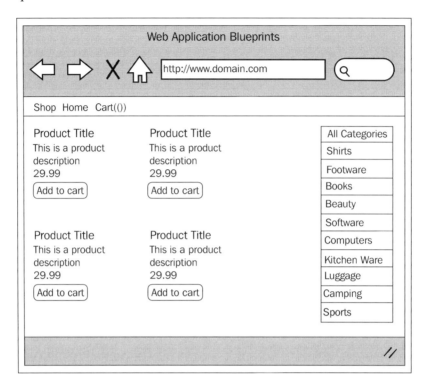

Add to cart – add()

The following screenshot shows you a user clicking and adding a product to their cart. This is done by clicking on an **Add to cart** button below a particular product. Clicking on this button will call the `shop` controller's `add()` function, which will then call the CodeIgniter `Cart` class' `$this->cart->insert()` function, which will add the product to the cart.

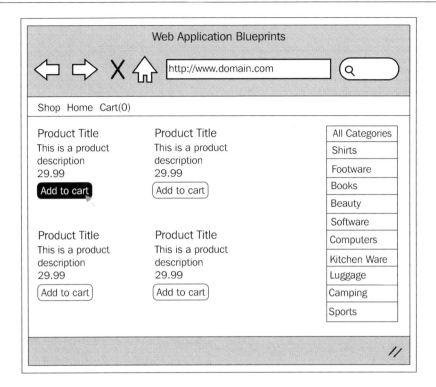

Cart – display_cart()

The following screenshot shows you a wireframe from point 3 (the Cart `display_cart()` item) in the site map. The user is presented with a list of items currently in the cart. The `display_cart()` function is accessed in two ways—either by clicking on the **Cart** link in the top navigation menu or immediately after clicking on **Add to cart** under a product displayed in point **1** (the Home `index()` item) in the site map. Adjusting the value in the text box under Quantity and pressing the **Update Cart** button will increase or decrease the number of that product in the cart.

Pressing Proceed to check out will call the `user_details()` function from point **4** (the Proceed to checkout item) in the site map.

User Details – user_details()

The following screenshot shows you a wireframe from point **4** (the Proceed to checkout `user_details()` item) in the site map. The user is presented with a form in which they can add their contact and delivery details for the order. Once the user enters their details and presses Go, their order (content of the cart) and contact details are written to the `orders` and `customer` tables, which are joined in the `orders` table by the customer ID.

File overview

This is a relatively small project, and all in all, we're only going to create seven files; these are as follows:

- /path/to/codeigniter/application/models/shop_model.php:
  This provides read/write access to the database.

- /path/to/codeigniter/application/views/shop/display_products.
  php: This displays a list of products to the user, allows them to add a
  product to the cart, and filters products by categories—as defined in the
  categories table.

- /path/to/codeigniter/application/views/shop/display_cart.php:
  This displays the contents of the cart to the user. There are form options to
  amend product quantities and proceed to the checkout.

- `/path/to/codeigniter/application/views/shop/user_details.php`: This displays a form to the user, allowing them to enter their contact details for their order fulfillment. User information is stored in the `customer` table, which is joined to the `orders` table—in the `orders` table—by the `customer` table's primary key.

- `/path/to/codeigniter/application/views/nav/top_nav.php`: This provides a navigation bar at the top of the page.

- `/path/to/codeigniter/application/controllers/shop.php`: This contains all the necessary functions to display products, add products to a cart, amend that cart, and process the customer details.

- `/path/to/codeigniter/application/language/english/en_admin_lang.php`: This provides language support for the application.

The file structure of the preceding seven files is as follows:

```
application/
├── controllers/
│   ├── shop.php
├── models/
│   ├── shop_model.php
├── views/shop/
│   ├── display_products.php
│   ├── display_cart.php
│   ├── user_details.php
├── views/nav/
│   ├── top_nav.php
├── language/english/
│   ├── en_admin_lang.php
```

Creating the database

Okay, you should have already set up CodeIgniter and Bootstrap as described in *Chapter 1, Introduction and Shared Project Resources*. If not, then you should know that the code in this chapter is specifically built with the setup from *Chapter 1, Introduction and Shared Project Resources*, in mind. However, it's not the end of the world if you haven't; the code can easily be applied to other situations.

First, we'll build the database. Copy the following MySQL code to your database:

```
CREATE DATABASE `shopdb`;
USE DATABASE `shopdb`;

CREATE TABLE `categories` (
```

```
  `cat_id` int(11) NOT NULL AUTO_INCREMENT,
  `cat_name` varchar(50) NOT NULL,
  `cat_url_name` varchar(15) NOT NULL,
  PRIMARY KEY (`cat_id`)
) ENGINE=InnoDB AUTO_INCREMENT=11 DEFAULT CHARSET=latin1;

INSERT INTO `categories` VALUES
  (1,'Shirts','shirts'),(2,'Footware','footware'),(3,'Books','
  books'),(4,'Beauty','beauty'),(5,'Software','software'),(6,'
  Computers','computers'),(7,'Kitchen Ware','kitchenware'),
  (8,'Luggage','luggage'),(9,'Camping','camping'),(10,'Sports','
  sports');

CREATE TABLE `ci_sessions` (
  `session_id` varchar(40) COLLATE utf8_bin NOT NULL DEFAULT '0',
  `ip_address` varchar(16) COLLATE utf8_bin NOT NULL DEFAULT '0',
  `user_agent` varchar(120) COLLATE utf8_bin DEFAULT NULL,
  `last_activity` int(10) unsigned NOT NULL DEFAULT '0',
  `user_data` text COLLATE utf8_bin NOT NULL
) ENGINE=MyISAM DEFAULT CHARSET=utf8 COLLATE=utf8_bin;

CREATE TABLE `customer` (
  `cust_id` int(11) NOT NULL AUTO_INCREMENT,
  `cust_first_name` varchar(125) NOT NULL,
  `cust_last_name` varchar(125) NOT NULL,
  `cust_email` varchar(255) NOT NULL,
  `cust_created_at` timestamp NOT NULL DEFAULT CURRENT_TIMESTAMP,
  `cust_address` text NOT NULL COMMENT 'card holder address',
  PRIMARY KEY (`cust_id`)
) ENGINE=InnoDB AUTO_INCREMENT=1 DEFAULT CHARSET=latin1;

CREATE TABLE `orders` (
  `order_id` int(11) NOT NULL AUTO_INCREMENT,
  `cust_id` int(11) NOT NULL,
  `order_details` text NOT NULL,
  `order_subtotal` int(11) NOT NULL,
  `order_created_at` timestamp NOT NULL DEFAULT CURRENT_TIMESTAMP,
  `order_closed` int(1) NOT NULL COMMENT '0 = open, 1 = closed',
  `order_fulfilment_code` varchar(255) NOT NULL COMMENT 'the
    unique code sent to a payment provider',
  `order_delivery_address` text NOT NULL,
  PRIMARY KEY (`order_id`)
) ENGINE=InnoDB AUTO_INCREMENT=1 DEFAULT CHARSET=latin1;

CREATE TABLE `products` (
```

```
  `product_id` int(11) NOT NULL AUTO_INCREMENT,
  `product_name` varchar(255) NOT NULL,
  `product_code` int(11) NOT NULL,
  `product_description` varchar(255) NOT NULL,
  `category_id` int(11) NOT NULL,
  `product_price` int(11) NOT NULL,
  PRIMARY KEY (`product_id`)
) ENGINE=InnoDB AUTO_INCREMENT=14 DEFAULT CHARSET=latin1;

INSERT INTO `products` VALUES (1,'Running Shoes',423423,'These are
  some shoes',2,50),(2,'Hawaiian Shirt',34234,'This is a shirt'
  ,1,25),(3,'Slippers',23134,'Nice comfortable  slippers',2,4),
  (4,'Shirt',2553245,'White Office Shirt',1,25),(5,'CodeIgniter
  Blueprints',5442342,'Some excellent projects to make and do (in
  CodeIgniter) - it\'s good value too!',3,25),(6,'Office Suite'
  ,34234123,'Writer, Calc, Presentation software',5,299),(7,'Anti-
  Virus',324142,'Get rid of those pesky viruses from your
  computer',5,29),(8,'Operating System',12341,'This can run your
  computer',5,30),(9,'Web Browser',42412,'Browse the web with a
  web browser (that\'s what they\'re for)',5,5),(10,'Dinner
  set',3241235,'6 dinner plates, 6 side plates, 6 cups',7,45),
  (11,'Champagne Glasses',1454352,'Crystal glasses to drink fizzy
  French plonk from ',7,45),(12,'Toaster',523234,'Capable of
  toasting 4 slices at once!',7,35),(13,'Kettle',62546245,'Heat
  water with this amazing kettle',7,25);
```

 Now take a look at that last bit of SQL code; it's quite big and fiddly. Don't panic; all SQL code is available online from this book's support page on the Packt website.

You'll see that the first table we create is `ci_sessions`. We need this to allow CodeIgniter to manage sessions, specifically, a customer's cart. However, this is just the standard session table available from the *CodeIgniter User Guide*, so I'll not include a description of that table as it's not technically specific to this application. However, if you're interested, there's a description at `http://ellislab.com/codeigniter/user-guide/libraries/sessions.html`.

Right, let's take a look at each item in each table and see what it means. First we will see the `categories` table.

Table: categories	
Element	**Description**
`cat_id`	This is the primary key
`cat_name`	This is the name of the category, and it is displayed as a title in the right-hand side category filter list in the `views/shop/display_products.php` file

Table: categories	
Element	**Description**
cat_url_name	This is the short version of the cat_name element; it is used as the third parameter of the URL when a user clicks on a category in the right-hand side category filter list in the views/shop/display_products.php file

Now take a look at the products table:

Table: products	
Element	**Description**
product_id	This is the primary key
product_name	This is the name of the product
product_code	This is a place where you can store your internal reference code for the product
product_description	This is the description of the product
category_id	This is the category that the product belongs to, and it is the primary key of the categories table
product_price	This is the price of the product

Next we will see the customer table:

Table: customer	
Element	**Description**
cust_id	This is the primary key
cust_first_name	This is the customer's first name
cust_last_name	This is the customer's last name
cust_email	This is the customer's e-mail address
cust_created_at	This is the MySQL timestamp of the date on which the row was created in the database
cust_address	This is the customer address (payment address)

Finally, let's see the `orders` table:

Table: orders	
Element	**Description**
`order_id`	This is the primary key
`cust_id`	This is the primary key of the customer from the `customer` table
`order_details`	This is a serialized dump of the `cart` table populated by the `serialize($this->cart->contents())` line
`order_subtotal`	This is the value of the order
`order_created_at`	This is the MySQL timestamp of the date the row that was created in the database
`order_closed`	The default value is 0 but can be 1. 0; it indicates that this is a new order, and 1 is that the order has been fulfilled
`order_fulfilment_code`	This is the value of the `$payment_code` generated in the `shop` controller's `user_details()` function, and it can be used to track the order through a payment system
`order_delivery_address`	This is the delivery address of the order

We'll also need to make amends to the `config/database.php` file, namely setting the database access details, username password, and so on.

Open the `config/database.php` file and find the following lines:

```
$db['default']['hostname'] = 'localhost';
$db['default']['username'] = 'your username';
$db['default']['password'] = 'your password';
$db['default']['database'] = 'shopdb';
```

Now edit the values in the preceding lines, ensuring you substitute these values with ones more specific to your setup and situation; so, enter your username, password, and so on.

Adjusting the config.php file

There are a few things in this file that we'll need to configure to support sessions and encryption. So open the `config/config.php` file and make the following changes:

1. We will need to set an encryption key; both sessions and CodeIgniter's encryption functionality require a encryption key to be set in the `$config` array, so find the following line:

   ```
   $config['encryption_key'] = '';
   ```

Replace it with the following:

```
$config['encryption_key'] = 'a-random-string-of-alphanum-
    characters';
```

 Now obviously, don't actually change the value to literally a-random-string-of-alphanum-characters; instead, change it to, er, a random string of alphanum characters—if that makes sense? Yeah, you know what I mean.

2. Find these lines:

```
$config['sess_cookie_name'] = 'ci_session';
$config['sess_expiration'] = 7200;
$config['sess_expire_on_close'] = FALSE;
$config['sess_encrypt_cookie'] = FALSE;
$config['sess_use_database'] = FALSE;
$config['sess_table_name'] = 'ci_sessions';
$config['sess_match_ip'] = FALSE;
$config['sess_match_useragent'] = TRUE;
$config['sess_time_to_update'] = 300;
```

Replace the lines with the following:

```
$config['sess_cookie_name'] = 'ci_session';
$config['sess_expiration'] = 7200;
$config['sess_expire_on_close'] = TRUE;
$config['sess_encrypt_cookie'] = TRUE;
$config['sess_use_database'] = TRUE;
$config['sess_table_name'] = 'ci_sessions';
$config['sess_match_ip'] = TRUE;
$config['sess_match_useragent'] = TRUE;
$config['sess_time_to_update'] = 300;
```

Adjusting the routes.php file

We want to redirect the user to the shop controller rather than the default CodeIgniter welcome controller. We will need to amend the default controller setting in the routes.php file to reflect this:

1. Open the config/routes.php file for editing and find the following lines (near the bottom of the file):

```
$route['default_controller'] = "welcome";
$route['404_override'] = '';
```

2. Firstly, we need to change the default controller. Initially in a CodeIgniter application, the default controller is set to `welcome`; however, we don't need that. Instead, we want the default controller to be `shop`. So, find the following line:

```
$route['default_controller'] = "welcome";
```

Change it to the following:

```
$route['default_controller'] = "shop";
$route['404_override'] = '';
```

Creating the model

There is only one model in this project—`shop_model.php`—which contains functions that are specific to searching and writing products to the database.

This is our one and only model for this project; let's briefly go over each function in it to give us a general idea of what it does, and then we will go into more detail in the code.

There are five main functions in this model, which are as follows:

- `get_product_details()`: This accepts one argument—the `$product_id`—of the product being added to the cart and returns a database result object that contains information about a specific product. This model function is used by the `shop` controller's `add()` function to fetch the correct details about a product before it is added to the cart.

- `get_all_products()`: This accepts no argument. This model function will return a list of products (as defined in the `products` table) to the `shop` controller's `index()` function.

- `get_all_products_by_category_name()`: This accepts one argument—`$cat_url_name` (defined in the database as `categories.cat_url_name`). This function is called if a user has clicked on a category filter link (displayed on the right-hand side of the wireframe in the *Home – index()* section of this chapter).

- `get_all_categories()`: This fetches categories from the `categories` table. It is used to populate the categories list (displayed on the right-hand side of the wireframe in the *Home – index()* section of this chapter).

- `save_cart_to_database()`: This accepts two arguments: `$cust_data` and `$order_data`. The `$cust_data` is data submitted by the user in point **4** (the Proceed to checkout `user_details()` item) in the site map, and `$order_data` is the contents of their cart. The customer data is added to the `customer` table and the primary key that's generated is used as a foreign key in the `orders` table.

That was a quick overview, so let's create the model and discuss how it functions.

Create the `/path/to/codeigniter/application/models/shop_model.php` file and add the following code to it:

```php
<?php if ( ! defined('BASEPATH')) exit('No direct script access
  allowed');

class Shop_model extends CI_Model {
  function __construct() {
    parent::__construct();
    $this->load->helper('url');
  }

  public function get_product_details($product_id) {
    $this->db->where('product_id', $product_id);
    $query = $this->db->get('products');
    return $query;
  }
```

The preceding `get_product_details()` function returns a list of all products. This function is called by the `shop` controller's `index()` function if the user hasn't filtered any results, that is, they haven't clicked on a category link in the `views/shop/display_products.php` file:`products() {`

```php
  $q
public function get_all_uery = $this->db->get('products');
  return $query;
}
```

The preceding `get_all_products()` function returns a list of products with a filter applied. This function is called by the `shop` controller's `index()` function if the user has filtered the products by a category, that, they have clicked on a category link in the `views/shop/display_products.php` file:

```php
public function get_all_products_by_category_name($cat_url_name =
  null) {
  if ($cat_url_name) {
    $this->db->where('cat_url_name', $cat_url_name);
    $cat_query = $this->db->get('categories');

    foreach ($cat_query->result() as $row) {
      $category_id = $row->cat_id;
    }

    $this->db->where('category_id', $category_id);
```

```
    }

    $query = $this->db->get('products');
    return $query;
  }
```

The preceding `get_all_products_by_category_name()` function returns a list of all categories in the `categories` table. This model function is called from the `shop` controller's `index()` function to supply data to the product categories list on the right-hand side of the `views/shop/display_products.php` file:

```
  public function get_all_categories($cat_url_name = null) {
    if ($cat_url_name) {
      $this->db->where('cat_url_name', $cat_url_name);
    }

    $query = $this->db->get('categories');
    return $query;
  }
```

The preceding `get_all_categories()` function returns a list of all categories in the `categories` table. This list is used in the `views/shop/display_products.php` file where a `foreach` loop iterates over the database object and displays the categories to the user. A user can then click on a category and filter their results.

Now, take a look at the following snippet:

```
    public function save_cart_to_database($cust_data, $order_data) {
      $this->db->insert('customer', $cust_data);
      $order_data['cust_id'] = $this->db->insert_id();
      if ($this->db->insert('orders', $order_data)) {
        return true;
      } else {
        return false;
      }
    }
  }
```

The preceding `save_cart_to_database()` function saves an order to the database; it converts the data in a cart, along with the data entered by the user in the `views/shop/user_details.php` file.

As you can see, the model is fairly straightforward and concise, so let's now take a look at the views.

Creating the views

There are four views in this project, and these are as follows:

- `/path/to/codeigniter/application/views/shop/display_products.php`: This displays a list of products to the user and allows them to add products to their cart and also filter products.

- `/path/to/codeigniter/application/views/shop/display_cart.php`: This displays all products in the user's cart, allows them to alter the quantities of products in their cart, and also gives an option to move to the checkout stage. This is a customized version of the cart template available from the CodeIgniter documentation.

- `/path/to/codeigniter/application/views/shop/user_details.php`: This displays a form to the user, allowing them to enter information about their order, such as their contact details and delivery address.

- `/path/to/codeigniter/application/views/nav/top_nav.php`: This displays the top-level menu. In this project, this is very simple, containing a project name and link to go to the shop` controller and a link named **Cart**; there is a variable positioned next to the word Cart, displaying the value (0 by default); however, this is in fact the number of items in the cart at any one time. If there were seven items in the cart, the link would say Cart (7).

That was a good overview of the views; now let's go over each one, build the code, and discuss how they function.

Create the `/path/to/codeigniter/application/views/shop/display_products.php` file and add the following code to it:

```
<div class="row row-offcanvas row-offcanvas-right">

  <div class="col-xs-12 col-sm-9">
    <div class="row">
      <?php foreach ($query->result() as $row) : ?>
        <div class="col-6 col-sm-6 col-lg-4">
          <h2><?php echo $row->product_name ; ?></h2>
          <p>&pound;<?php echo $row->product_price ; ?></p>
          <p><?php echo $row->product_description ; ?></p>
          <?php echo anchor('shop/add/'.$row->product_id, $this->
            lang->line('index_add_to_cart'), 'class="btn btn-
            default"') ; ?>
        </div>
      <?php endforeach ; ?>
    </div>
  </div>
```

The preceding block of code outputs a list of products and displays them with a description (`products.product_description`), price (`products.product_price`), and link to add to cart.

A `foreach` loop is used to iterate over the products in `$query`. The `$query` value is populated by data returned by the `get_all_products()` function of `Shop_model`; or, if the user has filtered by a category (explained in the following HTML), then `$query` is populated by the `get_all_products_by_category_name()` function of `Shop_model`:

```
<div class="col-xs-6 col-sm-3 sidebar-offcanvas" id="sidebar"
  role="navigation">
  <div class="list-group">
    <?php echo anchor(base_url(), $this->lang->
      line('index_all_categories'), 'class="list-group-item"') ;
      ?>
    <?php foreach ($cat_query->result() as $row) : ?>
      <?php echo anchor('shop/index/'.$row->cat_url_name, $row->
        cat_name, 'class="list-group-item"') ; ?>
    <?php endforeach ; ?>
  </div>
</div>
</div>
```

The preceding block of code outputs a list of categories that the user can use to filter results. We use a `foreach` loop to iterate over the `$cat_query` array. This array is supplied by the `get_all_categories()` function of `Shop_model`.

Create the `/path/to/codeigniter/application/views/shop/display_cart.php` file and add the following code to it:

```
<?php echo anchor('shop/user_details', $this->lang->
  line('display_cart_proceed_to_checkout'), 'type="button" class="btn
btn-primary btn-lg"') ; ?>
<br /><br />
<?php echo form_open('shop/update_cart'); ?>

<table class="table">

  <tr>
    <th><?php echo $this->lang->line('display_cart_quantity') ; ?>
      </th>
    <th><?php echo $this->lang->line('display_cart_description') ;
      ?></th>
    <th><?php echo $this->lang->line('display_cart_item_price') ;
      ?></th>
```

```
<th><?php echo $this->lang->line('display_cart_sub_total') ;
    ?></th>
</tr>
```

This view is responsible for displaying the contents of the cart to the user and also allowing the user to adjust item quantities in the cart.

Look at the following line of code; with it, we create the $i variable. This variable is incremented in the foreach loop. We use the $i variable to give the product quantity textbox a unique name, that is, 1, 2, 3, 4, and so on:

```
<?php $i = 1; ?>
```

This foreach loop iterates over each item in the CodeIgniter Cart class's $this->cart->contents() function. Each iteration is treated as the $item variable:

```
<?php foreach ($this->cart->contents() as $items): ?>

  <?php echo form_hidden($i . '[rowid]', $items['rowid']); ?>

  <tr>
    <td><?php echo form_input(array('name' => $i . '[qty]',
      'value' => $items['qty'], 'maxlength' => '3', 'size' =>
      '5')); ?></td>
    <td>
      <?php echo $items['name']; ?>

      <?php if ($this->cart->has_options($items['rowid']) ==
        TRUE): ?>

        <p>
          <?php foreach ($this->cart->product_options($items
            ['rowid']) as $option_name => $option_value): ?>

            <strong><?php echo $option_name; ?>:</strong> <?php
            echo $option_value; ?><br />

          <?php endforeach; ?>
        </p>

      <?php endif; ?>

    </td>
    <td><?php echo $this->cart->format_number($items['price']);
      ?></td>
    <td>&pound;<?php echo $this->cart->format_number($items
      ['subtotal']); ?></td>
```

```
    </tr>

    <?php $i++; ?>

  <?php endforeach; ?>

  <tr>
    <td colspan="2"> </td>
    <td><strong>Total</strong></td>
    <td>&pound<?php echo $this->cart->format_number($this->cart->
      total()); ?></td>
  </tr>

</table>
```

After the `foreach` loop, we display a button to the user. The following code is for the button that will submit the form along with any adjusted item quantities:

```
<p><?php echo form_submit('', $this->lang->line
  ('display_cart_update_cart'), 'class="btn btn-success"'); ?></p>
<?php echo form_close() ; ?>
```

Create the `/path/to/codeigniter/application/views/shop/user_details.php` file and add the following code to it:

```
<div class="row row-offcanvas row-offcanvas-right">
  <div class="col-xs-12 col-sm-9">
    <div class="row">
      <?php echo validation_errors(); ?>
      <?php echo form_open('/shop/user_details') ; ?>
      <?php echo form_input($first_name); ?><br />
      <?php echo form_input($last_name); ?><br />
      <?php echo form_input($email); ?><br />
      <?php echo form_input($email_confirm); ?><br />
      <?php echo form_textarea($payment_address); ?><br />
      <?php echo form_textarea($delivery_address); ?><br />
      <?php echo form_submit('', $this->lang->line
        ('common_form_elements_go'), 'class="btn btn-success"') ;
        ?><br />
      <?php echo form_close() ; ?>
    </div>
  </div>
</div>
```

The preceding block of code creates a form into which the user can enter contact details necessary for fulfilling their order.

Create the `/path/to/codeigniter/application/views/nav/top_nav.php` file and add the following code to it:

```
<!-- Fixed navbar -->
<div class="navbar navbar-inverse navbar-fixed-top"
  role="navigation">
  <div class="container">
    <div class="navbar-header">
      <button type="button" class="navbar-toggle" data-toggle=
        "collapse" data-target=".navbar-collapse">
        <span class="sr-only">Toggle navigation</span>
        <span class="icon-bar"></span>
        <span class="icon-bar"></span>
        <span class="icon-bar"></span>
      </button>
      <a class="navbar-brand" href="<?php echo base_url() ; ?>">
        <?php echo $this->lang->line('system_system_name'); ?></a>
    </div>
    <div class="navbar-collapse collapse">
      <ul class="nav navbar-nav">
        <li class="active"><?php echo anchor('shop', $this->lang->
          line('nav_home')) ; ?></li>
        <li><?php echo anchor('shop/display_cart', ($items > 0) ?
          $this->lang->line('nav_cart_count') . '(' . $items . ')'
          : $this->lang->line('nav_cart_count') .'(0)') ; ?></li>
      </ul>
    </div><!--/.nav-collapse -->
  </div>
</div>
<div class="container theme-showcase" role="main">
```

The preceding block of code creates the navigation menu at the top of the page. Take a look at the code in bold, shown again here (restructured):

```
<li>
  <?php
    echo anchor('shop/display_cart',
    ($items > 0) ? $this->lang->line('nav_cart_count') .
    '(' . $items . ')' : $this->lang->line
      ('nav_cart_count').'(0)') ;
  ?>
</li>
```

The preceding block of code displays the word Cart along with a value in brackets. This value is initially set to 0 (zero). However, this value is in fact the quantity of items in the cart—if no items are in the cart, that number will be zero by default.

To start with, we use a PHP ternary operator to switch between displaying zero and the actual number of items in the cart. If the number of items is greater than zero, then there must be some items in the cart. So, we display that number of items, otherwise we display zero.

The word Cart is set in the language file, but what about the value of the number of cart items? Where does that come from?

The number of items in the cart is calculated from several functions in the `shop` controller, which are `index()`, `update_cart()` and `user_details()`. Let's take a look at just one of these (as they all work the same) and see how it works in the `index()` function; check out the following code segment from the `index()` function:

```
...
$cart_contents = $this->session->userdata('cart_contents');
$data['items'] = $cart_contents['total_items'];

$this->load->view('common/header');
$this->load->view('nav/top_nav', $data);
...
```

We fetch the contents of the cart stored in the `cart_contents` session item and store it in the `$cart_contents` variable (to keep it simple).

The CodeIgniter `Cart` class automatically keeps a running total of the number of all items currently in the cart and conveniently stores it in the `total_items` item in the `$cart_contents` array.

We then assign `$data['items']` the value of `total_items` (which should be the number of items in the cart) and send it to the `nav/top_nav.php` view file where is it displayed next to the word Cart.

Creating the controllers

We're going to create only one controller in this project, which is `/path/to/codeigniter/application/controllers/shop.php`.

Let's go over that controller now, look at the code, and discuss how it functions.

Create the `/path/to/codeigniter/application/controllers/shop.php` file and add the following code to it:

```
<?php if (!defined('BASEPATH')) exit('No direct script access
  allowed');

class Shop extends MY_Controller {
  function __construct() {
    parent::__construct();
    $this->load->library('cart');
    $this->load->helper('form');
    $this->load->helper('url');
    $this->load->helper('security');
    $this->load->model('Shop_model');
    $this->load->library('form_validation');
    $this->form_validation->set_error_delimiters('<div class=
      "alert alert-danger">', '</div>');
  }

  public function index() {
```

We want to display the correct products and as such, we need to test whether the user has clicked on one of the filter links on the right-hand side of the `views/shop/display_products.php` file. We test for the presence of a third `uri` parameter.

If the third parameter does not exist, then we can safely assume the user does not want any filtering. So we call the `get_all_products()` function of `Shop_model`.

If a third parameter exists, then the user must be filtering their results. So we call the `get_all_products_by_category_name($this->uri->segment(3))` function, passing to it the third parameter.

The third parameter comes from the `categories.cat_url_name` column in the database, which is written out in the `views/shop/display_products.php` file by a `foreach` loop.

The loop iterates over the `cat_query` database object, which is populated by the `get_all_categories()` function of `Shop_model`, as shown here:

```
if (!$this->uri->segment(3)) {
  $data['query'] = $this->Shop_model->get_all_products();
} else {
  $data['query'] = $this->Shop_model->
    get_all_products_by_category_name($this->uri->segment(3));
}
```

As mentioned in the preceding paragraph, the `get_all_categories()` function of `Shop_model` is called, returning its result to `$data['cat_query']`. In the `views/shop/display_products.php` file, it is iterated over with a `foreach` loop to create a list of categories:

```
$data['cat_query'] = $this->Shop_model->get_all_categories();
```

Now we fetch the number of items in the cart from the `cart_contents` session item. A full explanation of this is in the *Creating the views* section of this chapter, specifically in the explanation for the `/path/to/codeigniter/application/views/nav/top_nav.php` view file:

```
$cart_contents = $this->session->userdata('cart_contents');
$data['items'] = $cart_contents['total_items'];

$this->load->view('common/header');
$this->load->view('nav/top_nav', $data);
$this->load->view('shop/display_products', $data);
$this->load->view('common/footer');
}
```

The following `add()` function adds an item to the cart. It is called from the `views/shop/display_products.php` file when a user clicks on Add to cart. The third parameter of the link in **Add to cart** is the product ID (`products.product_id`). We grab the product ID from the URI (it's the third segment) and pass it to the `get_product_details($product_id)` function of `Shop_model`. This will return the product details in the `$query` variable. We loop over `$query`, pulling out the individual details for the product and saving them to the `$data` array:

```
public function add() {
  $product_id = $this->uri->segment(3);
  $query = $this->Shop_model->get_product_details($product_id);
  foreach($query->result() as $row) {
    $data = array(
      'id'    => $row->product_id,
      'qty' => 1,
      'price'  => $row->product_price,
      'name' => $row->product_name,
    );
  }
```

We save the `$data` array to the cart using the CodeIgniter `Cart` class's `$this->cart->insert();` function:

```
$this->cart->insert($data);
```

We then fetch a list of all categories and the new number of items in the cart and send them to the `nav/top_nav.php` view file.

The `shop/display_cart.php` view file will loop over the contents of the cart using the CodeIgniter `Cart` class's `$this->cart->contents()` function:

```
$data['cat_query'] = $this->Shop_model->get_all_categories();
$cart_contents = $this->session->userdata('cart_contents');
$data['items'] = $cart_contents['total_items'];

$this->load->view('common/header');
$this->load->view('nav/top_nav', $data);
$this->load->view('shop/display_cart', $data);
$this->load->view('common/footer');
}
```

The `update_cart()` function is called when the user clicks on the **Update Cart** button in the `views/shop/display_cart.php` file. When it is called, it loops over the input posted from the form in `views/shop/display_cart.php` and saves it to the `$data` array; let's take a look:

```
public function update_cart() {
    $data = array();
    $i = 0;
```

First we create an array called `$data` in which we can store the adjusted cart data (we'll use this later). Then, we create a `$i` variable; we'll use this to create a multidimensional array, incrementing the value of `$i` on every iteration of the loop—with `$i` keeping the `rowid` value (the ID of the product in the cart) and `qty` value linked and related to each other.

We loop over the posted data (from the form in `views/shop/display_cart.php`), treating each iteration of the loop as `$item`.

Each `$item` has a `rowid` element (the position of the product in the cart) and `qty`, which is the adjusted product quantity:

```
foreach($this->input->post() as $item) {
    $data[$i]['rowid']  = $item['rowid'];
    $data[$i]['qty']    = $item['qty'];
    $i++;
}
```

Now that the cart data has been looped over and any quantity adjustments made, we'll use the CodeIgniter `Cart` class's `$this->cart->update()` function to update the cart. We then redirect the user using the `redirect()` function to the `shop` controller's `display_cart()` function, which will report the new values to the user:

```
    $this->cart->update($data);
    redirect('shop/display_cart');
}
```

The actual iteration over the cart data is done in the `views/shop/display_cart.php` view file, but the `display_cart()` function exists to offer a specific way to view items in the cart. Calling this function loads the `views/shop/display_cart.php` view:

```
public function display_cart() {
    $data['cat_query'] = $this->Shop_model->get_all_categories();
    $cart_contents = $this->session->userdata('cart_contents');
    $data['items'] = $cart_contents['total_items'];
    $this->load->view('common/header');
    $this->load->view('nav/top_nav', $data);
    $this->load->view('shop/display_cart', $data);
    $this->load->view('common/footer');
}

public function clear_cart() {
    $this->cart->destroy();
    redirect('index');
}
```

The `user_details()` function is responsible for displaying a form to the user, allowing them to enter their contact details, validating those details, and converting their cart to an order. Let's look in detail at how this works.

First off, we start by setting the validation rules for the form submission:

```
public function user_details() {
    // Set validation rules
    $this->form_validation->set_rules('first_name', $this->lang->
      line('user_details_placeholder_first_name'),
      'required|min_length[1]|max_length[125]');
    $this->form_validation->set_rules('last_name', $this->lang->
      line('user_details_placeholder_last_name'),
      'required|min_length[1]|max_length[125]');
    $this->form_validation->set_rules('email', $this->lang->
      line('user_details_placeholder_email'),
      'required|min_length[1]|max_length[255]|valid_email');
```

```
$this->form_validation->set_rules('email_confirm', $this->
    lang->line('user_details_placeholder_email_confirm'),
    'required|min_length[1]|max_length[255]|valid_email|
    matches[email]');
$this->form_validation->set_rules('payment_address', $this->
    lang->line('user_details_placeholder_payment_address'),
    'required|min_length[1]|max_length[1000]');
$this->form_validation->set_rules('delivery_address', $this->
    lang->line('user_details_placeholder_delivery_address'),
    'min_length[1]|max_length[1000]');
```

If this is the initial page load or there were errors with the submission of the form, then the `$this->form_validation->run()` function will return FALSE. If either of these happens, then we will begin to build the form elements, defining the settings for each form item:

```
if ($this->form_validation->run() == FALSE) {
  $data['first_name'] = array('name' => 'first_name', 'class' =>
      'form-control', 'id' => 'first_name', 'value' =>
      set_value('first_name', ''), 'maxlength' => '100', 'size' =>
      '35', 'placeholder' => $this->lang->
      line('user_details_placeholder_first_name'));
  $data['last_name'] = array('name' => 'last_name', 'class' =>
      'form-control', 'id' => 'last_name', 'value' =>
      set_value('last_name', ''), 'maxlength' => '100', 'size' =>
      '35', 'placeholder' => $this->lang->
      line('user_details_placeholder_last_name'));
  $data['email'] = array('name' => 'email', 'class' => 'form-
      control', 'id' => 'email', 'value' => set_value('email', ''),
      'maxlength'  => '100', 'size' => '35', 'placeholder' =>
      $this->lang->line('user_details_placeholder_email'));
  $data['email_confirm'] = array('name' => 'email_confirm',
      'class' => 'form-control', 'id' => 'email_confirm', 'value' =>
      set_value('email_confirm', ''), 'maxlength' => '100', 'size'
      => '35', 'placeholder' => $this->lang->
      line('user_details_placeholder_email_confirm'));
  $data['payment_address'] = array('name' => 'payment_address',
      'class' => 'form-control', 'id' => 'payment_address', 'value'
      => set_value('payment_address', ''), 'maxlength' => '100',
      'size' => '35', 'placeholder' => $this->lang->
      line('user_details_placeholder_payment_address'));
  $data['delivery_address'] = array('name' => 'delivery_address',
      'class' => 'form-control', 'id' => 'delivery_address', 'value'
      => set_value('delivery_address', ''), 'maxlength' => '100',
      'size' => '35', 'placeholder' => $this->lang->
      line('user_details_placeholder_delivery_address'));
```

Now we fetch the number of items in the cart from the `cart_contents` session item. A full explanation of this is in the *Creating the views* section of this chapter under the explanation for the `/path/to/codeigniter/application/views/nav/top_nav.php` view file. After we have the contents of the cart for the **Cart** link in the navigation bar, we'll load the `views/shop/user_details.php` file, which will do the job of displaying the form:

```
$cart_contents = $this->session->userdata('cart_contents');
$data['items'] = $cart_contents['total_items'];
$this->load->view('common/header');
$this->load->view('nav/top_nav', $data);
$this->load->view('shop/user_details', $data);
$this->load->view('common/footer');
} else {
```

If, however, there were no errors with the form when it was submitted, then we will arrive at the following code. We define two arrays—one called `$cust_data`, which will store the information submitted by the user in the form in the `views/shop/user_details.php` file and the other called `$order_details`, which will store a serialized dump of the cart. So, the following block of code saves the users' form data:

```
$cust_data = array(
'cust_first_name' => $this->input->post('cust_first_name'),
'cust_last_name' => $this->input->post('cust_last_name'),
'cust_email'=> $this->input->post('cust_email'),
'cust_address'  => $this->input->post('payment_address'));
```

The `$payment_code` value acts as a type of hook that you can use for payment processing. For example, most payment processing systems support the addition of a *code*—usually a string of text and/or numbers that are generated by the shop application, saved to the database, and sent off to the payment provider. After the payment, a webhook script will receive a signal from the payment processing system containing a success or error message (the success or error of the attempted payment from the customer's bank account), along with the *code*. This way, you can ensure that the correct order has been paid for (or not); anyway, `$payment_code` is the following method in the current project:

```
$payment_code = mt_rand();
```

The following block of code saves the cart data to the `$order_data` array. The contents of the cart are fetched from the cart by the CodeIgniter `Cart` class's `$this->cart->contents()` function. The retuned array is passed to the `serialize()` PHP function and is written to `$order_data['order_details':`

```
$order_data = array(
'order_details' => serialize($this->cart->contents()),
```

```
'order_delivery_address' => $this->input->
  post('delivery_address'),
'order_closed' => '0',
'order_fulfilment_code' => $payment_code,
'order_delivery_address' => $this->input->
  post('payment_address'));
```

Now that the customer's contact details and order details are in arrays, we can start to save them to the database. We call the save_cart_to_database() function of Shop_model, passing to it the $cust_data and $order_data array.

The save_cart_to_database() function of Shop_model first saves the customer to the customer table, returning the primary key of the insert and using that primary key as the foreign key value that goes in orders.cust_id:

```
if ($this->Shop_model->save_cart_to_database($cust_data,
  $order_data)) {
  echo $this->lang->line('user_details_save_success');
} else {
  echo $this->lang->line('user_details_save_error');
}
        }
      }
    }
```

Creating the language file

As with all the projects in this book, we're making use of the language file to serve text to users. This way, you can enable multiple region/multiple language support. Let's create the language file.

Create the /path/to/codeigniter/application/language/english/en_admin_lang.php file and add the following code to it:

```
<?php if (!defined('BASEPATH')) exit('No direct script access
  allowed');

// General
$lang['system_system_name'] = "Shop";

// nav
$lang['nav_cart_count'] = "Cart ";
$lang['nav_home'] = "Home";

// index()
```

```
$lang['index_all_categories'] = "All categories";
$lang['index_add_to_cart'] = "Add to cart";

// display_cart()
$lang['display_cart_proceed_to_checkout'] = "Proceed to checkout";
$lang['display_cart_quantity'] = "Quantity";
$lang['display_cart_description'] = "Description";
$lang['display_cart_item_price'] = "Item Price";
$lang['display_cart_sub_total'] = "Sub-Total";
$lang['display_cart_update_cart'] = "Update Cart";

// user_details()
$lang['user_details_placeholder_first_name'] = "First Name";
$lang['user_details_placeholder_last_name'] = "Last Name";
$lang['user_details_placeholder_email'] = "Email";
$lang['user_details_placeholder_email_confirm'] = "Confirm Email";
$lang['user_details_placeholder_payment_address'] = "Payment
  Address";
$lang['user_details_placeholder_delivery_address'] = "Delivery
  Address";
$lang['user_details_save_success'] = "Order and Customer saved to
  DB";
$lang['user_details_save_error'] = "Could not save to DB";
```

Putting it all together

Okay, here are a few examples that will help put everything together.

Filtering a search

When you filter a search, the following events take place:

1. The user visits the site and CodeIgniter routes them to the `shop` controller. The `shop` controller loads the `index()` function

2. The `index()` function recognizes that there is no third parameter in the URL, so it calls the `get_all_products()` function of `Shop_model`.

3. The `index()` function loads the `get_all_categories()` function of `Shop_model`, passing the retuned result to `$data['cat_query']`. This is passed to the `views/shop/display_products.php` file, which—using a `foreach` loop—echoes out the categories.

4. The user clicks on a category in the list. The URL calls the `index()` function, but this time with a third parameter.

5. The `index()` function recognizes this third parameter and loads the `get_all_products_by_category_name()` function of `Shop_model`, passing it the third `uri` segment.

6. The `get_all_products_by_category_name()` function of `Shop_model` then looks in the `categories` table for a category whose `categories.cat_url_name` value matches that supplied in the third parameter and returns the primary key of the category.

7. It then looks in the `products` table for all products whose `products.category_id` value matches the primary key of the category found in just the previous step using `get_all_products_by_category_name()` and then returns the query to the `shop` controller's `index()` function, where it is sent to the `views/shop/view_products.php` file.

Adding to cart

The sequence of events to add items to a cart is as follows:

1. The user visits the site and CodeIgniter routes them to the `shop` controller. The `shop` controller loads the `index()` function

2. The `index()` function recognizes that there is no third parameter in the URL, so it calls the `get_all_products()` function of `Shop_model`.

3. Using a `foreach` loop, the `views/shop/display_products.php` file iterates over the result object from `get_all_products()` and displays each product in turn.

4. The user clicks on the **Add to cart** button

5. CodeIgniter calls the `shop` controller's `add()` function

6. The `add()` function grabs the product ID from the third `uri` segment and sends it to the `get_product_details()` function of `Shop_model`.

7. The `get_product_details()` function looks in the `products` table for the product whose primary key matches that in the argument passed to it and returns it to the `$query` variable.

8. Using a `foreach` loop, we iterate over `$query`, fetching the details of the product, such as `product_name` and `product_price`, and saving them to an array called `$data`, which we will add to the cart. We also set the `qty` value to `1` (as they're only adding one item).

9. Using the CodeIgniter `Cart` class's `$this->cart->insert()` function, we add the product to the cart by passing it the `$data` array.

10. We then direct the user to `display_cart()` to make any amends should they wish.

Altering the product quantity

The user can access the cart in one of these two ways:

- By clicking on **Cart** in the navigation bar at the top of the page
- By being directed there automatically once they add an item to their cart

We'll pick up the story assuming that the user has used either of these methods (as they both drop us here):

1. CodeIgniter calls the `display_cart()` shop function.

2. The bulk of the work in displaying the cart occurs in the `views/shop/display_cart.php` file, which is a modified version of the template found in the CodeIgniter documentation.

3. A variable called `$i` is created and given the value of 1; this will increment as the loop iterates.

4. Using a `foreach` loop, we iterate ever the CodeIgniter `Cart` class's `$this->cart->contents()` function. For each iteration, we call `$item`.

5. An iteration writes the details of each product to an HTML table.

6. An HTML text input is created called `$i`, so if the current iteration is 1, then the name of the textbox will be 1, and if the current iteration is 4, the name of the textbox will be 4.

7. There are three items in the cart (three rows). Each row shows that there is one item of each of the three products in the cart. The user wishes to change the quantities of the product in the third row.

8. The user selects the value of the textbox named 3 and replaces the value in that textbox with the number 2 (which means that the user wishes to buy one item of product 1, one item of product 2, and two items of product 3).

9. The user presses the **Update Cart** button.

10. CodeIgniter calls the `update_cart()` shop function.

11. The `update_cart()` function adjusts the quantity of the third product in the cart.

For a detailed breakdown, check out the explanation in the *Creating the controllers* section of this chapter — look for the `update_cart()` function description.

Summary

In this project, you saw the beginnings of a great shop platform. As always, there are a few things you can do to expand upon the functionality, which are as follows:

- **Product CMS**: This project doesn't come with a CMS to manage products or categories—this is simply because adding such a functionality would have been far too big a topic to cover. However, perhaps you could add some sort of functionality to govern products, adding new ones, deleting old ones, and so on.

- **Product images**: You could add a column to the `products` table where an image file name can be stored and then echo out that value in an HTML `<img src="">` tag. You will, of course, need to add a folder somewhere in the filesystem to store the images.

- **Product pages**: You could add a link to the product title, opening a new page and displaying detailed information about that product, such as color, size, weight, "what's in the box", and so on. Of course, you'll need to add extra columns to the `products` table to support the new information, but this can be done quite easily.

- **BOGOFF**: Verb, British slang—an encouragement from one person to another to leave! Depart! Never to be seen again!

  Well, not quite, but you could add a **Buy One Get One Free** (erm, not sure about the last F) option. You could add logic so that if a certain number of products are selected, a discount is applied.

8
Creating a To-do List

This is a good little project; it's something nearly everyone might need in their day-to-day work: a to-do list. This project will give you a small application to create tasks and set them as complete. There's also a good level of scope for you to expand on the project and really make it your own.

In this chapter, we will cover the following topics:

- Design and wireframes
- Creating the database
- Creating the model
- Creating views
- Creating the controller
- Putting it all together

Introduction

Right; in this project, we will create an application that allows users to create tasks and view these tasks as a list. Tasks can also have a due date; late tasks will appear in red so that you know it's important to execute that task as soon as possible.

To create this app, we will create one controller; this will handle the displaying of tasks, creating these tasks, setting these tasks as done or still to do, and handling the deletion of these tasks.

We'll create a language file to store the text, allowing you to have multiple language support should that be required.

We'll create all the necessary view files and a model to interface with the database.

However, this app along with all the others in this book, relies on the basic setup we did in *Chapter 1, Introduction and Shared Project Resources*; although you can take large sections of the code and drop it into pretty much any app you might already have, please keep in mind that the setup done in the first chapter acts as a foundation for this chapter.

So without further ado, let's get on with it.

Design and wireframes

As always, before we start building, we should take a look at what we plan to build.

Firstly, a brief description of our intent: we plan to build an app that will allow people to add tasks that they need to do. It will also allow users to view these tasks as a list and set them as done. They can also delete old or unneeded tasks should they wish.

Anyway, to get a better idea of what's happening, let's take a look at the following site map:

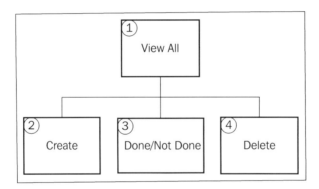

So that's the site map; the first thing to notice is how simple the site is. There are only four main areas to this project. Let's go over each item and get a brief idea of what it does:

- **View All**: This displays a form to create a task and also displays all tasks in a list
- **Create**: This processes the creation of tasks saved to the database
- **Done/Not Done**: This sets a task to either done or to-do
- **Delete**: This removes the task from the database

Now that we have a fairly good idea of the structure and form of the site, let's take a look at some wireframes of each page.

View All/Create

The following screenshot shows you a wireframe from point **1** (the View All item) and point **2** (the Create item) of the preceding site map. Initially, the user is shown a list of tasks. They are able to click on the **It's Done** or **Still Todo** button to go to point **3** (the Done/Not Done item) shown in the site map.

Delete

The following screenshot shows you a wireframe from point **4** (the Delete item) in the site map. The user views the task description (`tasks.task_desc`) and is given the option to delete (to process the deletion of the task from the database) or cancel to return to point **1** (the View All item) of the site map.

File overview

This is a relatively small project, and all in all, we're only going to create six files; these are as follows:

- `/path/to/codeigniter/application/models/tasks_model.php`:
  This provides read/write access to the `tasks` database table.

- `/path/to/codeigniter/application/views/tasks/delete.php`: This displays a form to the user, asking them to confirm the deletion of a task.

- `/path/to/codeigniter/application/views/tasks/view.php`: This is the view for the `tasks` controller's `index()` function. It displays a list of tasks to the user.

- `/path/to/codeigniter/application/views/nav/top_nav.php`:
  This provides a navigation bar at the top of the page.

- `/path/to/codeigniter/application/controllers/tasks.php`:
  This contains three main functions: `index()`, `apply()` and `create()`.

- `/path/to/codeigniter/application/language/english/en_admin_lang.php`: This provides language support for the application.

The file structure of the preceding six files is as follows:

```
application/
├── controllers/
│   ├── tasks.php
├── models/
│   ├── tasks_model.php
├── views/tasks/
│   ├── view.php
│   ├── delete.php
├── views/nav/
│   ├── top_nav.php
├── language/english/
│   ├── en_admin_lang.php
```

Creating the database

Okay, you should have already setup CodeIgniter and Bootstrap, as described in *Chapter 1, Introduction and Shared Project Resources*. If not, then you should know that the code in this chapter is specifically built with the setup from *Chapter 1, Introduction and Shared Project Resources*, in mind. However, it's not the end of the world if you haven't—the code can easily be applied to other situations.

Firstly, we'll build the database. Copy the following MySQL code to your database:

```sql
CREATE DATABASE `tasksdb`;
USE DATABASE `tasksdb`;

CREATE TABLE `ci_sessions` (
  `session_id` varchar(40) COLLATE utf8_bin NOT NULL DEFAULT '0',
  `ip_address` varchar(16) COLLATE utf8_bin NOT NULL DEFAULT '0',
  `user_agent` varchar(120) COLLATE utf8_bin DEFAULT NULL,
  `last_activity` int(10) unsigned NOT NULL DEFAULT '0',
  `user_data` text COLLATE utf8_bin NOT NULL
) ENGINE=MyISAM DEFAULT CHARSET=utf8 COLLATE=utf8_bin;

CREATE TABLE `tasks` (
  `task_id` int(11) NOT NULL AUTO_INCREMENT,
  `task_desc` varchar(255) NOT NULL,
  `task_due_date` datetime DEFAULT NULL,
  `task_created_at` timestamp NOT NULL DEFAULT CURRENT_TIMESTAMP,
  `task_status` enum('done','todo') NOT NULL,
  PRIMARY KEY (`task_id`)
) ENGINE=InnoDB AUTO_INCREMENT=1 DEFAULT CHARSET=utf8;
```

Now, take a look at that last bit of SQL code, it's quite big and fiddly. Don't panic; all SQL code is available online from this book's support page on the Packt website.

You'll see that the first table we create is `ci_sessions`, which we need to allow CodeIgniter to manage sessions, specifically logged-in users. However, this is just the standard session table available from the *CodeIgniter User Guide*, so I'll not include a description of that table as it's not technically specific to this application. However, if you're interested, there's a description at `http://ellislab.com/codeigniter/user-guide/libraries/sessions.html`.

Right, let's take a look at each item in each table, and see what it means:

Table: tasks	
Element	**Description**
`task_id`	This is the primary key.
`task_desc`	There is no title field or body to our tasks as such — only a brief description of what needs to be done; this is that description.
`task_due_date`	This is the date by which the task needs to be done. If a task is late, we will color the background of the table row red to indicate that a particular task remains to be done and is late.
`task_created_at`	as such MySQL timestamp of the date on which the row was created in the database.
`task_status`	This indicates whether the task still remains to be done or not. This is an enum field with the two values: `done` and `todo`. If a task is set to `done`, then we will use the `<strike>` HTML markup to strike through the text; if, however, is it set to `todo` (as it is by default), then the task isn't struck through and remains to be done.

We'll also need to make amends to the `config/database.php` file, namely setting the database access details, username password, and so on.

Open the `config/database.php` file and find the following lines:

```
$db['default']['hostname'] = 'localhost';
$db['default']['username'] = 'your username';
$db['default']['password'] = 'your password';
$db['default']['database'] = 'tasksdb';
```

Edit the values in the preceding lines, ensuring you substitute these values with ones more specific to your setup and situation; so, enter your username, password, and so on.

Adjusting the config.php file

There are a few things in this file that we'll need to configure to support sessions and encryption. So, open the `config/config.php` file and make the following changes:

1. We will need to set an encryption key—both sessions and CodeIgniter's encryption functionality require an encryption key to be set in the `$config` array, so find the following line:

    ```
    $config['encryption_key'] = '';
    ```

    Replace the preceding line with the following:

    ```
    $config['encryption_key'] = 'a-random-string-of-alphanum-
      characters';
    ```

    > Now obviously, don't actually change the preceding value to literally a-random-string-of-alphanum-characters but change it to, er, a random string of alphanum characters instead—if that makes sense? Yeah, you know what I mean.

2. Find the following lines:

    ```
    $config['sess_cookie_name'] = 'ci_session';
    $config['sess_expiration'] = 7200;
    $config['sess_expire_on_close'] = FALSE;
    $config['sess_encrypt_cookie'] = FALSE;
    $config['sess_use_database'] = FALSE;
    $config['sess_table_name'] = 'ci_sessions';
    $config['sess_match_ip'] = FALSE;
    $config['sess_match_useragent'] = TRUE;
    $config['sess_time_to_update'] = 300;
    ```

    Replace the preceding line with the following:

    ```
    $config['sess_cookie_name'] = 'ci_session';
    $config['sess_expiration'] = 7200;
    $config['sess_expire_on_close'] = TRUE;
    $config['sess_encrypt_cookie'] = TRUE;
    $config['sess_use_database'] = TRUE;
    $config['sess_table_name'] = 'ci_sessions';
    $config['sess_match_ip'] = TRUE;
    $config['sess_match_useragent'] = TRUE;
    $config['sess_time_to_update'] = 300;
    ```

Adjusting the routes.php file

We want to redirect the user to the `tasks` controller rather than the default CodeIgniter `welcome` controller. To do this, we will need to amend the default controller settings in the `routes.php` file:

1. Open the `config/routes.php` file for editing and find the following lines (near the bottom of the file):

   ```
   $route['default_controller'] = "welcome";
   $route['404_override'] = '';
   ```

2. First, we need to change the default controller. Initially in a CodeIgniter application, the default controller is set to `welcome`; however, we don't need this—instead, we want the default controller to be `tasks`. So find the following line:

   ```
   $route['default_controller'] = "welcome";
   ```

   Change it to the following:

   ```
   $route['default_controller'] = "tasks";
   $route['404_override'] = '';
   ```

Creating the model

There is only one model in this project, `tasks_model.php`, that contains functions that are specific to searching and writing tasks to the database.

This is our one and only model for this project. Let's briefly go over each function in it to give us a general idea of what it does, and then we will go into more detail in the code.

There are five main functions in this model, which are as follows:

- `get_tasks()`: This serves two functions: firstly, to display all tasks—for example, when a user first visits the site and when a user enters a new task in the form.

- `change_task_status()`: This changes the `tasks.task_status` value in the database from either `todo` or `done`. A task that is set to `done` appears struck through in the list, whereas tasks that are set to `todo` are not struck through and are displayed normally; this way, a user can easily work out what is done and not done.

- `save_task()`: This saves a task to the database when a user submits the form from point **3** (the Create item) of the site map.

- `get_task()`: This fetches an individual task from the `tasks` table.
- `delete()`: This deletes a task from the `tasks` table.

That was a quick overview, so let's create the model and discuss how it functions.

Create the `/path/to/codeigniter/application/models/tasks_model.php` file and add the following code to it:

```php
<?php if ( ! defined('BASEPATH')) exit('No direct script access
  allowed');

class Tasks_model extends CI_Model {
  function __construct() {
    parent::__construct();
  }
```

The `get_tasks()` function takes no argument. It returns all tasks from the database and returns it to the `tasks` controller's `index()` function. The `tasks/view.php` view file will loop over the database result object and display tasks in an HTML table:

```php
function get_tasks() {
  $query = "SELECT * FROM `tasks` ";

  $result = $this->db->query($query);
  if ($result) {
    return $result;
  } else {
    return false;
  }
}
```

The `change_task_status()` function changes the status of a task from either `todo` or `done`.

It takes two arguments: `$task_id` and `$save_data`. The `$task_id` and `$save_data` values are passed from the `tasks` controller's `status()` function.

The value of `$task_id` is set when the user clicks on either **It's Done** or **Still Todo** in the `views/tasks/view.php` view file; the fourth parameter of the `uri` segment of either option is the primary key (`tasks.task_id`) of the task in the `tasks` table and by using the CodeIgniter function `$this->uri->segment(4)`, we grab the value and store in a `$task_id` local variable.

The `$save_data` value is populated in the `tasks` controller. It contains only one item, `task_status`, that is populated in the `status()` function with the third parameter of the `uri` segment:

```
function change_task_status($task_id, $save_data) {
  $this->db->where('task_id', $task_id);
  if ($this->db->update('tasks', $save_data)) {
    return true;
  } else {
    return false;
  }
}
```

The `save_task()` function accepts one argument—an array of data. This data is supplied by the `tasks` controller's `index()` function. The function will save a task to the `tasks` table, returning `true` if successful and `false` if an error occurs:

```
function save_task($save_data) {
  if ($this->db->insert('tasks', $save_data)) {
    return true;
  } else {
    return false;
  }
}
```

The `get_task()` function takes one argument—`$task_id` (that is, the primary key of the task in the database). It is supplied by the `tasks` controller's `delete()` function, which uses it to supply information about the task in the delete confirmation form.

The user clicks on **Delete** in the `views/tasks/view.php` file, the third parameter of which is the task's primary key. The `tasks` controller's `delete()` function will then grab that ID from the URI with the `$this->uri->segment(3)` CodeIgniter function. This ID is passed to the `get_task()` model function, which will return the details of the task in the database or `false` if no ID was found:

```
function get_task($id) {
  $this->db->where('task_id', $id);
  $result = $this->db->get('tasks');
  if ($result) {
    return $result;
  } else {
    return false;
  }
}
```

The `delete()` function performs an operation on the database to remove a task. It accepts one argument — the ID of the task, which is the primary key of that task:

```
function delete($id) {
  $this->db->where('task_id', $id);
  $result = $this->db->delete('tasks');
  if ($result) {
    return true;
  } else {
    return false;
  }
}
}
```

Creating views

There are three views in this project, which are as follows:

- `/path/to/codeigniter/application/views/tasks/view.php`: This displays a list of current tasks to the user as well as a form that allows the user to create new tasks.

- `/path/to/codeigniter/application/views/tasks/delete.php`: This displays a confirmation message to the users, asking them to confirm whether they really want to delete the task.

- `/path/to/codeigniter/application/views/nav/top_nav.php`: This displays the top-level menu. In this project, this is very simple; it contains a project name and link to go to the `tasks` controller.

These are our three view files. Now let's go over each one, build the code, and discuss how they function.

Create the `/path/to/codeigniter/application/views/tasks/view.php` file and add the following code to it:

```
<div class="page-header">
    <?php echo form_open('tasks/index') ; ?>
      <div class="row">
        <div class="col-lg-12">
          <?php echo validation_errors() ; ?>
          <div class="input-group">
            <input type="text" class="form-control" name="
              task_desc" placeholder="<?php echo $this->lang->
              line('tasks_add_task_desc'); ?>">
            <span class="input-group-btn">
```

```php
              <button class="btn btn-default" type="submit"><?php
                echo $this->lang->line('tasks_add_task'); ?>
                </button>
            </span>
          </div><!-- /input-group -->
        </div><!-- /.col-lg-6 -->
      </div><!-- /.row -->

      <div class="row">
        <div class="form-group">
          <div class="col-md-2">
            <?php echo form_error('task_due_d'); ?>
            <select name="task_due_d" class="form-control">
              <option></option>
              <?php for ( $i = 1; $i <= 30; $i++) : ?>
                  <option value="<?php echo $i ; ?>"><?php echo
                    date('jS', mktime($i,0,0,0, $i, date('Y'))) ;
                    ?></option>
              <?php endfor ; ?>
            </select>
          </div>

          <div class="col-md-2">
            <?php echo form_error('task_due_m'); ?>
            <select name="task_due_m" class="form-control">
              <option></option>
              <?php for ( $i = 1; $i <= 12; $i++) : ?>
                  <option value="<?php echo $i ; ?>"><?php echo
                    date('F', mktime(0,0,0,$i, 1, date('Y'))) ;
                    ?></option>
              <?php endfor ; ?>
            </select>
          </div>

          <div class="col-md-2">
            <?php echo form_error('task_due_y'); ?>
            <select name="task_due_y" class="form-control">
              <option></option>
              <?php for ($i = date("Y",strtotime(date("Y"))); $i
                <= date("Y",strtotime(date("Y").' +5 year'));
                $i++) : ?>
                <option value="<?php echo $i;?>"><?php echo
                  $i;?></option>
              <?php endfor ; ?>
            </select>
```

```
        </div>
      </div>
    </div>
  <?php echo form_close() ; ?>
</div>
```

The preceding block of code is the form that the user can use to create a new task. Also in this block is the validation error code (`validation_errors()`) where we will display any errors with the data submitted form the form:

```
<table class="table table-hover">
  <?php foreach ($query->result() as $row) : ?>
  <?php if (date("Y-m-d",mktime(0, 0, 0, date('m'), date('d'),
    date('y'))) > $row->task_due_date) {echo ' <tr class="list-
    group-item-danger">';} ?>
  <?php if ($row->task_due_date == null) {echo ' <tr>';} ?>
    <td width="80%"><?php if ($row->task_status == 'done') {echo
      '<strike>'.$row->task_desc.'</strike>' ;} else {echo $row->
      task_desc;} ?>

    </td>
    <td width="10%">
      <?php if ($row->task_status == 'todo') {echo anchor ('
        tasks/status/done/'.$row->task_id, 'It\'s Done');} ?>
      <?php if ($row->task_status == 'done') {echo anchor ('
        tasks/status/todo/'.$row->task_id, 'Still Todo');} ?>
    </td>
    <td width="10%"><?php echo anchor ('tasks/delete/'.$row->
      task_id, $this->lang->line
      ('common_form_elements_action_delete')) ; ?>
    </td>
  </tr>
<?php endforeach ; ?>
</table>
```

The preceding table echoes out any tasks in the database. The actions are also in this block, that is, the PHP ternary operator that switches the status from **It's Done** to **Still Todo** and the **Delete** link.

Create the `/path/to/codeigniter/application/views/tasks/delete.php` file and add the following code to it:

```
<h2><?php echo $page_heading ; ?></h2>
<p class="lead"><?php echo $this->lang->
  line('delete_confirm_message');?></p>
<?php echo form_open('tasks/delete'); ?>
    <?php if (validation_errors()) : ?>
```

```
        <h3>Whoops! There was an error:</h3>
        <p><?php echo validation_errors(); ?></p>
    <?php endif; ?>
    <?php foreach ($query->result() as $row) : ?>
        <?php echo $row->task_desc; ?>
        <br /><br />
        <?php echo form_submit('submit', $this->lang->
          line('common_form_elements_action_delete'), 'class="btn
          btn-success"'); ?>
        or <?php echo anchor('tasks',$this->lang->
          line('common_form_elements_cancel'));?>
        <?php echo form_hidden('id', $row->task_id); ?>
    <?php endforeach; ?>
<?php echo form_close() ; ?>
```

The preceding block of code contains the form that asks the user to confirm whether they really wish to delete the task.

Create the /path/to/codeigniter/application/views/nav/top_nav.php file and add the following code to it:

```
<!-- Fixed navbar -->
<div class="navbar navbar-inverse navbar-fixed-top" role="navigation">
  <div class="container">
    <div class="navbar-header">
      <button type="button" class="navbar-toggle" data-
        toggle="collapse" data-target=".navbar-collapse">
      <span class="sr-only">Toggle navigation</span>
      <span class="icon-bar"></span>
      <span class="icon-bar"></span>
      <span class="icon-bar"></span>
      </button>
      <?php echo anchor('tasks', $this->lang->
        line('system_system_name'),'class="navbar-brand"') ; ?>
    </div>
    <div class="navbar-collapse collapse">
      <ul class="nav navbar-nav navbar-right">
      </ul>
    </div><!--/.nav-collapse -->
  </div>
</div>

<div class="container theme-showcase" role="main">
```

This view is quite basic but still serves an important role. It displays an option to return to the tasks controller's index() function.

Creating the controller

We're going to create only one controller in this project, which is `/path/to/codeigniter/application/controllers/tasks.php`.

Let's go over that controller now, look at the code, and discuss how it functions.

Create the `/path/to/codeigniter/application/controllers/tasks.php` file and add the following code to it:

```php
<?php if (!defined('BASEPATH')) exit('No direct script access
  allowed');

class Tasks extends MY_Controller {
  function __construct() {
  parent::__construct();
    $this->load->helper('string');
    $this->load->helper('text');
    $this->load->model('Tasks_model');
    $this->load->library('form_validation');
    $this->form_validation->set_error_delimiters('<div
      class="alert alert-danger">', '</div>');
  }
```

The `index()` function performs a couple of tasks: displaying a list of tasks and handling the form submission (validation, error checking, and so on).

Initially, we set the validation rules for the form, as follows:

```php
public function index() {
  $this->form_validation->set_rules('task_desc', $this->lang->
    line('tasks_task_desc'), 'required|min_length[1]|
    max_length[255]');
  $this->form_validation->set_rules('task_due_d', $this->lang->
    line('task_due_d'), 'min_length[1]|max_length[2]');
  $this->form_validation->set_rules('task_due_m', $this->lang->
    line('task_due_m'), 'min_length[1]|max_length[2]');
  $this->form_validation->set_rules('task_due_y', $this->lang->
    line('task_due_y'), 'min_length[4]|max_length[4]');
```

If there were errors in the form or if it is the first time the page is accessed, then we'll build the form elements, defining their settings and be ready to draw them in the view:

```php
if ($this->form_validation->run() == FALSE) {
  $page_data['job_title'] = array('name' => 'job_title', 'class'
    => 'form-control', 'id' => 'job_title', 'value' => set_value
    ('job_title', ''), 'maxlength' => '100', 'size' => '35');
```

```
$page_data['task_desc'] = array('name' => 'task_desc', 'class'
    => 'form-control', 'id' => 'task_desc', 'value' => set_value
    ('task_desc', ''), 'maxlength' => '255', 'size' => '35');
$page_data['task_due_d'] = array('name' => 'task_due_d', 'class'
    => 'form-control', 'id' => 'task_due_d', 'value' => set_value
    ('task_due_d', ''), 'maxlength' => '100', 'size' => '35');
$page_data['task_due_m'] = array('name' => 'task_due_m', 'class'
    => 'form-control', 'id' => 'task_due_m', 'value' => set_value
    ('task_due_m', ''), 'maxlength' => '100', 'size' => '35');
$page_data['task_due_y'] = array('name' => 'task_due_y', 'class'
    => 'form-control', 'id' => 'task_due_y', 'value' => set_value
    ('task_due_y', ''), 'maxlength' => '100', 'size' => '35');
```

Next, we'll fetch all tasks in the database and store them in the `$page_data['query']` array. We will send this array to the `tasks/view.php` file where it will be looped over using `foreach($query->result as $row)` — where each task will be written out in a table along with the **It's Done**, **Still Todo**, and **Delete** options:

```
$page_data['query'] = $this->Tasks_model->get_tasks();

$this->load->view('common/header');
$this->load->view('nav/top_nav');
$this->load->view('tasks/view', $page_data);
$this->load->view('common/footer');
} else {
```

If there were no errors with the form, then we try to create the task in the database. First, we look to see whether the user has tried to set a due date for the task. We do this by looking for the date fields in the `post` array.

We require all three (day, month, and year) items to create a due date, so we check to see whether all three have been set. If all three are set, then we build a string that will be the date. This is saved in the `$task_due_date` variable. If all three date items haven't been set (perhaps only two were), then we just set the `$task_due_date` value to `null`:

```
if ($this->input->post('task_due_y') && $this->input->
    post('task_due_m') && $this->input->post('task_due_d')) {
    $task_due_date = $this->input->post('task_due_y') .'-'. $this->
        input->post('task_due_m') .'-'. $this->input->
        post('task_due_d');
} else {
    $task_due_date = null;
}
```

We then create an array to pass to the `save_task()` function of `Tasks_model`. The `$save_data` array contains the task description, any date that might have been applied (or `null` value), and a default value for `task_status`; this is initially set to `todo`:

```
$save_data = array(
  'task_desc' => $this->input->post('task_desc'),
  'task_due_date' => $task_due_date,
  'task_status' => 'todo'
);
```

The `$save_data` array is then sent to the `save_task()` function of `Tasks_model`. This function will return `true` if the save operation was successful or `false` if there was an error. Whatever the outcome, we'll set a message using the `$this->session->set_flashdata()`CodeIgniter function with a success message or an error message (the content for these messages is in the language file) and redirect to the `tasks` controller's `index()` function, which will display all tasks (and hopefully, the one just created) to the user:

```
if ($this->Tasks_model->save_task($save_data)) {
  $this->session->set_flashdata('flash_message', $this->lang->
    line('create_success_okay'));
} else {
  $this->session->set_flashdata('flash_message', $this->lang->
    line('create_success_fail'));
}
redirect ('tasks');
}
}
```

The `status()` function is used to change a task status from `done` to `todo`. If you hover over either the **It's Done** or **Still Todo** links, you'll see the URI. The format will look something like `http://www.domain.com/tasks/status/todo/1` (if the task is set to `done` in the database) or `http://www.domain.com/tasks/status/done/1` (if the task is set to `todo` in the database). The third parameter is always the opposite to whatever is the current status of the task, so if a task is set to `done`, the URI will display `todo`, and if it is set to `todo`, the URI will display `done`.

The fourth parameter is the primary key (in the preceding example, this is 1).

When the user clicks on either **It's Done** or **Still Todo**, the `status()` function grabs the third and fourth parameters and sends them to the `status()` function of `Tasks_model`:

```
public function status() {
  $page_data['task_status'] = $this->uri->segment(3);
  $task_id = $this->uri->segment(4);
```

We take the third and fourth parameters and send them to the `change_task_status()` function of `Tasks_model`. The `change_task_status()` function will return `true` if the update was successful or `false` if there was an error. We set a message to the user using the `$this->session->set_flashdata()` CodeIgniter function and redirect to the `tasks` controller's `index()` function:

```
if ($this->Tasks_model->change_task_status($task_id,
  $page_data)) {
  $this->session->set_flashdata('flash_message', $this->lang->
    line('status_change_success'));
} else {
  $this->session->set_flashdata('flash_message', $this->lang->
    line('status_change_fail'));
}
redirect ('tasks');
}
```

The `delete()` function does two things. It displays information about the task to the user so that they are able to decide whether they really want to delete the task, and it also processes the deletion of that task should it be confirmed by the user. First off, we set the validation rules for the form. This is the form that the user uses to confirm the deletion:

```
public function delete() {
  $this->form_validation->set_rules('id', $this->lang->
    line('task_id'), 'required|min_length[1]|max_length[11]|
    integer|is_natural');
```

Because the function can be accessed by the user by clicking on **Delete** or submitting the form, the task ID can be supplied either from the URI (in the case of **Delete**) or in a hidden form element in the form. So, we check whether the form is being posted or accessed for the first time and grab the ID from either `post` or `get`:

```
if ($this->input->post()) {
  $id = $this->input->post('id');
} else {
  $id = $this->uri->segment(3);
}

$data['page_heading'] = 'Confirm delete?';
if ($this->form_validation->run() == FALSE) {
```

We then send the ID to the `get_task()` function of `Tasks_model`, which will return the details of the task as a database object. This is saved in `$data['query']` and sent to the `tasks/delete.php` view file, where the user is asked to confirm whether they wish to really delete the task:

```
$data['query'] = $this->Tasks_model->get_task($id);
$this->load->view('common/header', $data);
$this->load->view('nav/top_nav', $data);
$this->load->view('tasks/delete', $data);
$this->load->view('common/footer', $data);
} else {
```

If there were no errors with the form submission, then we call the `delete()` function of `Tasks_model` so that the task is deleted:

```
    if ($this->Tasks_model->delete($id)) {
      redirect('tasks');
    }
  }
 }
}
```

Creating the language file

As with all the projects in this book, we're making use of the language file to serve text to users. This way, you can enable multiple region/multiple language support. Let's create the language file.

Create the `/path/to/codeigniter/application/language/english/en_admin_lang.php` file and add the following code to it:

```php
<?php if (!defined('BASEPATH')) exit('No direct script access
  allowed');

// General
$lang['system_system_name'] = "Todo";

// Tasks - view.php
$lang['tasks_add_task'] = "Add";
$lang['tasks_add_task_desc'] = "What have you got to do?";
$lang['tasks_task_desc'] = "Task Description";
$lang['tasks_set_done'] = "Mark as done";
$lang['tasks_set_todo'] = "Mark as todo";
$lang['task_due_d'] = "Due Day";
$lang['task_due_m'] = "Due Month";
$lang['task_due_y'] = "Due Year";
$lang['status_change_success'] = "Task updated";
$lang['status_change_fail'] = "Task not updated";
```

Putting it all together

Okay, here are a few examples that will help put everything together.

User adds a task

The sequence of events in order to add a task is as follows:

1. The user visits the site and CodeIgniter routes them to the `tasks` controller.

2. The `tasks` controller loads (by default) the `index()` function. The `index()` function checks whether the form validation is false:

   ```
   if ($this->form_validation->run() == FALSE) {
   ...
   ```

3. As this is the first load and the form has not been submitted, it will equal `false`. The `index()` function then defines the settings for the `task_desc` text field, calls the `get_tasks()` function of `Tasks_model` (which returns all tasks from the database), and then loads the view files, passing the database object to the `views/tasks/view.php` file.

4. The user enters the `Chase meeting room booking` string, selects a date three days into the future, and clicks on **Add** to submit the form.

5. The form is submitted and `index()` validates the `task_desc` form elements and the three date dropdowns' values. The validation is now passed.

   The three date fields are strung together to form a date string to be entered into the database and saved as `$task_due_date`:

   ```
   $task_due_date = $this->input->post('task_due_y') .'-'. $this->input->post('task_due_m') .'-'. $this->input->post('task_due_d');
   ```

6. These `$task_due_date` and `task_desc` values are saved to an array called `$save_data`. Also saved is a default value for the `task_status` field in the `tasks` table. This value is set to `todo`.

7. After a successful save operation to the database. the user is redirected to `index()`, where their new task is displayed.

User changes the task status

The events performed while a user changes the task status are as follows:

1. The user visits the site and CodeIgniter routes them to the `tasks` controller.

2. The `tasks` controller loads (by default) the `index()` function. The `index()` function checks whether the form validation is false:

   ```
   if ($this->form_validation->run() == FALSE) {
   ...
   ```

3. As this is the first load and the form has not been submitted, it will equal false. The `index()` function then defines the settings for the `task_desc` text field, calls the `get_tasks()` function of `Tasks_model` (which returns all tasks from the database), and then loads the view files, passing the database object to the `views/tasks/view.php` file.

4. The user sees the task "Chase meeting room booking" and (knowing that this task is done) clicks on **It's Done**.

5. CodeIgniter loads the `status()` task function.

6. The `status()` function takes the third (`todo` or `done`) and fourth (the task's primary key) parameters of the URI and sets them to the `$page_data['task_status']` and `$task_id` local variables.

7. These two variables are sent to the `change_task_status()` function of `Tasks_model`.

8. The `change_task_status()` function takes the `$task_id` value and the new status and performs an Active Record update on this task, returning true or false values if successful or if an error occurred.

9. The `status()` function looks at the return value and sets a session flash message accordingly: a success message if successful and an error if not.

10. The user is then redirected to `index()`, where they can see the updated task status.

Summary

So. this is a fairly small application—perhaps one of the smallest in the book—but it's by no means not useful. You can use this to-do list as a really easy way to manage any tasks you might have on your plate; however, there's always room for improvement. There are a few things that you can do to add greater functionalities to the project, and these might include the following:

- **Adding a sorting feature**: You could add sorting functions to only display late (overdue), done, or still-to-do tasks.

- **Adding a category**: You could add a dropdown to the form that creates the tasks. This dropdown could (for example) have the colors Red, Green, Blue, Yellow, Orange, and so on. A task can be assigned a color and this color could be displayed in the table that displays each task. You could use the Bootstrap label markup; for example, the `span` warning label (`<span class="label label-warning">Warning</span>`) would give you a great block of color—change the word `Warning`, though!

- **Adding progress and progress bar**: You could add an HTML dropdown with set percentage values: 25 percent, 50 percent 75 percent, 100 percent, and so on, which allow you to define how much of the task has been completed.

9
Creating a Job Board

There are some quite complex job boards out there and some that are woefully designed. There are some that I can think of that simply don't work as you would think they should and some that don't function properly at all. I'm sure they all have a heap of VC funding and probably turn some sort of profit, so it is beyond me why they don't manage to get it together and make something that actually works; the thing is that it's not actually that difficult a thing to do.

The job board in this project is small and concise, but there is scope to expand upon—if you skip ahead to the *Summary* section, you'll see some things you can add to make it more feature-rich, but I'm sure you have your own.

In this chapter, we will cover the following topics:

- Design and wireframes
- Creating the database
- Creating the model
- Creating views
- Creating the controller
- Putting it all together

Introduction

So what are we going to do for this project anyway? We'll create an application that allows users to create job adverts that will be displayed on a "board". Users can search for specific terms and some results will be returned.

Other users can create adverts that will be displayed in these boards.

To create this app, we will create one controller; this will handle the display of jobs, creation of new jobs, and applying for jobs.

We'll create a language file to store text, allowing you to have multiple language support should that be required.

We'll create all the necessary view files and a model to interface with the database.

However, this app along with all the others in this book relies on the basic setup we did in *Chapter 1*, *Introduction and Shared Project Resources*; although you can take large sections of the code and drop it into pretty much any app you might already have, please keep in mind that the setup done in the first chapter acts as a foundation for this chapter.

So without further ado, let's get on with it.

Design and wireframes

As always, before we start building, we should take a look at what we plan to build.

Firstly, a brief description of our intent: we plan to build an app that will allow people to browse job adverts in the form of a job board.

People will be able to create job adverts that will appear on search listings. Others will be allowed to apply for these advertised jobs, and applications are sent in an e-mail to the advertiser with details of the job and applicant.

Anyway, to get a better idea of what's happening, let's take a look at the following site map:

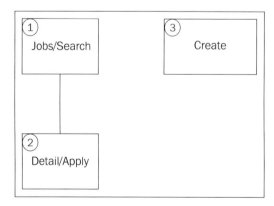

So that was the site map; the first thing to notice is how simple the site is. There are only three main areas to this project. Let's go over each item and get a brief idea of what it does:

- **Jobs/Search**: Imagine this as the start point. The user is presented with a list of active jobs available on the site. The user is able to view the job details and apply (taking them to point **2** of the site map), or click on **Create** on the navigation bar and go to point **3** (the Create item) of the site map.

- **Detail/Apply**: The user is presented with the details of the job advertised, such as the start date, location and the job description, and advertiser's contact details. There is also a form below the job details that allows a user to apply for the job. Details of the application are sent in an e-mail to the job advertiser (`jobs.job_advertiser_email`).

- **Create**: This will display a form to the user, allowing them to create a job advert. Once that advert is created, it will be displayed in search listings.

Now that we have a fairly good idea of the structure and form of the site, let's take a look at some wireframes of each page.

Job/Search

The following screenshot shows you a wireframe from point **1** (the Create item) in the site map. Initially, the user is shown a list of current jobs. The job title and description are shown. The description is kept at a set length—that of the first 50 words of a job description. They are able to click on the job title or an **Apply** link to go to point **2** (the Detail/Apply item) of the site map.

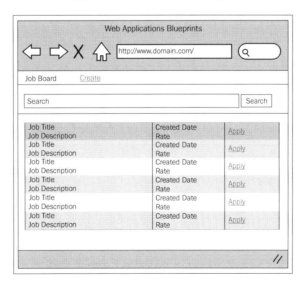

Detail/Apply

The following screenshot shows you a wireframe from point **2** (the Detail/Apply item) in the site map. The user views the detailed description of the job advertised and a form that enables the user to enter their details and send off an application for the job—the details of this application are e-mailed to the job advertiser.

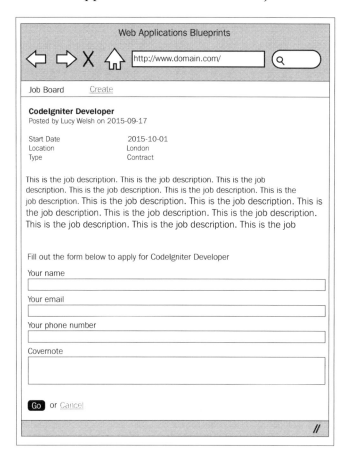

Create

The following screenshot shows you a wireframe from point **3** (the Create item) of the site map. Any user can post a job advert. This displays a form to the user, allowing them to enter the details of their job advert and save it to the database.

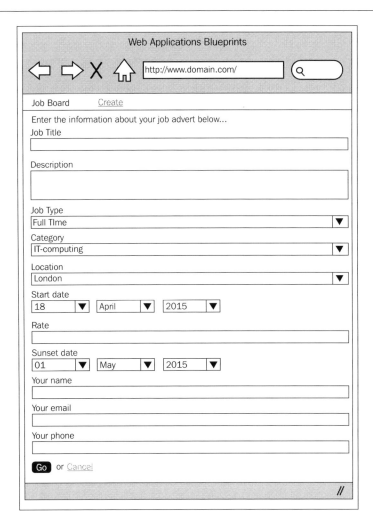

File overview

This is a relatively small project, and all-in-all, we're only going to create seven files; these are as follows:

- `/path/to/codeigniter/application/models/jobs_model.php`: This provides read/write access to the `jobs` database table.

- `/path/to/codeigniter/application/views/jobs/apply.php`: This provides us an interface that allows the user to view a job advert's details and also a form that allows any user to apply for a job.

- `/path/to/codeigniter/application/views/jobs/create.php`: This displays a form to the user, allowing the user to create a job advert.

- `/path/to/codeigniter/application/views/jobs/view.php`: This is the view for the `jobs` controller's `index()` function. It displays the search form and lists any results.

- `/path/to/codeigniter/application/views/nav/top_nav.php`: This provides a navigation bar at the top of the page.

- `/path/to/codeigniter/application/controllers/jobs.php`: This contains three main functions: `index()`, `apply()` and `create()`.

- `/path/to/codeigniter/application/language/english/en_admin_lang.php`: This provides language support for the application.

The file structure of the preceding seven files is as follows:

```
application/
├── controllers/
│   ├── jobs.php
├── models/
│   ├── jobs_model.php
├── views/create/
│   ├── create.php
│   ├── apply.php
│   ├── view.php
├── views/nav/
│   ├── top_nav.php
├── language/english/
│   ├── en_admin_lang.php
```

Creating the database

Okay, you should have already set up CodeIgniter and Bootstrap as described in *Chapter 1, Introduction and Shared Project Resources*; if not, then you should know that the code in this chapter is specifically built with the setup from *Chapter 1, Introduction and Shared Project Resources*, in mind. However, it's not the end of the world if you haven't—the code can easily be applied to other situations.

First, we'll build the database. Copy the following MySQL code to your database:

```sql
CREATE DATABASE `jobboarddb`;
USE `jobboarddb`;

DROP TABLE IF EXISTS `categories`;
CREATE TABLE `categories` (
```

```
  `cat_id` int(11) NOT NULL AUTO_INCREMENT,
  `cat_name` varchar(25) NOT NULL,
  PRIMARY KEY (`cat_id`)
) ENGINE=InnoDB AUTO_INCREMENT=5 DEFAULT CHARSET=utf8;

INSERT INTO `categories` VALUES (1,'IT'),(2,'Legal'),(3,'Management'),
(4,'Purchasing');

DROP TABLE IF EXISTS `ci_sessions`;
CREATE TABLE `ci_sessions` (
  `session_id` varchar(40) COLLATE utf8_bin NOT NULL DEFAULT '0',
  `ip_address` varchar(16) COLLATE utf8_bin NOT NULL DEFAULT '0',
  `user_agent` varchar(120) COLLATE utf8_bin DEFAULT NULL,
  `last_activity` int(10) unsigned NOT NULL DEFAULT '0',
  `user_data` text COLLATE utf8_bin NOT NULL
) ENGINE=MyISAM DEFAULT CHARSET=utf8 COLLATE=utf8_bin;

DROP TABLE IF EXISTS `jobs`;
CREATE TABLE `jobs` (
  `job_id` int(11) NOT NULL AUTO_INCREMENT,
  `job_title` varchar(50) NOT NULL,
  `job_desc` text NOT NULL,
  `cat_id` int(11) NOT NULL,
  `type_id` int(11) NOT NULL,
  `loc_id` int(11) NOT NULL,
  `job_start_date` datetime NOT NULL,
  `job_rate` int(5) NOT NULL,
  `job_advertiser_name` varchar(50) NOT NULL,
  `job_advertiser_email` varchar(50) NOT NULL,
  `job_advertiser_phone` varchar(20) NOT NULL,
  `job_sunset_date` datetime NOT NULL,
  `job_created_at` timestamp NULL DEFAULT CURRENT_TIMESTAMP,
  PRIMARY KEY (`job_id`)
) ENGINE=InnoDB AUTO_INCREMENT=4 DEFAULT CHARSET=utf8;

INSERT INTO `jobs` VALUES (1,'PHP Developer','PHP Developer
  required for a large agency based in London.  Must have MVC
  experience\n',1,1,1,'2014-09-24 00:00:00',400,'Rob Foster',
  'rob@bluesuncreative.com','01234123456','2015-09-26 00:00:00',
  '2014-09-17 09:00:18'),(2,'CodeIgniter Developer','Small London
  agency urgently requires a CodeIgniter developer to work on
  small eCommerce project.',1,1,1,'0000-00-00 00:00:00',
  350,'Lucy','lucy@londonagencycomain.com','01234123456','2015-09-
  26 00:00:00','2014-09-17 11:22:19'),(3,'Flash Developer','Paris
  based agency requires Flash Developer to work on new built
```

```
        project',1,1,2,'0000-00-00 00:00:00',
        350,'Brian','brian@frenchdesignagenct.fr','2015-
        09-26 00:00:00','2014-09-17 11:23:39');


DROP TABLE IF EXISTS `locations`;

CREATE TABLE `locations` (
   `loc_id` int(11) NOT NULL AUTO_INCREMENT,
   `loc_name` varchar(25) NOT NULL,
   PRIMARY KEY (`loc_id`)
) ENGINE=InnoDB AUTO_INCREMENT=5 DEFAULT CHARSET=utf8;

INSERT INTO `locations` VALUES (1,'England'),(2,'France'),(3,'Germany'
),(4,'Spain');

DROP TABLE IF EXISTS `types`;
CREATE TABLE `types` (
   `type_id` int(11) NOT NULL AUTO_INCREMENT,
   `type_name` varchar(25) NOT NULL,
   PRIMARY KEY (`type_id`)
) ENGINE=InnoDB AUTO_INCREMENT=4 DEFAULT CHARSET=utf8;

INSERT INTO `types` VALUES (1,'Contract'),(2,'Full Time'),(3,'Part
Time');
```

 Now, take a look at that last bit of SQL code, it's quite big and fiddly. Don't panic, all SQL code is available online from this book's support page on the Packt website.

You'll see that the first table we create is `ci_sessions`. We need this to allow CodeIgniter to manage sessions, specifically, logged-in users. However, this is just the standard session table available from *CodeIgniter User Guide*, so I'll not include a description of that table as it's not technically specific to this application. However, if you're interested, there's a description at `http://ellislab.com/codeigniter/user-guide/libraries/sessions.html`.

Right, let's take a look at each item in each table, and see what it means. First, we will take a look at the `categories` table:

Table: categories	
Element	Description
cat_id	This is the primary key.
cat_name	This stores the name of the category.

Next up, we will see the `types` table:

Table: types	
Element	**Description**
`type_id`	This is the primary key.
`type_name`	This stores the name of the type.

Now, let's see the `locations` table:

Table: locations	
Element	**Description**
`loc_id`	This is the primary key.
`loc_name`	This stores the name of the location.

Finally, we will see the `jobs` table:

Table: jobs	
Element	**Description**
`job_id`	This is the primary key.
`job_title`	This is the title of the position advertised.
`job_desc`	This is the general job specification for the position advertised.
`cat_id`	This is foreign key from the `categories` table, indicating the category of the position—IT, Management, Manufacturing, Health Care, and so on
`type_id`	This is the foreign key from the `types` table, indicating the type of the position—full time, part time, contract, and so on
`loc_id`	This is the foreign key from the `locations` table, indicating the location that the position is to be based in.
`job_start_date`	This is the starting date of the position advertised.
`job_rate`	This is the money offered (remuneration)—salary, day rate, and so on.
`job_advertiser_name`	This is the name of the person advertising the position so that the applicant knows who to contact to chase their application.
`job_advertiser_email`	This is the contact e-mail of the person who is advertising the position. It is to this e-mail address that an application is sent. The application is sent when a user fills in and submits the form in `views/jobs/apply.php`.

Table: jobs	
Element	**Description**
job_advertiser_phone	This is the phone number of the person advertising the position. This is included if the applicant wishes to call the job advertiser.
job_sunset_date	This is the date at which the job will no longer be displayed in searches. This is required as jobs will not be advertised forever and applying a date that limits the time jobs can be applied for prevents people from applying for jobs that have either been filled or no longer exist.
job_created_at	This is the MySQL timestamp that's applied when a new record is added to the database.

We'll also need to make amends to the `config/database.php` file, namely setting the database access details, username password and so on.

Open the `config/database.php` file and find the following lines:

```
$db['default']['hostname'] = 'localhost';
$db['default']['username'] = 'your username';
$db['default']['password'] = 'your password';
$db['default']['database'] = 'jobboarddb';
```

Edit the values in the preceding lines, ensuring you substitute these values with ones more specific to your setup and situation; so, enter your username, password, and so on.

Adjusting the config.php file

There are a few things in this file that we'll need to configure to support sessions and encryption. So, open the `config/config.php` file and make the following changes.

1. We will need to set an encryption key; both sessions and CodeIgniter's encryption functionality require an encryption key to be set in the `$config` array, so find the following line:

   ```
   $config['encryption_key'] = '';
   ```

   Change it to the following:

   ```
   $config['encryption_key'] = 'a-random-string-of-alphanum-
   characters';
   ```

Now obviously, don't actually change this value to literally
a-random-string-of-alphanum-characters but change it to, er, a
random string of alphanum characters instead — if that makes sense?
Yeah, you know what I mean.

2. Find these lines:

```
$config['sess_cookie_name'] = 'ci_session';
$config['sess_expiration'] = 7200;
$config['sess_expire_on_close'] = FALSE;
$config['sess_encrypt_cookie'] = FALSE;
$config['sess_use_database'] = FALSE;
$config['sess_table_name'] = 'ci_sessions';
$config['sess_match_ip'] = FALSE;
$config['sess_match_useragent'] = TRUE;
$config['sess_time_to_update'] = 300;
```

Change them to the following:

```
$config['sess_cookie_name'] = 'ci_session';
$config['sess_expiration'] = 7200;
$config['sess_expire_on_close'] = TRUE;
$config['sess_encrypt_cookie'] = TRUE;
$config['sess_use_database'] = TRUE;
$config['sess_table_name'] = 'ci_sessions';
$config['sess_match_ip'] = TRUE;
$config['sess_match_useragent'] = TRUE;
$config['sess_time_to_update'] = 300;
```

Adjusting the routes.php file

We want to redirect the user to the `jobs` controller rather than the default
CodeIgniter `welcome` controller. To do this, we will need to amend the default
controller setting in the `routes.php` file:

1. Open the `config/routes.php` file for editing and find the following lines
   (near the bottom of the file):

```
$route['default_controller'] = "welcome";
$route['404_override'] = '';
```

2. First, we need to change the default controller. Initially in a CodeIgniter application, the default controller is set to `welcome`; however, we don't need this—instead, we want the default controller to be `jobs`. So, find the following line:

```
$route['default_controller'] = "welcome";
```

Replace it with the following:

```
$route['default_controller'] = "jobs";
$route['404_override'] = '';
```

Creating the model

There is only one model in this project—`jobs_model.php`—that contains functions that are specific to searching and writing job adverts to the database.

This is our one and only model for this project, so let's create the model and discuss how it functions.

Create the `/path/to/codeigniter/application/models/jobs_model.php` file and add the following code to it:

```php
<?php if ( ! defined('BASEPATH')) exit('No direct script access
  allowed');

class Jobs_model extends CI_Model {
  function __construct() {
    parent::__construct();
  }

  function get_jobs($search_string) {
    if ($search_string == null) {
      $query = "SELECT * FROM `jobs` WHERE DATE(NOW()) <
        DATE(`job_sunset_date`) ";
    } else {
      $query = "SELECT * FROM `jobs` WHERE `job_title` LIKE
        '%$search_string%'
                OR `job_desc` LIKE '%$search_string%' AND
                  DATE(NOW()) < DATE(`job_sunset_date`)";
    }

    $result = $this->db->query($query);
    if ($result) {
      return $result;
    } else {
```

```
      return false;
    }
  }

  function get_job($job_id) {
    $query = "SELECT * FROM `jobs`, `categories`, `types`,
      `locations` WHERE
              `categories`.`cat_id` = `jobs`.`cat_id` AND
              `types`.`type_id` = `jobs`.`type_id` AND
              `locations`.`loc_id` = `jobs`.`loc_id` AND
              `job_id` = ? AND
              DATE(NOW()) < DATE(`job_sunset_date`) ";

    $result = $this->db->query($query, array($job_id));
    if ($result) {
      return $result;
    } else {
      return flase;
    }
  }

  function save_job($save_data) {
    if ($this->db->insert('jobs', $save_data)) {
      return $this->db->insert_id();
    } else {
      return false;
    }
  }

  function get_categories() {
    return $this->db->get('categories');
  }

  function get_types() {
    return $this->db->get('types');
  }

  function get_locations() {
    return $this->db->get('locations');
  }
}
```

There are six main functions in this model, which are as follows:

- `get_jobs()`: This serves two functions: firstly, displaying all jobs—for example, when a user first visits the site—and secondly, when a user enters a search term, the query is then changed to look for the specific search term in `job_title` and `job_desc`.
- `get_job()`: This fetches the details of a specific job advert for point **2** (the Details/Apply item) of the site map.
- `save_job()`: This saves a job advert to the database when a user submits the form from point **3** (the Create item) of the site map.
- `get_categories()`: This fetches categories from the `categories` table. It is used to populate the categories dropdown for the create process.
- `get_types()`: This fetches types from the `types` table. It is used to populate the types dropdown for the create process.
- `get_locations()`: This fetches locations from the `locations` table. It is used to populate the locations dropdown for the create process.

Taking the `get_jobs()` function first, as mentioned, this function has two purposes:

- To return all results, that is, to list all jobs
- To return results (jobs) that match a user's search

When a user visits the site, they are routed to `jobs/index`. This will cause the `get_jobs()` model function to search the database. On this initial visit, the `$search_string` variable will be empty (as the user isn't searching for anything). This will cause the first part of the `if` statement to be run, basically returning every valid job.

However, if the user is searching for something, then the `$search_string` variable will not be empty; it will contain the search term the user entered in the `views/jobs/view.php` form.

This will cause the second part of the `if` statement to run, adding `$search_term` to the database query:

```
function get_jobs($search_string) {
  if ($search_string == null) {
    $query = "SELECT * FROM `jobs` WHERE DATE(NOW()) <
      DATE(`job_sunset_date`) ";
  } else {
    $query = "SELECT * FROM `jobs` WHERE `job_title` LIKE
      '%$search_string%'
            OR `job_desc` LIKE '%$search_string%' AND
              DATE(NOW()) < DATE(`job_sunset_date`)";
  }
```

```
    $result = $this->db->query($query);
    if ($result) {
      return $result;
    } else {
      return false;
    }
  }
```

Both queries will only return results whose sunset date has not passed. The `jobboarddb.job_sunset_date` field contains a date on which the job advert will stop being displayed in search terms.

Next, we'll look at the `get_job()` function. This function is passed the `$job_id` value from the `jobs` controller. The `jobs` controller gets the ID of the job advert from `$this->uri->segment(3)` when the user clicks on the **Apply** link in `views/jobs/view.php`.

The `get_job()` function simply returns all the data for point **2** (the Details/Apply item) of the site map.

It joins the `categories`, `types`, and `locations` tables to the `jobs` table in order to ensure that the correct category, type, and location is displayed in the `views/jobs/apply.php` view along with the specific job advert details.

We then move down to the `save_job()` function. This accepts an array of data from the `jobs` controller. The `jobs` controller's `create()` function sends the `$save_data` array to the `save_job()` model function. The `$save_data` array contains the input from the form in the `views/jobs/create.php` view file.

On a successful save, the primary key of the insert is returned.

Now we will cover the three functions—`_categories()`, `get_types()` and `get_locations()`—at the same time (as they do pretty similar things). These three functions fetch all categories, types, and locations from their respective tables. These functions are called by the `jobs` controller's `create()` function to ensure that the dropdowns are populated with the correct data.

Creating views

There are four views in this project, and these are as follows:

- `/path/to/codeigniter/application/views/jobs/view.php`: This displays a list of current jobs to the user.

- `/path/to/codeigniter/application/views/jobs/create.php`: This view allows the job advertiser to enter the job advert details. The form submits to the `jobs` controller's `create()` function.

- /path/to/codeigniter/application/views/jobs/apply.php: This displays a form to the user allowing them to enter information to apply for the job. It also displays validation errors.

- /path/to/codeigniter/application/views/nav/top_nav.php: This displays the top-level menu. In this project, this is very simple as it contains a project name and link to go to the jobs controller.

These are our four view files. Now, let's go over each one, build the code, and discuss how it functions.

Create the /path/to/codeigniter/application/views/jobs/view.php file and add the following code to it:

```php
<div class="page-header">
  <h1>
    <?php echo form_open('jobs/index') ; ?>
      <div class="row">
        <div class="col-lg-12">
          <div class="input-group">
            <input type="text" class="form-control" name="
              search_string" placeholder="<?php echo $this->lang->
              line('jobs_view_search'); ?>">
            <span class="input-group-btn">
              <button class="btn btn-default" type="submit"><?php
                echo $this->lang->line('jobs_view_search');
                ?></button>
            </span>
          </div><!-- /input-group -->
        </div><!-- /.col-lg-6 -->
      </div><!-- /.row -->
    <?php echo form_close() ; ?>
  </h1>
</div>

<table class="table table-hover">
  <?php foreach ($query->result() as $row) : ?>
  <tr>
    <td><?php echo anchor ('jobs/apply/'.$row->job_id, $row->
      job_title) ; ?><br /><?php echo word_limiter($row->job_desc,
      50) ; ?>
    </td>
    <td>Posten on <?php echo $row->job_created_at ; ?><br />Rate
      is &pound;<?php echo $row->job_rate ; ?>
    </td>
```

```
      <td><?php echo anchor ('jobs/apply/'.$row->job_id, $this->
        lang->line('jobs_view_apply')) ; ?>
      </td>
    </tr>
<?php endforeach ; ?>
</table>
```

This view serves two functions:

- To display a simple search form at the top of the page. This is where a user can search for jobs that match a search term.

- To display a list of jobs in an HTML table. These are the current active jobs in the database. A job is considered active if the job's sunset date (`jobs.job_sunset_date`) has not passed.

The search form is submitted to the `jobs` controller's `index()` function—this controller function will pass the search term to the `get_jobs($search_term)` function of `Jobs_model`. It will be added to the database query; this query will look in `jobs.job_title` and `jobs.job_desc` for text that matches the term.

Create the `/path/to/codeigniter/application/views/jobs/create.php` file and add the following code to it:

```php
<?php if ($this->session->flashdata('flash_message')) : ?>
  <div class="alert alert-info" role="alert"><?php echo $this->
    session->flashdata('flash_message');?></div>
 <?php endif ; ?>

  <p class="lead"><?php echo $this->lang->line
    ('job_create_form_instruction_1');?></p>
  <div class="span8">
  <?php echo form_open('jobs/create','role="form" class="form"') ;
    ?>
    <div class="form-group">
      <?php echo form_error('job_title'); ?>
      <label for="job_title"><?php echo $this->lang->
        line('job_title');?></label>
      <?php echo form_input($job_title); ?>
    </div>

    <div class="form-group">
      <?php echo form_error('job_desc'); ?>
      <label for="job_desc"><?php echo $this->lang->
        line('job_desc');?></label>
      <?php echo form_textarea($job_desc); ?>
    </div>
```

The type dropdown is populated by the `get_types()` function in `Jobs_model`. It returns a result object that we loop over, allowing the user to select the type:

```
<div class="form-group">
  <?php echo form_error('type_id'); ?>
  <label for="type_id"><?php echo $this->lang->
    line('type');?></label>
  <select name="type_id" class="form-control">
  <?php foreach ($types->result() as $row) : ?>
    <option value="<?php echo $row->type_id ; ?>"><?php echo $row-
      >type_name ; ?></option>
  <?php endforeach ; ?>
  </select>
</div>
```

The category dropdown is populated by the `get_categories()` function in `Jobs_model`. It returns a result object that we loop over, allowing the user to select the category:

```
<div class="form-group">
  <?php echo form_error('cat_id'); ?>
  <label for="cat_id"><?php echo $this->lang->
    line('cat');?></label>
  <select name="cat_id" class="form-control">
  <?php foreach ($categories->result() as $row) : ?>
    <option value="<?php echo $row->cat_id ; ?>"><?php echo $row->
      cat_name ; ?></option>
  <?php endforeach ; ?>
  </select>
</div>
```

The location dropdown is populated by the `get_locations()` function in `Jobs_model`. It returns a result object that we loop over, allowing the user to select the location:

```
<div class="form-group">
  <?php echo form_error('loc_id'); ?>
  <label for="loc_id"><?php echo $this->lang->
    line('loc');?></label>
  <select name="loc_id" class="form-control">
  <?php foreach ($locations->result() as $row) : ?>
    <option value="<?php echo $row->loc_id ; ?>"><?php echo
      $row->loc_name ; ?></option>
  <?php endforeach ; ?>
  </select>
</div>
```

```php
<label for="sunset_d"><?php echo $this->lang->line
  ('job_start_date');?></label>
<div class="row">
  <div class="form-group">
    <div class="col-md-2">
      <?php echo form_error('startd'); ?>
      <select name="startd" class="form-control">
      <?php for ( $i = 1; $i <= 30; $i++) : ?>
        <?php if (date('j', time()) == $i) : ?>
          <option selected value="<?php echo $i ; ?>"><?php
            echo date('jS', mktime($i,0,0,0, $i, date('Y'))) ;
            ?></option>
        <?php else : ?>
          <option value="<?php echo $i ; ?>"><?php echo date
            ('jS', mktime($i,0,0,0, $i, date('Y'))) ; ?>
            </option>
        <?php endif ; ?>
      <?php endfor ; ?>
      </select>
    </div>

    <div class="col-md-2">
      <?php echo form_error('startm'); ?>
      <select name="startm" class="form-control">
      <?php for ( $i = 1; $i <= 12; $i++) : ?>
        <?php if (date('m', time()) == $i) : ?>
          <option selected value="<?php echo $i ; ?>"><?php
            echo date('F', mktime(0,0,0,$i, 1, date('Y'))) ;
            ?></option>
        <?php else : ?>
          <option value="<?php echo $i ; ?>"><?php echo date
            ('F', mktime(0,0,0,$i, 1, date('Y'))) ; ?>
            </option>
        <?php endif ; ?>
      <?php endfor ; ?>
      </select>
    </div>

    <div class="col-md-2">
      <?php echo form_error('starty'); ?>
      <select name="starty" class="form-control">
      <?php for ($i = date("Y",strtotime(date("Y"))); $i <=
        date("Y",strtotime(date("Y").' +3 year')); $i++) : ?>
        <option value="<?php echo $i;?>"><?php echo $i;?>
          </option>
```

```php
        <?php endfor ; ?>
        </select>
      </div>
    </div>
</div>

<div class="form-group">
  <?php echo form_error('job_rate'); ?>
  <label for="job_rate"><?php echo $this->lang->line
    ('job_rate');?></label>
  <?php echo form_input($job_rate); ?>
</div>

<div class="form-group">
  <?php echo form_error('job_advertiser_name'); ?>
  <label for="job_advertiser_name"><?php echo $this->lang->
    line('job_advertiser_name');?></label>
  <?php echo form_input($job_advertiser_name); ?>
</div>

<div class="form-group">
  <?php echo form_error('job_advertiser_email'); ?>
  <label for="job_advertiser_email"><?php echo $this->lang->
    line('job_advertiser_email');?></label>
  <?php echo form_input($job_advertiser_email); ?>
</div>

<div class="form-group">
  <?php echo form_error('job_advertiser_phone'); ?>
  <label for="job_advertiser_phone"><?php echo $this->lang->
    line('job_advertiser_phone');?></label>
  <?php echo form_input($job_advertiser_phone); ?>
</div>

<label for="sunset_d"><?php echo $this->lang->line
  ('job_sunset_date');?></label>
<div class="row">
  <div class="form-group">
    <div class="col-md-2">
      <?php echo form_error('sunset_d'); ?>
      <select name="sunset_d" class="form-control">
      <?php for ( $i = 1; $i <= 30; $i++) : ?>
        <?php if (date('j', time()) == $i) : ?>
```

```
    <option selected value="<?php echo $i ; ?>"><?php
      echo date('jS', mktime($i,0,0,0, $i, date('Y'))) ;
      ?></option>
  <?php else : ?>
    <option value="<?php echo $i ; ?>"><?php echo date
      ('jS', mktime($i,0,0,0, $i, date('Y'))) ; ?>
      </option>
  <?php endif ; ?>
  <?php endfor ; ?>
  </select>
</div>

<div class="col-md-2">
  <?php echo form_error('sunset_m'); ?>
  <select name="sunset_m" class="form-control">
  <?php for ( $i = 1; $i <= 12; $i++) : ?>
    <?php if (date('m', time()) == $i) : ?>
      <option selected value="<?php echo $i ; ?>"><?php
        echo date('F', mktime(0,0,0,$i, 1, date('Y'))) ;
        ?></option>
    <?php else : ?>
      <option value="<?php echo $i ; ?>"><?php echo date
        ('F', mktime(0,0,0,$i, 1, date('Y'))) ; ?>
        </option>
    <?php endif ; ?>
  <?php endfor ; ?>
  </select>
</div>

<div class="col-md-2">
  <?php echo form_error('sunset_y'); ?>
  <select name="sunset_y" class="form-control">
  <?php for ($i = date("Y",strtotime(date("Y"))); $i <=
    date("Y",strtotime(date("Y").' +3 year')); $i++) : ?>
    <option value="<?php echo $i;?>"><?php echo $i;?>
      </option>
  <?php endfor ; ?>
  </select>
</div>
  </div>
</div>

<span class="help-block"><?php echo $this->lang->line
  ('job_sunset_date_help') ; ?></div>
<div class="form-group">
```

```
        <button type="submit" class="btn btn-success"><?php echo
            $this->lang->line('common_form_elements_go');?></button>
            or <? echo anchor('jobs',$this->lang->
            line('common_form_elements_cancel'));?>
        </div>
<?php echo form_close() ; ?>
    </div>
</div>
```

Any error messages related to the validation process—such as a missing form field that's required—are also displayed in this view file next to the form field, triggering an error. To do this, we use the `form_error()` CodeIgniter validation function.

Create the `/path/to/codeigniter/application/views/jobs/apply.php` file and add the following code to it:

```
<?php if ($this->session->flashdata('flash_message')) : ?>
    <div class="alert alert-info" role="alert"><?php echo $this->
        session->flashdata('flash_message');?></div>
<?php endif ; ?>


<div class="row">
    <div class="col-sm-12 blog-main">
        <div class="blog-post">
            <?php foreach ($query->result() as $row) : ?>
                <h2 class="blog-post-title"><?php echo $row->job_title ;
                    ?></h2>
                <p class="blog-post-meta">Posted by <?php echo $row->
                    job_advertiser_name . ' on ' . $row->job_created_at ;
                    ?></p>
                <table class="table">
                    <tr>
                        <td>Start Date
                        </td>
                        <td><?php echo $row->job_start_date ; ?>
                        </td>
                        <td>Contact Name
                        </td>
                        <td><?php echo $row->job_advertiser_name ; ?>
                        </td>
                    </tr>
                    <tr>
                        <td>Location
                        </td>
                        <td><?php echo $row->loc_name ; ?>
                        </td>
```

```
            <td>Contact Phone
            </td>
            <td><?php echo $row->job_advertiser_phone ; ?>
            </td>
          </tr>
          <tr>
            <td>Type
            </td>
            <td><?php echo $row->type_name ; ?>
            </td>
            <td>Contact Email
            </td>
            <td><?php echo $row->job_advertiser_email ; ?>
            </td>
          </tr>
        </table>
        <p><?php echo $row->job_desc ; ?></p>
      <?php endforeach ; ?>
    </div>
  </div>
</div>

<p class="lead"><?php echo $this->lang->line
  ('apply_instruction_1') . $job_title ;?></p>
<div class="span12">
<?php echo form_open('jobs/apply','role="form" class="form"') ;
  ?>
  <div class="form-group">
    <?php echo form_error('app_name'); ?>
    <label for="app_name"><?php echo $this->lang->line
      ('app_name');?></label>
    <?php echo form_input($app_name); ?>
  </div>

  <div class="form-group">
    <?php echo form_error('app_email'); ?>
    <label for="app_email"><?php echo $this->lang->line
      ('app_email');?></label>
    <?php echo form_input($app_email); ?>
  </div>

  <div class="form-group">
    <?php echo form_error('app_phone'); ?>
    <label for="app_phone"><?php echo $this->lang->line
      ('app_phone');?></label>
```

```php
    <?php echo form_input($app_phone); ?>
  </div>

  <div class="form-group">
    <?php echo form_error('app_cover_note'); ?>
    <label for="app_cover_note"><?php echo $this->lang->line
      ('app_cover_note');?></label>
    <?php echo form_textarea($app_cover_note); ?>
  </div>

  <input type="hidden" name="job_id" value="<?php echo $this->
    uri->segment(3) ; ?>" />

  <div class="form-group">
    <button type="submit" class="btn btn-success"><?php echo
      $this->lang->line('common_form_elements_go');?></button>
      or <? echo anchor('jobs',$this->lang->line
      ('common_form_elements_cancel'));?>
  </div>
<?php echo form_close() ; ?>
  </div>
</div>
```

Take a look at the top of the view file, specifically, the code in the `foreach($query->result() as $row)` loop that displays the details of the job. It is arranged as an HTML table, clearly separating the main points of the job advert, such as the start date, job location, and contact details. The only thing that's not in the table is the job description.

Below the `foreach()` loop is an HTML form that allows the user to enter their contact details and a small cover note explaining their interest in the role. The form is submitted when the user clicks on **Go**.

There is a hidden field element called `job_id`, and it looks like this:

```php
<input type="hidden" name="job_id" value="<?php echo $this->uri->
  segment(3) ; ?>" />
```

This hidden field that's populated with the ID of the job advert ensures that when the form is submitted, the `jobs/apply()` function can query the database with the correct ID and fetch the correct e-mail address (`jobs.job_advertiser_email`) associated with the job, and using PHP's `mail()` function, it will send an e-mail to the job advertiser with the applicants details.

Create the `/path/to/codeigniter/application/views/nav/top_nav.php` file and add the following code to it:

```
<!-- Fixed navbar -->
<div class="navbar navbar-inverse navbar-fixed-top" role
  ="navigation">
  <div class="container">
    <div class="navbar-header">
      <button type="button" class="navbar-toggle" data-
        toggle="collapse" data-target=".navbar-collapse">
        <span class="sr-only">Toggle navigation</span>
        <span class="icon-bar"></span>
        <span class="icon-bar"></span>
        <span class="icon-bar"></span>
      </button>
      <a class="navbar-brand" href="<?php echo base_url() ;
        ?>"><?php echo $this->lang->line
        ('system_system_name'); ?></a>
    </div>
    <div class="navbar-collapse collapse">
      <ul class="nav navbar-nav">
        <li class="active"><?php echo anchor('jobs/create',
          'Create') ; ?></li>
      </ul>
    </div><!--/.nav-collapse -->
  </div>
</div>

<div class="container theme-showcase" role="main">
```

This view is quite basic but still serves an important role. It displays an option to return to the `jobs` controller's `index()` function.

Creating the controller

We're going to create only one controller in this project, which is `/path/to/codeigniter/application/controllers/jobs.php`.

There is only one controller in this project, so let's go over it now. We will look at the code and discuss how it functions.

There are three main functions in this controller, and these are as follows:

- `index()`: This displays the initial list of job adverts to the user. It also displays the search box and displays any results that might be returned.

- `create()`: This displays a form to the any user, allowing the users create a job advert.

- `apply()`: This is accessed if the user clicks on the **Apply** button or the job title.

Create the `/path/to/codeigniter/application/controllers/jobs.php` file and add the following code to it:

```php
<?php if (!defined('BASEPATH')) exit('No direct script access
  allowed');

class Jobs extends MY_Controller {
  function __construct() {
  parent::__construct();
    $this->load->helper('string');
    $this->load->helper('text');
    $this->load->model('Jobs_model');
    $this->load->library('form_validation');
    $this->form_validation->set_error_delimiters('<div
      class="alert alert-danger">', '</div>');
  }
```

Looking at `index()` first, you'll see that one of the first things this function does is call the `get_jobs()` function of `Jobs_model`, passing to it the search string. If no search string was entered by the user in the search box, then this post array item will be empty, but that's okay because we test for it in the model.

The result of this query is stored in `$page_data['query']`, which is ready to be passed to the `views/jobs/view.php` file, where a `foreach()` loop will display each job advert:

```php
public function index() {
  $this->form_validation->set_rules('search_string', $this->lang->
    line('search_string'), 'required|min_length[1]|
    max_length[125]');
  $page_data['query'] = $this->Jobs_model->get_jobs($this->input->
    post('search_string'));
```

We set the validation rules for `search_string`. If this is the first time the page is viewed or if the validation fails, then `$this->form_validation()` will return a false value:

```
if ($this->form_validation->run() == FALSE) {
  $page_data['search_string'] = array('name' => 'search_string',
    'class' => 'form-control', 'id' => 'search_string', 'value' =>
    set_value('search_string', $this->input->post
    ('search_string')), 'maxlength'  => '100', 'size' => '35');
```

To display a list of jobs to the user, we call the `get_jobs()` function of `Jobs_model`, passing to it any search string entered by the user and storing the database result object in the `$page_data` array's item query. We pass the `$page_data` array to the `views/jobs/view.php` file:

```
    $page_data['query'] = $this->Jobs_model->get_jobs($this->
      input->post('search_string'));
    $this->load->view('common/header');
    $this->load->view('nav/top_nav');
    $this->load->view('jobs/view', $page_data);
    $this->load->view('common/footer');
  } else {
    $this->load->view('common/header');
    $this->load->view('nav/top_nav');
    $this->load->view('jobs/view', $page_data);
    $this->load->view('common/footer');
  }
}
```

The `create()` function is a little more meaty; initially, we set out the form validation rules—nothing really interesting to see there—but just after, we call three model functions: `get_categories()`, `get_types()`, and `get_locations()`, the results of which are stored in their own `$save_data` array items, as follows:

```
$page_data['categories'] = $this->Jobs_model->get_categories();
$page_data['types'] = $this->Jobs_model->get_types();
$page_data['locations'] = $this->Jobs_model->get_locations();
```

We'll loop over these results in the `view/jobs/create.php` file and populate the HTML select dropdowns.

Anyway, after this, we check whether the form has been submitted and if so, whether it's submitted with errors. We build the form elements, specifying each element's settings and sending them in the `$page_data` array to the `views/jobs/create.php` view.

If there were no errors after the form was submitted, we package up all the post inputs and send them to the `save_job()` function of `Jobs_model`.

If the save operation worked, we'll set a success message flash data, indicating to the user that their job has been saved so that they know it will now appear in searches. However, if it hasn't, we'll return an error message:

```
public function create() {
    $this->form_validation->set_rules('job_title', $this->lang->
        line('job_title'), 'required|min_length[1]|max_length[125]');
    $this->form_validation->set_rules('job_desc', $this->lang->
        line('job_desc'), 'required|min_length[1]|max_length[3000]');
    $this->form_validation->set_rules('cat_id', $this->lang->
        line('cat_id'), 'required|min_length[1]|max_length[11]');
    $this->form_validation->set_rules('type_id', $this->lang->
        line('type_id'), 'required|min_length[1]|max_length[11]');
    $this->form_validation->set_rules('loc_id', $this->lang->
        line('loc_id'), 'required|min_length[1]|max_length[11]');
    $this->form_validation->set_rules('start_d', $this->lang->
        line('start_d'), 'min_length[1]|max_length[2]');
    $this->form_validation->set_rules('start_m', $this->lang->
        line('start_m'), 'min_length[1]|max_length[2]');
    $this->form_validation->set_rules('start_y', $this->lang->
        line('start_y'), 'min_length[1]|max_length[4]');
    $this->form_validation->set_rules('job_rate', $this->lang->
        line('job_rate'), 'required|min_length[1]|max_length[6]');
    $this->form_validation->set_rules('job_advertiser_name', $this->
        lang->line('job_advertiser_name'), 'required|
        min_length[1]|max_length[125]');
    $this->form_validation->set_rules('job_advertiser_email', $this-
        >lang->line('job_advertiser_email'), 'min_length[1]|
        max_length[125]');
    $this->form_validation->set_rules('job_advertiser_phone', $this-
        >lang->line('job_advertiser_phone'), 'min_length[1]|
        max_length[125]');
    $this->form_validation->set_rules('sunset_d', $this->lang->
        line('sunset_d'), 'min_length[1]|max_length[2]');
    $this->form_validation->set_rules('sunset_m', $this->lang->
        line('sunset_m'), 'min_length[1]|max_length[2]');
    $this->form_validation->set_rules('sunset_y', $this->lang->
        line('sunset_y'), 'min_length[1]|max_length[4]');

    $page_data['categories'] = $this->Jobs_model->get_categories();
    $page_data['types'] = $this->Jobs_model->get_types();
    $page_data['locations'] = $this->Jobs_model->get_locations();

    if ($this->form_validation->run() == FALSE) {
```

```php
$page_data['job_title']              = array('name' =>
  'job_title', 'class' => 'form-control', 'id' => 'job_title',
  'value' => set_value('job_title', ''), 'maxlength'   =>
  '100', 'size' => '35');
$page_data['job_desc']               = array('name' =>
  'job_desc', 'class' => 'form-control', 'id' => 'job_desc',
  'value' => set_value('job_desc', ''), 'maxlength'   =>
  '3000', 'rows' => '6', 'cols' => '35');
$page_data['start_d']                = array('name' =>
  'start_d', 'class' => 'form-control', 'id' => 'start_d',
  'value' => set_value('start_d', ''), 'maxlength'   => '100',
  'size' => '35');
$page_data['start_m']                = array('name' =>
  'start_m', 'class' => 'form-control', 'id' => 'start_m',
  'value' => set_value('start_m', ''), 'maxlength'   => '100',
  'size' => '35');
$page_data['start_y']                = array('name' =>
  'start_y', 'class' => 'form-control', 'id' => 'start_y',
  'value' => set_value('start_y', ''), 'maxlength'   => '100',
  'size' => '35');
$page_data['job_rate']               = array('name' =>
  'job_rate', 'class' => 'form-control', 'id' => 'job_rate',
  'value' => set_value('job_rate', ''), 'maxlength'   =>
  '100', 'size' => '35');
$page_data['job_advertiser_name']    = array('name' =>
  'job_advertiser_name', 'class' => 'form-control', 'id' =>
  'job_advertiser_name', 'value' => set_value(
  'job_advertiser_name', ''), 'maxlength'   => '100', 'size'
  => '35');
$page_data['job_advertiser_email']   = array('name' =>
  'job_advertiser_email', 'class' => 'form-control', 'id' =>
  'job_advertiser_email', 'value' => set_value(
  'job_advertiser_email', ''), 'maxlength'   => '100', 'size'
  => '35');
$page_data['job_advertiser_phone']   = array('name' =>
  'job_advertiser_phone', 'class' => 'form-control', 'id' =>
  'job_advertiser_phone', 'value' => set_value(
  'job_advertiser_phone', ''), 'maxlength'   => '100', 'size'
  => '35');
$page_data['sunset_d']               = array('name' =>
  'sunset_d', 'class' => 'form-control', 'id' => 'sunset_d',
  'value' => set_value('sunset_d', ''), 'maxlength'   =>
  '100', 'size' => '35');
$page_data['sunset_m']               = array('name' =>
  'sunset_m', 'class' => 'form-control', 'id' => 'sunset_m',
  'value' => set_value('sunset_m', ''), 'maxlength'   =>
  '100', 'size' => '35');
```

```
    $page_data['sunset_y']              = array('name' =>
      'sunset_y', 'class' => 'form-control', 'id' => 'sunset_y',
      'value' => set_value('sunset_y', ''), 'maxlength'    =>
      '100', 'size' => '35');

    $this->load->view('common/header');
    $this->load->view('nav/top_nav');
    $this->load->view('jobs/create', $page_data);
    $this->load->view('common/footer');
  } else {
```

At this point, the data has passed validation and is stored in the $save_data array in preparation for saving it to the database:

```
$save_data = array(
  'job_title' => $this->input->post('job_title'),
  'job_desc' => $this->input->post('job_desc'),
  'cat_id' => $this->input->post('cat_id'),
  'type_id' => $this->input->post('type_id'),
  'loc_id' => $this->input->post('loc_id'),
  'job_start_date' => $this->input->post('start_y') .'-'.$this->
    input->post('start_m').'-'.$this->input->post('start_d'),
  'job_rate' => $this->input->post('job_rate'),
  'job_advertiser_name' => $this->input->
    post('job_advertiser_name'),
  'job_advertiser_email' => $this->input->
    post('job_advertiser_email'),
  'job_advertiser_phone' => $this->input->
    post('job_advertiser_phone'),
  'job_sunset_date' => $this->input->post('sunset_y') .'-'.$this->
    input->post('sunset_m').'-'.$this->input->post('sunset_d'),
);
```

The $save_data array is then sent to the save_job() function of Jobs_model, which will use set_flashdata() to generate a confirmation message if the save operation was successful or an error message if it failed:

```
    if ($this->Jobs_model->save_job($save_data)) {
      $this->session->set_flashdata('flash_message', $this->lang->
        line('save_success_okay'));
      redirect ('jobs/create/');
    } else {
      $this->session->set_flashdata('flash_message', $this->lang->
        line('save_success_fail'));
      redirect ('jobs');
    }
  }
}
```

Finally, we arrive at the `apply()` function. This is a little simpler. Like `create()`, we start off by defining our form item validation rules, and then we check whether the form is being posted (submitted) or not. We do this because the job ID can be passed to it in two ways.

The first way is using `$this->uri->segment(3)`. The ID is passed to the `apply()` function via the third `uri` segment if a user clicks on the **Apply** link or the job title in the `views/jobs/view.php` file.

The second way is `$this->input->post('job_id')`. The ID is passed to the `apply()` function via the post array if the form has been submitted. There is a hidden form element in the `views/jobs/view.php` file named `job_id`, the value of which is populated with the actual ID of the job being viewed:

```
public function apply() {
  $this->form_validation->set_rules('job_id', $this->lang->
    line('job_title'), 'required|min_length[1]|max_length[125]');
  $this->form_validation->set_rules('app_name', $this->lang->
    line('app_name'), 'required|min_length[1]|max_length[125]');
  $this->form_validation->set_rules('app_email', $this->lang->
    line('app_email'), 'required|min_length[1]|max_length[125]');
  $this->form_validation->set_rules('app_phone', $this->lang->
    line('app_phone'), 'min_length[1]|max_length[125]');
  $this->form_validation->set_rules('app_cover_note', $this->lang-
    >line('app_cover_note'), 'required|min_length[1]|
    max_length[3000]');

  if ($this->input->post()) {
```

The ID is stored in the `$page_data` array's `job_id` item and passed to the `get_job()` function of `Jobs_model`:

```
    $page_data['job_id'] = $this->input->post('job_id');
  } else {
    $page_data['job_id'] = $this->uri->segment(3);
  }

  $page_data['query'] = $this->Jobs_model->
    get_job($page_data['job_id']);
```

We then test to see whether anything is returned. We use the `num_rows()` CodeIgniter function to see whether there are any rows in the returned database object. If there aren't, then we just set a flash message saying that the job is no longer available.

It might be that in the time between the user clicking on the **Apply** link and the time when they actually submit their application, the job advert has become unavailable; that is, its `job_sunset_date` has passed, or someone might have manually typed a random ID and it just so happens that that ID doesn't exist. Anyway, whatever the reason, if no results are returned, a flash message is shown to the user. If, however, it is been found, we pull out the data from the database and store it as local variables:

```
if ($page_data['query']->num_rows() == 1) {
  foreach ($page_data['query']->result() as $row) {
    $page_data['job_title'] = $row->job_title;
    $page_data['job_id'] = $row->job_id;
    $job_advertiser_name = $row->job_advertiser_name;
    $job_advertiser_email = $row->job_advertiser_email;
  }
} else {
  $this->session->set_flashdata('flash_message', $this->lang->
    line('app_job_no_longer_exists'));
  redirect('jobs');
}
```

We then move on to the form validation process. If this is the initial page view or if there were errors with the submit, then `$this->form_validation->run()` will have retuned FALSE; if so, then we build our form items, defining their settings:

```
if ($this->form_validation->run() == FALSE) {
  $page_data['job_id']        = array('name' => 'job_id', 'class'
    => 'form-control', 'id' => 'job_id', 'value' =>
    set_value('job_id', ''), 'maxlength'   => '100', 'size' =>
    '35');
  $page_data['app_name']      = array('name' => 'app_name',
    'class' => 'form-control', 'id' => 'app_name', 'value' =>
    set_value('app_name', ''), 'maxlength'   => '100', 'size' =>
    '35');
  $page_data['app_email']     = array('name' => 'app_email',
    'class' => 'form-control', 'id' => 'app_email', 'value' =>
    set_value('app_email', ''), 'maxlength'   => '100', 'size' =>
    '35');
  $page_data['app_phone']     = array('name' => 'app_phone',
    'class' => 'form-control', 'id' => 'app_phone', 'value' =>
    set_value('app_phone', ''), 'maxlength'   => '100', 'size' =>
    '35');
  $page_data['app_cover_note'] = array('name' => 'app_cover_note',
    'class' => 'form-control', 'id' => 'app_cover_note', 'value'
    => set_value('app_cover_note', ''), 'maxlength'   => '3000',
    'rows' => '6', 'cols' => '35');

  $this->load->view('common/header');
```

```
$this->load->view('nav/top_nav');
$this->load->view('jobs/apply', $page_data);
$this->load->view('common/footer');
```

If there was no error with the submit, then we will build an e-mail to be sent to the advertiser of the job; this e-mail will be sent to the e-mail address contained in `jobs.job_advertiser_email`.

```
} else {
```

We substitute the variables in the e-mail using the `str_replace()`; PHP function, replacing the variables with the details pulled from the database or form submit, such as the applicant's contact details and cover note:

```
$body = "Dear %job_advertiser_name%,\n\n";
$body .= "%app_name% is applying for the position of
  %job_title%,\n\n";
$body .= "The details of the application are:\n\n";
$body .= "Applicant:  %app_name%,\n\n";
$body .= "Job Title:  %job_title%,\n\n";
$body .= "Applicant Email:  %app_email%,\n\n";
$body .= "Applicant Phone:  %app_phone%,\n\n";
$body .= "Cover Note:  %app_cover_note%,\n\n";

$body = str_replace('%job_advertiser_name%', $job_advertiser_name,
  $body);
$body = str_replace('%app_name%', $this->input->post('app_name'),
  $body);
$body = str_replace('%job_title%', $page_data['job_title'],
  $body);
$body = str_replace('%app_email%', $this->input->
  post('app_email'), $body);
$body = str_replace('%app_phone%', $this->input->
  post('app_phone'), $body);
$body = str_replace('%app_cover_note%', $this->input->
  post('app_cover_note'), $body);
```

If the e-mail is sent successfully, we send a flash message to the applicant, informing them that their application has been sent as shown in the following code; this isn't the same as a validation error. Validation errors have been handled earlier and we wouldn't be this far into the processing of the form if validating had not been passed. Really, what we're saying is if the e-mail had not been sent correctly—perhaps `mail()` failed for some reason—the application would not have been sent. This is what we are indicating:

```
if (mail($job_advertiser_email, 'Application for ' .
  $page_data['job_title'], $body)) {
  $this->session->set_flashdata('flash_message', $this->
    lang->line('app_success_okay'));
```

```
      } else {
        $this->session->set_flashdata('flash_message', $this->
          lang->line('app_success_fail'));
      }

      redirect ('jobs/apply/'.$page_data['job_id']);
    }
  }
}
```

Creating the language file

As with all the projects in this book, we're making use of the language file to serve text to users. This way, you can enable multiple region/multiple language support. Let's create the language file.

Create the /path/to/codeigniter/application/language/english/en_admin_ lang.php file and add the following code to it:

```php
<?php if (!defined('BASEPATH')) exit('No direct script access
  allowed');

// General
$lang['system_system_name'] = "Job Board";

// Jobs - view.php
$lang['jobs_view_apply'] = "Apply";
$lang['jobs_view_search'] = "Search";

// Jobs - create.php
$lang['job_create_form_instruction_1'] = "Enter the information
  about your job advert below...";

$lang['job_title'] = "Title";
$lang['job_desc'] = "Description";
$lang['type'] = "Job type";
$lang['cat'] = "Category";
$lang['loc'] = "Location";
$lang['job_start_date'] = "Start date";
$lang['job_rate'] = "Rate";
$lang['job_advertiser_name'] = "Your name (or company name)";
$lang['job_advertiser_email'] = "Your email address";
$lang['job_advertiser_phone'] = "Your phone number";
$lang['job_sunset_date'] = "Sunset date";
```

```
$lang['job_sunset_date_help'] = "Your job advert will be live up
    to this date, after which it will not appear in searches and
    cannot be applied for";

$lang['save_success_okay'] = "Your advert has been saved";
$lang['save_success_fail'] = "Your advert cannot be saved at this
    time";

// Jobs - Apply
$lang['apply_instruction_1'] = "Fill out the form below to apply
    for ";
$lang['app_name'] = "Your name ";
$lang['app_email'] = "Your email ";
$lang['app_phone'] = "Your phone number ";
$lang['app_cover_note'] = "Cover note ";
$lang['app_success_okay'] = "Your application has been sent ";
$lang['app_success_fail'] = "Your application cannot be sent at
    this time ";
$lang['app_job_no_longer_exists'] = "Unfortunately we are unable
    to process your application as the job is no longer active";
```

Putting it all together

Okay, here are a couple of examples that will help put everything together.

User creates a job advert

Let's see how the process of creating a job advert exactly works:

1. The user visits the site and is presented with a list of jobs, a search box, and a navigation bar.

2. The user wishes to create a new job so they click on the **Create** link contained in the `views/nav/top_nav.php` file.

3. CodeIgniter loads the `jobs` controller's `create()` function.

4. The `create()` function displays the form in the `views/jobs/create.php` view file. There are three HTML dropdown form elements that allow the user to choose a job type, category, and location. These dropdowns are populated by the `get_types()`, `get_categories()` and `get_locations()` functions of `Jobs_model`, respectively.

5. The user fills in the form and clicks on **Go** to submit the form.

6. The form is submitted to the `jobs` controller's `create()` function; it is validated and passed.

7. The `jobs` controller's `create()` function sends the validated form input to the `save_job()` function of `Jobs_model` where it is saved to the `jobs` database table.

User looks at a job

Now we will see how does a user looks at a job:

1. The user visits the site and is presented with a list of jobs, a search box, and a navigation bar.

2. The user clicks on the job title of the first job in the list.

3. CodeIgniter loads the `jobs` controller's `apply()` function.

4. The `apply()` function looks at the third segment in the URI (this is the `job_id` value passed in the URL of the job title in the previous step) and passes this to the `get_job()` function in `Jobs_model`.

5. The `get_job()` function pulls the details of the job from the database and returns a database result object to the `jobs` controller.

6. The `jobs` controller sends the database result object to the `views/jobs/apply.php` view file where a `foreach()` loop runs over the object, echoing out the details of the job.

User searches for a job

The flow of steps followed when a user searches for a job is as follows:

1. The user visits the site and is presented with a list of jobs, a search box, and a navigation bar.

2. The user types the word `CodeIgniter` into the search box and hits the *Enter* key.

3. The CodeIgniter framework then calls the `jobs` controller's `index()` function.

4. The `index()` function calls the `get_jobs` function of `Jobs_model` and passes to it the `search_string` post item:

```
$page_data['query'] = $this->Jobs_model->get_jobs($this->
    input->post('search_string'));
```

5. The `get_jobs()` function of `Jobs_model` recognizes that there is a search string as input and runs the correct database query, looking at `jobs.job_title` and `jobs.job_desc` to see whether a string of text matches the user's search string.

6. A job advert is found to match.

7. The result object is returned to the `views/jobs/view.php` file, where a `foreach()` loop runs over the result object, displaying the summary details of the job.

8. The user is free to click on the **Apply** link to study the details further or apply for the job.

User applies for a job

When a user wants to apply for a job, the following steps are performed:

1. The user visits the site and is presented with a list of jobs, a search box and navigating bar.

2. The user clicks on the job title of the first job in the list.

3. CodeIgniter loads the `jobs` controller's `apply()` function.

4. The `apply()` function looks at the third segment in the URI (this is the `job_id` value passed in the URL of the job title in the previous step) and passes this to the `get_job()` function in `Jobs_model`.

5. The `get_job()` function pulls the details of the job from the database and returns a database result object to the `jobs` controller.

6. The `jobs` controller sends the database result object to the `views/jobs/apply.php` view file where a `foreach()` loop runs over the object, echoing out the details of the job.

7. The user enters their details in the form below the job description and clicks on **Go**.

8. The form is submitted to the `jobs` controller's `apply()` function where it is validated; once passed, the `jobs` controller queries the `get_job()` function of `Jobs_model` to find the `jobs.job_advertiser_email` and `jobs.job_advertiser_name` values in order to e-mail the application to the advertiser.

Summary

So, here we have a basic job board application; it is capable of allowing people to create jobs, displaying those jobs, searching for jobs, and it also allows people to apply for these jobs. However, there are still areas of improvement and scope to add greater functionality; perhaps you could do the following:

- Add e-mail confirmation for the applicant. You could add a functionality to the `jobs/apply()` function to send a confirmation e-mail to the applicant when they apply for a job.

- Limit the number of applications. You could add a functionality to limit the number of job applications per job; logic would be needed to calculate which came first: the sunset date or the application limit.

- You could paginate the results. Currently, all active jobs are displayed in the `jobs/index()` function. You might wish to add pagination to this, limiting the number of jobs per page to a set number — 25 per page, for example.

- You can have detailed search options. You could add a more complex search, perhaps a dropdown specifying locations or job types, and so on.

- You can delete old job adverts. You could create a small Cron script, deleting jobs that are beyond their sunset date (`jobs.job_sunset_date`). This would reduce the database to a more reasonable size and ensure that only jobs that are active are kept there.

So there we are, then — we're at the end! What have we learned… erm, well, you should have a whole bunch of projects to be ready to work with — best of all, they're all really simple, so you can easily expand upon them and build more features and functions as you require; at the very least, you should have a *base* platform on which you can build any number of applications.

Be sure to check out the CodeIgniter website (`http://www.codeigniter.com/`) for regular updates and new releases. Don't forget that the code in this book is available online from the Packt website, so you don't have to painfully copy from page to screen, and the SQL for each project is there too.

Right — that's it, the end!

Index

Symbols

A

W

Thank you for buying
CodeIgniter Web Application Blueprints

About Packt Publishing

Packt, pronounced 'packed', published its first book, *Mastering phpMyAdmin for Effective MySQL Management*, in April 2004, and subsequently continued to specialize in publishing highly focused books on specific technologies and solutions.

Our books and publications share the experiences of your fellow IT professionals in adapting and customizing today's systems, applications, and frameworks. Our solution-based books give you the knowledge and power to customize the software and technologies you're using to get the job done. Packt books are more specific and less general than the IT books you have seen in the past. Our unique business model allows us to bring you more focused information, giving you more of what you need to know, and less of what you don't.

Packt is a modern yet unique publishing company that focuses on producing quality, cutting-edge books for communities of developers, administrators, and newbies alike. For more information, please visit our website at www.packtpub.com.

About Packt Open Source

In 2010, Packt launched two new brands, Packt Open Source and Packt Enterprise, in order to continue its focus on specialization. This book is part of the Packt Open Source brand, home to books published on software built around open source licenses, and offering information to anybody from advanced developers to budding web designers. The Open Source brand also runs Packt's Open Source Royalty Scheme, by which Packt gives a royalty to each open source project about whose software a book is sold.

Writing for Packt

We welcome all inquiries from people who are interested in authoring. Book proposals should be sent to author@packtpub.com. If your book idea is still at an early stage and you would like to discuss it first before writing a formal book proposal, then please contact us; one of our commissioning editors will get in touch with you.

We're not just looking for published authors; if you have strong technical skills but no writing experience, our experienced editors can help you develop a writing career, or simply get some additional reward for your expertise.

Codelgniter 2 Cookbook

ISBN: 978-1-78216-230-8   Paperback: 306 pages

Over 80 recipes to help you create Codelgniter-powered applications and solve common coding problems

1. Customizable code that can be used in your own applications right away.

2. Recipes that will help you solve your Codelgniter issues efficiently and effectively.

3. Each recipe comes with a full code example, and where necessary, the model and view files are included too.

Programming with Codelgniter MVC

ISBN: 978-1-84969-470-4   Paperback: 124 pages

Build feature-rich web applications using the Codelgniter MVC framework

1. Build feature-rich web applications using the Codelgniter MVC framework.

2. Master the concepts of maximum simplicity, separation, flexibility, reusability, and performance efficiency.

3. A quick guide to programming using the Codelgniter MVC framework.

Please check **www.PacktPub.com** for information on our titles

CodeIgniter 1.7 Professional Development

ISBN: 978-1-84951-090-5   Paperback: 300 pages

Become a CodeIgniter expert with professional tools, techniques, and extended libraries

1. Learn expert CodeIgniter techniques and move beyond the realms of the user guide.

2. Create mini applications that teach you a technique and allow you to easily build extras on top of them.

3. Create CodeIgniter libraries to minimize code bloat and allow for easy transitions across multiple projects.

CodeIgniter 1.7

ISBN: 978-1-84719-948-5   Paperback: 300 pages

Improve your PHP coding productivity with the free, compact, open source, MVC CodeIgniter framework!

1. Clear, structured tutorial on working with CodeIgniter for rapid PHP application development.

2. Careful explanation of the basic concepts of CodeIgniter and its MVC architecture.

3. Use CodeIgniter with databases, HTML forms, files, images, sessions, and e-mail.

Please check **www.PacktPub.com** for information on our titles

6245095R00192

Printed in Germany
by Amazon Distribution
GmbH, Leipzig